THE 'HEAVEN' AND 'HELL' OF WILLIAM BLAKE

'To Annihilate the Self-hood of Deceit & False Forgiveness'
From Blake's poem, Milton

THE 'HEAVEN' AND 'HELL'
OF
WILLIAM BLAKE

G. R. Sabri-Tabrizi

INTERNATIONAL PUBLISHERS

NEW YORK

PR
4147
S2
1973

PRINTED BY Unwin Brothers Limited

THE GRESHAM PRESS, OLD WOKING, SURREY, ENGLAND

Produced by Letterpress

PREFACE

The following book is the result of ten years' reading of William Blake. I became interested in Blake while studying in Istanbul in 1959, and while pursuing the problem of 'what is literature for?'. I had this question in mind ever since graduating in 1956 from the University of Tabriz, Iran. What are the human values of literature and what is its use for society? I found the answer, among English writers, in Blake: true literature and art are concerned with people and their practical life, and it is with this that literature must be mainly concerned.

> 'Can I see another's woe,
> And not be in sorrow too?'

These simple lines from the *Songs of Innocence* seemed to echo a profound truth. True literature, and, indeed, all art must be concerned, directly or indirectly, with another human being's woe or joy. In other words, art is closely linked with social conditions. Can writings which are dominated by the author's selfish and limited memories care about another's woe? To Blake, they could not:

> 'He who sees the Ratio only, sees himself only.'

Thus I found Blake's art humane and practical.

A second question that arose after reading his 'prophetic' books was why Blake had not carried on writing with the relative simplicity of his early works. Again, although not religious in the orthodox sense, why did he seem preoccupied with the terms 'Heaven' and 'Hell'? This was a mystery to me, but believing that Blake was against mysticism and all mystifications I sought the solution in his social circumstances. I studied the society and conditions in which Blake worked and lived.

I have chosen *The Marriage of Heaven and Hell* as the starting point of my study for three reasons. Firstly, I found in it material relevant to my search for the reason why Blake used

v

particular religious terms and such a variety of 'unheard-of' symbols in his radical writings. Secondly, a comparison with Swedenborg's *Heaven and Hell*, a comparison which I found absorbing, presented a contrast between two opposite types of literature, one representing abstract and passive memories and the other practical and active life. Thirdly, the idea of 'contraries' and *The Marriage* as a whole still remain a controversial subject among Blake scholars.

From Chapter Two onwards, where the analysis of the works of Blake begins, all reference Notes in each chapter are numbered and refer to Notes at the end of the book. Some abbreviations are used: M.H.H. stands for Blake's *The Marriage of Heaven and Hell*, H.H. for Swedenborg's *Heaven and Hell*, and K for *Blake Complete Writings* edited by Geoffrey Keynes.

In this research I owe much to my wife who has been my first critic. Among Blake Scholars I must express my gratitude to Sir Geoffrey Keynes, the editor of *The Complete Writings of William Blake*, for his reading my book and his encouragement. I would also like to acknowledge the assistance of Professor V. G. Kiernan (of the Department of History, University of Edinburgh), and express my gratitude for his constructive comments on reading a part of my book. I owe a special word of thanks to Colin Nicholson and David Tittensor (Department of English, University of Edinburgh) who read the typescript. I should finally make it clear that I hold only myself responsible for the ideas and any shortcomings in this book.

INTRODUCTION

The main aim of this book is to present the whole of Blake in a coherent and comprehensible way. Books on Blake are mostly either very specialized and detailed or very shallow, discussing only some of the simple poems. I have attempted to bridge these extremes by presenting Blake as a whole, discussing and giving examples from both the apparently simple works and the so-called 'Prophetical Writings'. Some Blake critics (e.g. Kathleen Raine and Martin K. Nurmi) have generally classed Blake with such mystic and apocalyptic thinkers as Swedenborg and Jacob Boehme, and have suggested that Blake's ideas were derived from these traditions and philosophies. But Blake, as I shall demonstrate, was a social critic and revolutionary poet who opposed class society and its philosophical systems. Indeed, very important and valuable researches of scholars, such as J. Bronowski's *A Man Without a Mask* (1944), David V. Erdman's *Blake: Prophet Against Empire* (1954) and A. L. Morton's *The Everlasting Gospel* (1958) have rediscovered Blake as a social thinker. My work primarily stresses the consistent materialism of Blake in his opposition against Church and State and all forms of exploitation.

The book has seven chapters, in the first of which I have taken Blake's writings as a first-hand experience of and a source of information about social and political life in the eighteenth century. An attempt has been made to sketch an outline of social conditions and relationships in the England of that time. There are two reasons for doing this. First, Blake's writings are the product of the contemporary social conditions and class conflicts. When he attacks Swedenborg, Newton and Locke, for example, he is attacking, as most radical poets and writers did, the whole social order that they represented. From the evidence thus obtained one may conclude that Blake's *Songs of Innocence* and *Songs of Experience*, *Marriage of Heaven and Hell* and other works must be studied in this social context.

Blake is a dialectical thinker, and in Chapter Two I have

attempted to present a new interpretation of *Songs of Innocence* and *Songs of Experience* in this light, suggesting that the *Songs of Innocence* are not simply a recollection of childhood memories and the *Songs of Experience* are not the experience of adulthood. The *Songs* are a deep social satire and criticism in which the true 'innocence' and 'experience', for example, of 'The Little Vagabond' or 'The Chimney Sweeper', both instances of a powerfully political poetry, revolt against the false and passive 'innocence' and 'experience' of priestcraft and the ruling interest. Thus the idea of 'Two Contrary States of the Human Soul' is political and should be seen within a social context. Blake's writings must be studied in their particular context. Every poem and line that he writes is deliberate and well thought out. For example, the term 'Imagination', which is very central in Blake, is generally treated by scholars (Kathleen Raine and others) as denoting an abstract mental activity; but 'Imagination' is, for Blake, the true representation of reality—'My Streets are my Ideas of Imagination'. The definition and particular meaning of 'Imagination', in Blake's philosophy, is illustrated in the second part of Chapter Two.

In Chapter Three I have attempted to demonstrate how Blake's *Marriage of Heaven and Hell* has been misinterpreted in the past. The work is a powerful challenge and criticism of class society and its philosophical systems. This is shown by a close and comparative examination of Swedenborg's *Heaven and Hell* and Blake's *Marriage of Heaven and Hell*. 'Heaven' and 'Hell' are not abstract terms. They represent social classes and conditions. 'Heaven' represents the rich and propertied or higher clerical class epitomized by Swedenborg. 'Hell' represents the poor and working class epitomized by Blake. Those who are in 'Heaven' are called Angels, and those in 'Hell' Devils. Thus Swedenborg's *Heaven and Hell* and Blake's *Marriage of Heaven and Hell* represent two contrasting philosophies, two types of social outlook and literature in defence of two opposing interests.

Chapter Four discusses Blake's idea of 'Poetic Genius' or the creative mind as opposed to one relying on passive memories derived from sense-perception, and consideration is given to his conclusion that Priesthood began by the abstraction of 'mental deities' from objects and environment. Deities are the

imaginative or mental forms of sensible objects. The major
difference between the mind of human beings and that of the
lower animals is a difference in creativity. The mind of man
has an unchangeable power which he can apply to his particu-
lar environment. Swedenborg had potentially as creative a
mind as Blake but he set his limited and passive memories
against unlimited and universal or creative man, whereas
Blake stressed the unchangeable and creative mind:

'The true Man is the source, he being the Poetic Genius.'

'Poetic Genius' is the source because it is unchangeable. It
applies its unchangeable power to changeable objects or the
environment.

In Chapter Five, while examining the Prophetical writings,
I attempt to demonstrate that these writings are not the
product of a different mind. The voice of true 'Innocence' or
creative 'Imagination' is heard throughout the Prophetical
works as well. The poet did not change his principle, though
he had to change his language because of the darkening condi-
tions in which he lived and wrote. (The book of *Vala, or The
Four Zoas* exemplifies the darkening social condition.) The
change of characters and symbols in Blake is due to the change
of context and the characters' relationships with others rather
than a change in the poet's heart. Rintrah, for instance, is a
dual character. One is the prophetic character and another
the Urizenic character or false prophet. In order to understand
the so-called 'Romantic movement' and the social conflict in
the eighteenth century, an understanding of Blake and his
dialectics is essential.

In Chapter Six, I have further examined Blake's symbolism.
In order to show his consistency and social intention fully, I
have included his paintings and engravings in my arguments.
I have suggested that symbols in Blake are social personalities
or characters who represent one class or the other. The 'worm'
symbol, for example, is a devouring and parasitic social being
which should be 'cut' in order that the land may be fertile and
productive: 'the cut worm forgives the plow'. This can prove
Blake to be a revolutionary poet whose Jerusalem was neither
a religious fantasy nor a Utopia but a social vision of human
brotherhood which he hoped would take place on earth.

An illustration of this is the subject of Chapter Seven. In his *Milton*, repudiating the interference of any superhuman power in human affairs and history, Blake asserts the importance of man as creator and builder of 'Jerusalem' or new society. In other words, to Blake 'Jerusalem' is a social resurrection which will take place in England and all over the world by replacing 'Babylon' or class society.

CONTENTS

CONTENTS

ILLUSTRATIONS

The original engraving of 'Albion' is in the Alverthorpe Gallery, Pennsylvania, who kindly supplied a photograph. The engravings from 'The Gates of Paradise' are reproduced from Blake, Complete Writings, edited by Sir Geoffrey Keynes, by kind permission of Oxford University Press.

Chapter One

SWEDENBORG AND BLAKE:
THE SOCIAL CONTEXT

I. EIGHTEENTH-CENTURY BACKGROUND

Writers 'cannot escape', says Shelley, 'from subjection to a common influence which arises out of an infinite combination of circumstances belonging to the time in which they live. . . .'* The personality of a writer or poet is mainly formed by his social circumstances and experience. He derives his convictions and ideas from his own experiences of practical life which are both private and public. George Eliot remarked in her *Felix Holt* that '. . . there is no private life which has not been determined by a wider public life . . .'†

This chapter is an attempt to sketch a necessarily schematic outline of social conditions and relationships in eighteenth-century England, and its purpose is twofold. Firstly it aims to demonstrate that the writings of Blake reflect the contemporary social conditions and class structure, and leads on to the conclusion that Blake's *Marriage of Heaven and Hell* and Swedenborg's *Heaven and Hell* must be studied in their respective social contexts. Secondly it attempts to show that *Heaven and Hell* and *The Marriage of Heaven and Hell* reflect two contrasting philosophies, types of social outlook and of literature. Although Blake and Swedenborg represent two opposing personalities or mentalities, they are not individuals isolated from history. *Heaven and Hell* mirrors the drive of a conservative class to keep the social system static, while *The Marriage of Heaven and Hell* presents a revolutionary notion of society struggling to be freed from self-interest.

---

* Preface to *The Revolt of Islam*, *The Complete Poetical Works* of P. B. Shelley (Oxford University Press, 1945), p. 35.
† George Eliot, *Felix Holt* (Chapter III).

Eighteenth-century England inherited and augmented the late seventeenth century's traditions and social order against which the Romantic movement was to rebel. 'Wordsworth and Coleridge', says T. S. Eliot, 'are not merely demolishing a debased tradition, but revolting against a whole social order';* Blake's reaction against such men as Swedenborg, Locke and Newton is not against them as individuals but rather against the social order which they supported and represented. To fully understand Blake he must be examined in his social context.

The late eighteenth century was a time of revolution, though geographically limited: the French and American political revolutions abroad, and the Industrial Revolution in Britain.† The Romantic poets and radical thinkers in England came under the influence of these political revolutions abroad, but the social and political movement did not spring solely from foreign sources. It had social roots at home.

The Industrial Revolution did not, in its earlier phases, change the social order but aggravated the social relationships against which poets and writers rebelled. They did not all indeed rebel against industrialization as such but rather against the industrial exploitation of man. For the same reason Blake opposed the machine. The revolution was, basically, 'no more than a powerful way of drawing . . . industry together'.‡ Between 1760 and 1830 small industries were brought together and great industrial enterprises were created. But the social order remained the same. The old family connections, for example, as Asa Briggs and Dorothy Marshall have indicated, were still important,§ and the landowner was still the most influential element in society: 'much of the mediaeval foundations of society still remained . . . Power was still in the hands of the man who possessed land. The merchant and the financier, . . . had still . . . to operate within the framework of a society that had been shaped by landowner for landowners'.‖

---

* T. S. Eliot, *The use of Poetry and the use of Criticism* (London, Faber ed.), p. 25.
† For details see E. J. Hobsbawm, *The Age of Revolution* (London 1964), pp. 78, 243 and 262–7.
‡ J. Bronowski, *William Blake, A Man Without a Mask* (London 1947), p. 19.
§ Asa Briggs, *The Age of Improvement* (London 1960), pp. 9–20.
‖ Dorothy Marshall, *English People in the Eighteenth Century* (London 1962), pp. 39–40.

As Blake wrote at this time:

'For Commerce, tho' the child of Agriculture,
Fosters his parent . .'*

These landowners held their position only by inheritance,
rarely by merit. The majority of the people, the poor, lived in
misery, for the 'increasing opulence on the one hand was
matched by increasing distress on the other'.† The labourers,
Cobbett said, became 'real slaves'.‡ and declined as their
masters prospered. They flocked to the cities to be swallowed
by factories whose owners needed cheap labour, and there
they became 'poorer, hungrier and restless'.§ Blake writes in his
Poetical Sketches (1769–1778):

'The Nobles of the land did feed
    Upon the hungry Poor;
  They tear the poor man's lamb, and drive
    The needy from their door!

"The land is desolate; our wives
  "And children cry for bread; . . ."

The husbandman does leave his plow,
    To wade thro' fields of gore;
  The merchant binds his brows in steel,
    And leaves the trading shore:'‖.

During his own lifetime (1757–1827) Parliament failed to
take any effective measures to improve the conditions of the
poor, but passed numerous laws to combat the rising crime rate
that resulted from poverty. The law as a whole was rigid and
inhumane, protecting only the interest and wealth of the rich
against the poor. The list of offences punishable by death
numbered one hundred and fifty by 1767 and the number was
growing. As Blake judged it, the cause of these capital crimes

* The page references in all citations from Blake are *The Complete Writings of
William Blake* with all the variant Readings. Edited by Geoffrey Keynes (London
1957), p. 19.
  † *The Georgians at Home* 1714–1830, by Elizabeth Burton (London 1967),
published by Longmans, p. 119.
  ‡ William Cobbett, *Rural Rides* (Macdonald ed., London 1958), p. 219.
  § Elizabeth Burton, *op. cit.*, p. 205.
  ‖ *Poetical Sketches* (K. pp. 11–12).

was 'the Miser's passion, not the Thief's'.* Stealing forty
shillings' worth of goods from a house, five shillings' worth
from a shop, or a handkerchief from a person were all capital
crimes.†

This was Blake's society, and his life's 'experience' was of its
injustice and its intolerance. His 'London' poem in the *Songs
of Experience* (1789–94) is one reaction to the misery and
inequality:

> 'I wander thro' each charter'd street,
> Near where the charter'd Thames does flow,
> And mark in every face I meet
> Marks of weakness, marks of woe.
>
> In every cry of every Man,
> In every Infant's cry of fear,
> In every voice, in every ban,
> The mind-forg'd manacles I hear.
>
> How the Chimney-sweeper's cry
> Every black'ning Church appalls;
> And the hapless Soldier's sigh
> Runs in blood down Palace walls.
>
> But most thro' midnight streets I hear
> How the youthful Harlot's curse
> Blasts the new born Infant's tear,
> And blights with plagues the Marriage hearse.'‡

This poem is a social history of the time. When Blake was born,
it was a 'year of dearth' and from 1757 throughout Blake's life,
the years of dearth grew common. Malnutrition was most
marked in the cities where rickets, the 'English disease', also
prevailed and gin was 'the principal sustenance . . . of more
than 100 thousand people': § 'weakness' and 'woe' were indeed
etched on every face. The streets were 'chartered' by laws and
social conventions that attempted to stifle and clap manacles
on action and original thought. 'Charter'd' also suggests the
monopolies and exploitation by the Chartered city corporations.

---

* Letter to Dr. Trusler, August 23, 1799 (K. p. 793).
† J. Bronowski, *op. cit.*, pp. 23–4.
‡ *Songs of Experience* (K. p. 216).
§ E. Burton, *op. cit.*, p. 214.

Eighteenth-century England repeatedly suffered the 'dislocating change from peace to war and war to peace'.* In war or peace the military was used by the government 'to prevent a distressed people from committing acts of violence'.† But in peace time the soldiers themselves were 'hapless'. Wounded or discharged, they were sent penniless to swell the ranks of the starving unemployed.

Poverty and lack of opportunity drove young girls to the streets where they quickly became infected and in turn passed on their 'blight' to others and to their children. These infants were abandoned in the streets by mothers to whom they meant only expense and shame.

Social inequality and low wages forced children of the poor to start work at a very early age.‡ They were cheap labour, easily replacable and thus readily exploited. Some were ' "ready to dispose of their children under the influence of a glass of gin".'§ No apprentice fee was expected, and the master sweep was even prepared to pay the parents for the services of a child who was thus literally bought and sold. Blake's chimney sweeper is a typical example of a child labourer.

> 'When my mother died I was very young,
> And my Father sold me while yet my tongue
> Could scarcely cry " 'weep! 'weep! 'weep! 'weep!"
> So your chimneys I sweep, and in soot I sleep.'‖

It was, as E. P. Thompson has noted, in the immediate aftermath of the French Revolution that the 'Kingdom within' in the 'Dissent of the poor' changed to the 'Kingdom without' and 'the millennarial current, so long underground, burst into the open with unexpected force'.¶ In the *Songs of Innocence* Tom, a chimney sweeper, dreams of an angel who has a 'bright Key' and sets all chimney sweepers free and tells Tom that 'if he'd be a good boy, He'd have God for his father'. But in the *Songs*

---

* M. D. George, *England in Transition* (A Pelican Book, 1953), p. 53.
† William Cobbett, *op. cit.*, p. 382.
‡ M. D. George, *op. cit.*, p. 123.
§ M. D. George, *London Life* (1925), p. 244.
‖ *Songs of Innocence*, 1789 (K. p. 117).
¶ E. P. Thompson, *The Making of the English Working Class*, Pelican ed., 1968, pp. 54–5.

of Experience (1789–94) 'God and his priest and King' are held responsible as the cause of social inequality and misery:

> 'A little black thing among the snow,
> Crying " 'weep! 'weep!" in notes of woe!
> "Where are thy father and mother? say?"
> "They are both gone up to the church to pray . . .
> "And are gone to praise God & his Priest & King,
> "Who make up a heaven of our misery." '*

The poverty and misery indeed were not peculiar to the eighteenth century. The poor suffered for centuries.

But '. . . little is known about the poor', Elizabeth Burton writes, 'well on in the eighteenth century. The poor held no offices, being illiterate they wrote no letters. . . They are the anonymous, faceless ones and they made up probably seventy-five per cent of the population. . . . But about the poor as people, as human beings, we know nearly nothing. They do not, for they could not, tell us themselves what they felt and suffered. Others had to speak for them—and others began to do so.'† Blake was one of the people who spoke on behalf of the poor and the working class.

These conditions were not, of course, exclusive to Britain; the same misery and the gulf between rich and poor existed all over Europe. Swedenborg's *Heaven and Hell*, as we shall see later, reflects the unjust social conditions that existed at the time in Sweden. Although the concentration of labour known as the industrial revolution did not occur in Sweden until as late as 1850, the living conditions of the miners were already oppressive and the social structure rigid and inhuman.

This preliminary sketch of the eighteenth-century social scene will help to put Blake's works into perspective. It shows how they were closely related to the social context, and why Blake revolted against the whole order of society in defence of human values, as opposed to Swedenborg who attempted to justify and support the position and interest of a leisured class (the mine owners) by turning against human values. The study involved will lead to the conclusion that critics are erroneous who attempt to identify Blake with Swedenborg or give a

* *Songs of Experience* (1789–94) (K. p. 212).
† Elizabeth Burton, *op. cit.*, p. 33.

metaphysical and apocalyptic interpretation to the works of Blake by abstracting them from their social context.

Blake's criticism of philosophical, scientific and religious thought is inseparable from his social criticism. The intellectual and philosophical atmosphere of the eighteenth century strengthened the class structure in which everyone had his allotted place. Locke's philosophy of the human understanding, according to which the mind was a *tabula rasa* receiving sense impressions, and his friend Newton's mechanical laws of the universe, were felt to have a relevance to every aspect of social life. It became fashionable, as Peter Brown and Asa Briggs have pointed out, to apply the principles of 'rational' enquiry to all fields of knowledge.* The social constitution was regarded as a living application of Newtonian principles to the art of government, its clockwork mechanism a smaller version of the clockwork of the universe as a whole.† Religion, ethics, politics, law and art were all based on nature. Social relationships were based on the universal system in which every planet had its fixed and proper place. The clockmaker God had created a balanced universe and given it to us in perfect working order. We must, it was felt, keep the mechanism working perfectly by respecting and practising its laws. The universe became increasingly regarded as the 'Great Machine' working by rigidly determined laws. Blake's 'dark Satanic Mills' are apparently the symbol of this mechanical social order where each institution such as Church, University and Industry is like a 'Mill' within the mechanical social system which suppresses man. Because of their suppressive relationship they are regarded as 'Satanic'. While Newton's mechanical laws of the universe naturalized the social order, Locke's philosophy served religion under the name of Deism. Orthodox religion related social events and changes to divine Providence or supernatural power, and Natural religion related them to a nature discoverable by 'Reason'. All were equal according to the laws of nature. Everyone had an assigned and fixed position. In other words everyone was born into his predestined position as are the stars. It was the Architect of the Universe who had

* Peter Brown, *The Chathamites* (Macmillan ed., 1967), p. 422.
† Asa Briggs, *op. cit.*, pp. 75–88.

'distributed men into different ranks, and at the same time
united them into one society, in such sort as men are united'.
By Divine Decree the poor were placed under 'the superin-
tendency and patronage of the rich'. In turn, the rich were
charged by 'natural providence, as much as by revealed
appointment, with the care of the poor'.* Blake in his poem
'King Edward The Third' (1769–78) satirizes this mechanical
system:

> '. . . Our names are written equal
> In fame's wide trophied hall; 'tis ours to gild
> The letters, and to make them shine with gold
> That never tarnishes: whether Third Edward,
> Or the Prince of Wales, or Montacute, or Mortimer,
> Or ev'n the least by birth, shall gain the brightest fame,
> Is in his hand to whom all men are equal.
> The world of men are like the num'rous stars,
> That beam and twinkle in the depth of night,
> Each clad in glory according to his sphere; . . .'†

And the insecurity stemming from this form of dependence and
social injustice was directly experienced by Blake. He fought
against self-interest and abstract moral laws as well as the state
religion of the time. He knew that the evil must be fought
within society. In his book *Vala, or The Four Zoas* (1795–1804),
when, as E. P. Thompson notes, 'the Jacobin current went
into more hidden underground channels' and when he would
have been glad to find work and salvage 'something less than a
life',‡ Blake writes:

> ' "It is an easy thing to talk of patience to the afflicted,
> "To speak the laws of prudence to the houseless wanderer,
> "To listen to the hungry raven's cry in wintry season
> "When the red blood is fill'd with wine & with the marrow
>   of lambs." '§

The story of Blake was not uncommon and 'it is not even a
personal story'.‖ His poetry and art are directly linked with

* *The Works of Joseph Butler* (ed. W. E Gladstone), Vol. II (1896), p. 305.
† *Poetical Sketches* (K. p. 18).
‡ J. Bronowski, pp. 1–9.
§ *The Four Zoas*, Night the Second, lines 404–7 (K. p. 290).
‖ J. Bronowski, p. 1.

the social circumstances of his time. The difficulty of understanding Blake's art is the difficulty of understanding this link. 'The difficulty comes', says D. V. Erdman, 'at least as much from a failure to enter imaginatively into Blake's times as it does from a failure to enter Blake's imagination'.*

Blake used his poetry and art as a means of social criticism which was a product of what T. S. Eliot calls his peculiar honesty. 'It is an honesty against which the whole world conspires, because it is unpleasant. Blake's poetry has the unpleasantness of great poetry.'† This peculiar honesty was not exclusive to Blake. Other Romantics also shared it. 'It is sometimes suggested', says R. W. Harris, 'that the Romantics were social misfits, weak and vapid in their idealism, beautiful and ineffectual angels, beating in the void their luminous wings in vain'. But this suggestion 'remains both an inaccurate and an uncharitable judgment'.‡

The growth of discontent in society, and creative vigour and revolutionary spirit in literature, progressed rapidly against the static and rigid social orders in Britain and Europe. In Germany the Pietists, for example, represented one of these movements. Rejecting traditional scholastic theology and the rigid social system, they mainly supported the lower classes of society and propounded the view that social justice and recognition of human values were the bases upon which true Christianity stood. Pietism and similar movements against the static social system were widespread and powerful in Germany during the seventeenth and eighteenth centuries.§

In Sweden they were opposed by Swedenborg. Swedenborg's own position is an interesting one. In England he enjoyed some popularity which led to the establishment of the so-called 'New Church' which was against the teachings of the Orthodox Church. It made its greatest impact in northern England. The first meeting of the New Church took place on December 7, 1788, attended by Blake and his wife, apparently as a matter

---

* David V. Erdman, *Blake: Prophet Against Empire* (Princeton 1954), pp. 4–5.
† T. S. Eliot, *The Sacred Wood*, Univ. Paperbacks ed., 1967, p. 161.
‡ R. W. Harris, *Romanticism and the Social Order*, 1780–1830 (London 1969), pp. 36–7.
§ Koppel S. Pinson, *Pietism as a Factor in the Rise of German Nationalism* (New York, 1934), pp. 14–16 and p. 27.

of interest.* But in his own country, 'where his beliefs never
enjoyed much popularity . . .',† Swedenborg identified himself
with the established Church. His *Last Judgement* and *Heaven
and Hell*, which we shall discuss later, are in fact an attempt to
justify the position of the established social system against its
opponents. In the section concerning the 'Spiritual World' he
cast out into the desert Quakers and Moravians who preached
equality and brotherhood. Swedenborg described the Quakers
as 'devoid of understanding' and the Moravians seduced men
'by their flattering speeches'.‡

The discourses of the Quakers and Moravians were based
on practical Christianity as opposed to the orthodox theolo-
gians who preached abstract religion and indifference to social
issues. The Quakers flourished mainly in England and the
United States, while the Pietists and Moravians were more
influential in Germany. In 1720, when Swedenborg was
thirty-one years of age, the Pietists created a great stir in
Sweden. Calling themselves 'radical Pietists' they wished to
sever ties with the traditional Church which bitterly opposed
them.§ One of their leaders was a student called Sven Rosén
who had been influenced by Moravian teaching and who
founded the Renewed Church of the United Brethren at
Herrnhut in 1727. The Moravians, although they did not
advocate separation from the established Church, attracted
the workers and lower classes generally and so were also
considered a threat to Church and State which were united in
the face of a common danger. Consequently in 1726 the
'Conventicle Edict' in Sweden prohibited 'all . . . private
worship'.‖

The Moravians, nevertheless, continued to flourish. They
offered some hope to the working poor who were severely
oppressed as Sweden struggled to build up her industries. The
mine workers suffered worst of all and their conditions are
reflected in Swedenborg's *Heaven and Hell*.

A close examination of the teaching of the Moravians and

* See for details Minutes of the New Church (London 1885), pp. xix, xx, 19.
† Stewart Oakley, *The Story of Sweden* (London 1966), p. 180.
‡ E. Swedenborg, *The Last Judgement*, Amsterdam (London 1810), 1763,
pp. 56–9, nos. 83–7.
§ Robert Murray, *A Brief History of the Church of Sweden* (Stockholm 1961), p. 51–2.
‖ *Ibid.*, p. 53.

Pietists and their influence on progressive thought throughout Europe will help to explain why they presented such a threat to the traditional structure of Church and State and, consequently, why Swedenborg stood in opposition to them. The Moravians believed in an individual's 'deep, emotional personal relationship' with Jesus. They advocated a practical brotherhood under the figurehead of the historical human Jesus.* Thus they sought to unify the widely separated social classes and in doing so to raise the position of the poor. In his *Pia Desideria* Spener condemns the traditional churches' emphasis on abstract learning. The Church should instead concentrate on practical good works.

We can at least see that reaction against the established social system and Church was widespread in both England and Europe, and can thus put the relationship between Swedenborg and Blake into perspective. Swedenborg linked himself with the established orthodox clergy on the one hand, and with the mine-owners and nobles on the other, while Blake sympathized with humanitarian and religious thinkers like Lavater and revolutionary thinkers like Tom Paine.†

Blake's sympathy with Lavater and Paine, if proof is needed, is clearly demonstrated in his 'Annotations'. About Lavater he writes:

'I hope no one will call what I have written cavilling because he may think my remarks of small consequence. For I write from the warmth of my heart, & cannot resist the impulse I feel to rectify what I think false in a book I love so much & approve so generally.

Man is bad or good as he unites himself with bad or good spirits: tell me with whom you go & I'll tell you what you do.

As we cannot experience pleasure but by means of others . . . , who experience either pleasure or pain thro'

* K. S. Pinson, *op. cit.*, p. 25. The Moravian Brethren represented the last great outburst of Pietism in the eighteenth century (*ibid.*, p. 22). Pietism may be said to have begun officially with the publication of Spener's *Pia Desideria oder Wahren evangelischen Kirche* in 1675. Philipp Jakob Spener is perhaps the father of Pietism (*ibid.*, p. 15).

† About Blake's sympathy with Paine see, for example, Blake's *Annotations to Watson*.

us, And as all of us on earth are united in thought, for it is impossible to think without images of somewhat on earth—So it is impossible to know God and heavenly things; therefore all who converse in the spirit, converse with spirits. [& They converse with the spirit of God. del.]

For these reasons I say that this Book is written by consultation with Good Spirits, because it is Good, & that the name Lavater is the amulet of those who purify the heart of man.'*

Blake believed in universal brotherhood and equality and considered this the true Christian philosophy. As opposed to Swedenborg's rigid class system, Blake agreed with such characteristic utterances of Lavater as:

'Know, in the first place, that mankind agree in essence, as they do in limbs and senses.'

'Mankind differ as much in essence as they do in form, limbs, and senses—and only so, and not more.'

Blake commented: 'This is true Christian philosophy far above all abstraction.'† Blake also applauded Lavater's practical Christianity. Lavater wrote:

'. . . As the interest of man, so his God—as his God, so he.'
'. . . The object of your love is your God.'

Blake commented 'All Gold!' and 'This should be written in gold letters on our temples.'‡

Defending Tom Paine against Bishop Watson in his *Annotations To Watson's Apology for the Bible* (1798), Blake wrote:

'To defend the Bible in this year 1798 would cost a man his life.

The Beast & the Whore rule without control.
It is an easy matter for a Bishop to triumph over Paine's attack, but it is not so easy for one who loves the Bible.

The Perversions of Christ's words & acts are attack'd

* *Annotations to Lavater* (K. p. 88).
† *Ibid.* (K. p. 65).
‡ *Ibid.*, pp. 65–6.

by Paine & also the perversions of the Bible; Who dare defend either the Acts of Christ or the Bible Unperverted?

But to him who sees this mortal pilgrimage in the light that I see it, Duty to his country is the first consideration & safety the last . . .' (K. p. 383).

'Men who give themselves to their Energetic Genius in the manner that Paine does are no Examiners . . .' (K. p. 386).

Blake was warned by his friends against the publication of this Annotation: 'I have been commanded from Hell not to print this, as it is what our Enemies wish' (K. p. 383). The warning seems justified. Through the years, as E. P. Thompson records, imprisonments went on: Kyd Wake, a Gosport bookbinder, was sentenced at the end of 1796 to five years hard labour, and to the pillory, for saying 'No George, no war' (in 1803 Blake was himself to escape narrowly from such a charge): Johnson, the bookseller and friend of Blake, and Godwin were imprisoned; prosecutions for sedition in Lancashire and Lincolnshire took place.* It is interesting to observe how Blake uses 'Hell' to signify the poor and suppressed class and how he supports one religious thinker and attacks another not on the ground of religion but in respect of their human and social values.

It is a mistake to view Blake's works either as the product of a mystical experience or of a personal crisis. He did indeed experience crises, but their root was neither mental nor physical but was in the social conditions and relationships in which he lived. The following quotations from Blake scholars may clarify our viewpoint. Geoffrey Keynes writes about *Visions of the Daughters of Albion*:

'The theme of this poem has been related by some writers to crises in Blake's own life, such as his realization that he was tied legally and morally to a barren wife. But this is pure conjecture, and it is better to regard the book as a poet's view of the evils of organized religion, compulsory morals, oppressed womanhood, and, in addition of slavery . . .'†

* E. P. Thomson, *op. cit.*, pp. 191–3.
† Geoffrey Keynes, *William Blake, Poet, Printer, Prophet* (Trianon Press, 1964), p. 26.

This view is also true of the other symbolic and prophetical works of Blake, including *The Marriage of Heaven and Hell*, which was written in opposition to the static, unjust and inhuman social order that Swedenborg represents in his *Heaven and Hell*. Bronowski remarks:

'Blake speaks the discontent of his time. Until we know the discontent, we do not begin to read his writings; because we do not speak their language.'*

The terms 'Heaven' and 'Hell' and all Blake's symbols likewise must be studied within society and its language of discontent.

2. SWEDENBORG'S SOCIAL BACKGROUND

Swedenborg's *Heaven and Hell* is a reflection of two different social experiences. It is the outcome of the feelings he had experienced during his dependence on his father until 35 years of age, and then during his years with the Board of Mines, among the Royal family, Church officials and the House of Nobles.

Heaven and Hell has been treated as a mystical or religious work. Swedenborgians, like other religious followers, have taken the terms 'Heaven' and 'Hell' literally. But, as we shall show, Swedenborg's 'Heaven' and 'Hell' correspond to social and economic conditions and relationships which Swedenborg recognized within society. By the word 'Heaven' Swedenborg indicates that social grouping which possesses material wealth, intelligence and wisdom. These people, as Swedenborg states, are called Angels:

'I converse freely, and am in friendship with all the Bishops of my country, which are ten in number, and also with the sixteen Senators, and the rest of the Grandees, who love and honour me, as knowing that I am in fellowship with *angels*. The King and Queen themselves, as also the three Princes, their sons, show me all kind countenance; and I was once invited to eat with the King and Queen at

* J. Bronowski, *op. cit.*, p. 133.

their table (an honour granted only to the Peers of the realm,) and likewise since with the hereditary prince.'*

By the word 'Hell' he indicates the condition of those who work in mines and do manual work, or those who do not possess the glory and the wealth of Angels. These people he calls Devils. Blake adopts Swedenborg's terminology in *The Marriage of Heaven and Hell*. Thus 'Heaven' represents those who live in delight and receive the necessities of life 'gratis' from the Lord. 'Hell' represents those who depend on their own work or energy.

When Swedenborg was born in 1688 his father, Jasper Swedberg, was the Swedish Court chaplain. He was also appointed President of Swedish Churches in Pennsylvania and London by King Charles XII. The change of the family name from Swedberg to Swedenborg is explained in a letter (1769) by Emanuel Swedenborg:

> 'In 1719 I was ennobled by Queen Ulrica Eleonora, and named *Swedenborg*; from which time I have taken my seat with the Nobles of Equestrian Order' in the Triennial Assemblies of the States.†

Swedenborg was brought up in a theological atmosphere on the one hand, and amid the luxury of palaces and royal gardens on the other.‡ His grandfathers on both sides of the family were 'connected with the great mining industry of Sweden'. Daniel Issacsson, the father of Bishop Swedenborg, was a mine owner at Fahlum. Albrecht Behm, Swedenborg's maternal grandfather, had occupied at the Board of Mines a position similar to that which Swedenborg himself later held (Swedenborg, of course, also inherited these mining estates).§ To both Swedenborg and his father, living amid material comfort, the spiritual world seemed very real. Swedenborg's father, his biographer tells us, 'had an assured faith in the

---

* 'Letter by the Author' (London 1769), *Heaven and Hell* (London 1896), pp. xlix–l (italics are mine in all citations from Swedenborg, unless otherwise stated).

† *Heaven and Hell*, *op. cit.*, p. xliii.

‡ See George Trobridge, *Life of Emanuel Swedenborg* (London 1912), pp. 10–15.

§ *Ibid.*, p. 15 and p. 42. The variety of names in the same family is explained by E. Swedenborg in The 'letter by the Author' (London 1769), H.H., *op. cit.*

presence of angels among men, and of the helpful offices they fulfil as "ministering spirits, sent forth to minister into them who shall be heirs of salvation".'* Alongside this spiritualism and 'faith in the presence of angels among men' Swedenborg's father, at this time, was investing 'all available money on his own enterprises'.†

In the face of his rather abstract spiritualism, it is instructive to recall that there were times when Swedenborg's concerns were more directly involved in the material world. Writing to his brother-in-law (Benzelius) from London in April 1711 he complains:

'I am kept back here on account of *"want of money"*. I wonder my father does not show greater care for me. . . . It is hard to live without food or drink like some poor drudge in Schonen.'‡

Swedenborg was, of course, dependent on his father and expected money from him as a right, yet, as his biographer notes, always seemed afraid 'to approach his father with demands' for it.§ 'I believe', he concludes his letter to Benzelius, that

Your 'advice and your letters will induce my father to be so favourable towards me, as to send me the funds which . . . will infuse into me new spirit for the prosecution of my studies'.‖

When he writes his *Heaven and Hell*, however, Swedenborg is 'funding' his spirit rather differently, rejecting the body as evil in favour of 'soul', and the material world in favour of the spiritual.

A period of weary waiting and discouragement followed young Swedenborg's return to his native country. Full of the theories and new ideas of Newton and Flamstead he had 'many schemes for his country's good and the enlargement of

* *Life of Emanuel Swedenborg*, p. 18. For information about the Church of Sweden and its development and great influence on the whole affairs of the country while Charles XII was at war with Russia, see Robert Murray, *A Brief History of the Church of Sweden* (Stockholm 1961), pp. 46–8 and p. 110.
† *Ibid.*, pp. 28–9.   ‡ *Ibid.*, p. 28.   § *Ibid.*, p. 36.   ‖ *Ibid.*, pp. 38–9.

his own reputation'. But they were all frustrated. At a time when position was more important than ability, his father tried to find Swedenborg employment by using his influence at Court, but was unsuccessful until 1716 when Swedenborg was appointed 'Extraordinary Assessor' at the Board of Mines. He later became an 'ordinary assessor' and received payment for his work (1724), but did not receive the full salary until 1730.* This appointment was made, as Swedenborg himself tells us, through the favour of Charles XII:

> 'In the year 1716, and afterwards, I frequently conversed with Charles XII, King of Sweden, who was pleased to bestow on me a large share of his favour, and in that year appointed me to the office of Assessor in the Metallic College, in which office I continued from that time till the year 1747, when I quitted the office, but still retain the salary annexed to it as an appointment for life.'†

It is fascinating to correlate more fully this change of social situation with corresponding changes in Swedenborg's philosophical outlook. As his biographer records, before 1719 he is writing to Benzelius: 'It seems to me there is little reward for the trouble of advancing the cause of science . . . on account of the lack of funds, which prevents our going as far into it as we ought, . . .' In sending Benzelius his treatise on the decimal system, he renews his complaint:

> ' "This is the last",' he vows, ' "that I will publish myself, . . . because I have already worked myself poor by them. I have been singing long enough, let us see whether anyone will come forward, and hand me some bread in return!" '‡

By 1747, after he inherits the mines and ironworks from his mother's and stepmother's families and receives a salary for life, he is writing: The Angel's life stems from 'one single fountain of life, the Lord'.§ Angels 'are clothed, fed, and

---

* George Trobridge, *op. cit.* (p. 36).
† 'Letter by the Author', *op. cit.* (p. xlix).
‡ George Trobridge, *op. cit.*, pp. 41–2.
§ Emanuel Swedenborg, *Heaven and Hell* (Manchester 1817: originally published in London in the year 1758); references in all citations from *Heaven and Hell* are this edition unless stated otherwise, p. 10, no. 9.

housed gratuitously'.* ('As a man is, So he Sees', said Blake, K. p. 793).

Upon the assumption of his duties at the Board of Mines the passive life of 'leisure', of ideas and theories, is confronted by the 'active' life of coal-mines and miners. Swedenborg at last came face to face with reality. He had to visit the mining areas and to play an active part in the duties of the Board of Mines, which were many and varied.† It is interesting to see how these real events have been dressed up in apparently spiritual and moral terms. Symbols, images and emotive words such as 'smoke', 'fire', 'cloud', 'valley', 'deep', 'wilds', 'wilderness', 'caverns', 'rage', 'anger', and so on, redolent of the coal mines, are used to portray Swedenborg's 'Hell', while their condition seems 'torment' and 'insanity' to the man from the comfortable background of court and church. By studying the reports that Swedenborg had to make on the areas he visited we can follow him day by day, driving for miles through interminable forests, 'we can even picture him risking his life in steep descents into the gloomy subterranean caverns . . . a dangerous feat for one not daily accustomed to such work'.‡

Swedenborg's contemporary, Carl Linnaeus, while visiting the Great Copper Mine at Fahlun, near to Swedenborg's own mines, was struck by the appalling aspects of the pit. An extract from his account will give a good idea of the kind of sights which met Swedenborg's eyes and, as we see in his 'Hell', left a deep impression on him. (Linnaeus, of course, did not know that Swedenborg would give a theological interpretation to the scene.)

> 'From this mine arose a continual smoke, and the whole effect of it gave one the idea that the descriptions of hell, which the theologians use to make an impression upon the mind of the man to be saved, is taken from this or similar pits. Never could any poet describe the Kingdom of the underworld, never could any theologian describe a hell, more horrible than pits like these.

* *Heaven and Hell* (London 1958), p. 127, no. 266.
† Cyril Odhner Sigstedt, *The Swedenborg Epic, The Life and Works of Emanuel Swedenborg* (New York 1952), pp. 93–5.
‡ *Ibid.*, p. 96.

From its mouth goes up a poisonous, corrosive, sulphurous smoke, which poisons the air round about so that one gets there not without pain. The smoke eats into the earth so that no plants can grow thereabout. Below the surface are innumerable dark cells, never seen by the sun, filled with the smell of smoke and dust and heat to a depth of 450 yards, under the hard heavy earth. In these cells over 1,200 sun-shy workers go about, doomed to mine work, black as very devils on all sides surrounded with darkness and soot, smoke and smell. The walls are dark with soot, and the floor is slippery from wet stones, the passages are narrow as if dug by moles, and the roofs drip corrosive, vitriolic water. Cave-ins are continually dreaded. What awful anxiety grips one at the lowly portal of this underground kingdom, I know not, or what incredible longing to ascend! There the condemned souls work, naked to the waist, their mouths tied around with a woollen rag, so that the smoke and dust will not seep in too much. No room here for taking a clean breath. The sweat runs from their bodies like water from a bag. How easy to take a wrong step, and plunge into the bottomless chasm below! How easily might you be overtaken with a fainting spell as you cling to the swaying ladders, two or three fastened together!'

Linnaeus, however, unlike Swedenborg who condemns the miners' love of work as 'love of self and of the world', admires the labourers' energy: '. . . however black and horrible it is, there never are lacking labourers and men with zeal and enthusiasm seeking work there to win their dearly bought bread . . .'*

If we turn to Swedenborg's 'Hell' we see how the mines become 'Hell', and the mine-workers the inhabitants of 'Hell'.

'The apertures or gates to the hells', which are, says Swedenborg, 'beneath the plains and valleys, appear of different aspects . . . all are covered, nor are they opened except when evil spirits from the world of spirits are cast in thither; and when they are opened, there is an exhalation

---

* Sigstedt, *op. cit.*, pp. 96–7.

B

thence either like that of fire with smoke . . . or like flame
without smoke, or like soot, . . . or like a mist and thick
cloud: I have heard that the infernal spirits do not see those
things, . . . because when they are in them they are as in
their own atmosphere, and thus in the delight of their life,
and this by reason that those things correspond to the evils
and falses in which they are principled . . .'

Swedenborg, priest and mine owner, visits the mines. So:

'It hath also been granted me to look into the hells, and
to see what is their quality within, for when it is well-
pleasing to the Lord, a spirit and angel, who is above, may
penetrate by sight into the places beneath . . . Some hells
appear to the view like caverns and dens in rocks tending
inwards . . . into the deep obliquely . . . some hells appear
to the view like caves and dens, such as wild beasts inhabit
in forests: . . . such as are seen in mines . . .'*

These considerations help us to understand the nature of
Swedenborg's *Heaven and Hell* and so to appreciate the powerful
effect of Blake's critique.

In *Heaven and Hell* three distinct worlds or realms are
delineated, corresponding to the classes in contemporary
society. There is 'Heaven', inhabited by beings called Angels,
who enjoy pleasant homes and garments, and plenty to eat
and drink—the wealthy ruling class. There is the world of
'spirits', the spirits of people who after death have come to
occupy an intermediate position between 'Heaven' and 'Hell'—
the middle class. And there is 'Hell', where the infernal
spirits—the workers—live.

The clothes the Angels wear are more perfect, the food they
eat more delicate and their habitations more beautiful than
those on earth. This outward magnificence corresponds to
their inward wisdom. For example, according to the degree of
their intelligence, so the Angels wear different garments. The
most intelligent have garments 'glittering as from flame and
light'. The less intelligent have merely white garments.†

These garments can be seen and felt in the world because
the Angels wear clothes as men in the world do. They change

* *Heaven and Hell, op. cit.*, nos. 584–6, pp. 508–9.
† *Ibid.*, no. 178, p. 132.

them regularly and receive them 'from the Lord'.* Because every being's garments correspond to his intelligence which is derived from the divine truth, the less fortunate, infernal spirits also dwell 'in hells, since they are without truths, appear indeed clothed with garments, but with such as are tattered, dirty and hideous, everyone according to his insanity'.†

If it was hardly common belief before Swedenborg's writings appeared that Angels wore clothes, similarly it was not realized that there are 'houses and gardens' in the spiritual world as in the natural. The Angels, remarks Swedenborg, 'are well aware that such ignorance prevails at this day in the world.'‡ But again, the habitations of Angels are vastly superior to those on earth, and vary according to the dignity of the occupier. When Swedenborg's 'interior sight' was open he was able to wander through these heavenly dwellings in which 'are chambers, inner rooms, and bed-chambers . . . there are courts, and round about are gardens'.§ Their magnificence exceeds all description 'being ornamented with such decorations as neither expressions of language, nor science are able to describe'. These magnificences are 'presented by the Lord' before the Angels' eyes; 'nevertheless they delight their minds more than their eyes'.‖ In other words, these objects are perceived by the five senses first, and then delight the Angels' minds. Thus Swedenborg gives an account of his natural impressions—the wealth, property and leisure in 'Heaven' as opposed to the condition of the poor and the miners in 'Hell'. Blake later denounces the Angels' 'abyss of the five senses'.¶

Swedenborg gives a spiritual interpretation to the material wealth in 'Heaven'. In other words he attempts to justify the position of the wealthy Angels in 'Heaven'. He argues that external situation represents internal condition. Those in 'Hell' cannot have beautiful houses and gardens because their interiors are closed and blackened. Angels, however, are accommodated in palaces and houses, which correspond 'to the good and truths appertaining to them from the Lord'.** The highest Angels dwell in mountains, the Angels in the

* *Heaven and Hell*, p. 135, no. 181, see 'Garments', pp. 131–5.
† *Ibid.*, p. 135, no. 182.   ‡ *Ibid.*, p. 136, no. 183.
§ *Ibid.*, p. 137, no. 184.   ‖ *Ibid.*, p. 138, no. 185.
¶ *The Marriage of Heaven and Hell* (K. p. 150).
** *Ibid.*, p. 138, no. 186.

lower spiritual kingdoms dwell in less elevated places. But
again, even these last are superior to the human situation.
They are more perfect 'because in a more perfect state: for as
angelic wisdom exceeds human wisdom . . . so . . . do all things
which are perceived by them . . .'*

Their houses are given to them 'gratis' by the Lord, and
'according to their reception of good and truth . . .' and they
are 'gifted with whatsoever things they have need of'.†

Thus those in 'Heaven' receive their possessions free by
reason of their moral superiority. But those in 'Hell', who have
to work for whatever they want, are condemned because their
possessions spring from the 'infernal love' of self and the world.
But 'the things done from the man himself are all in them-
selves evil'.‡

To Blake such a degraded idea of human 'energy' and work
dishonours the human 'genius' which is love and desire to make
and create. Only in this context can we fully appreciate the
honesty of Blake's irony. In Swedenborg's Angelic society the
Devil seems to be more honest than the Angel, so Blake's
'Devil' must be in good company.

3. BLAKE'S SOCIAL BACKGROUND

Blake's life was much more humble than Swedenborg's and his
background totally different. At fourteen, Blake chose to be an
engraver; and he held to that choice until he died. He had not
chosen to be a poet and a painter, partly because he could not
afford to and partly because he did not separate art or litera-
ture from practical life. He believed that 'Heaven & Hell are
born together'.§ He worked daily and depended on his own
'energy'.

His apprenticeship had ended when he was twenty-one
years of age, and he made a successful marriage in 1782 when
believing, as he later said, that 'Peace & Plenty & Domestic
Happiness' are the 'Source of Sublime Art', proving 'to the
Abstract Philosophers that Enjoyment & not Abstinence is the

---

* *Heaven and Hell*, p. 132, no. 177.
† *Ibid.*, p. 141, no. 190.   ‡ *Ibid.*, p. 410, no. 484.
§ *Annotations to Swedenborg's Divine Love* (K. ed. p. 96).

food of Intellect'.* He was twenty-five years old. He did not look to his father for his keep, but earned his living by engraving. After his father's death in 1784, Blake opened a printshop with a fellow engraver and took his brother Robert in with him.† Meanwhile, self-taught, he was reading widely, including the works of Swedenborg.

Concerning the question of how Blake came to know about Swedenborg, David Erdman has suggested that it was the engraver Sharp who first interested Blake in him.‡ Whether Blake was attracted to Swedenborgian teaching through his parents or through his friends is not our concern. What really interests us is that he read most of Swedenborg's writings as they were issued by the Society of Swedenborg in London. He annotated Swedenborg's *Wisdom of Angels Concerning Divine Love and Divine Wisdom* in 1788, and *Providence* in 1790. He annotated *Heaven and Hell*, the second edition, 1784, the annotations being written in 1790.§

Friends of Blake like John Flaxman and Thomas Butts, who were earnest Swedenborgians, ‖ did not possess Blake's own vision and consciousness. For Blake realized that Swedenborg's teachings were an attempt to justify the existing social system. He was aware of what Swedenborg meant by 'Heaven' and 'Hell'. But although he rejected Swedenborg he always kept on friendly terms with Flaxman and Butts.

Blake's consciousness of the meaning of Swedenborg's philosophy and its implied class division stems from the fact that Blake was a common man—an engraver, working among his fellow men, loving them in his heart and feeling at one with them. *The Songs of Innocence* are one expression of this sympathy.

> 'Can I see another's woe
> And not be in sorrow too?'

Swedenborg looked on the mine workers as beings from

---

* *Letter to George Cumberland 6 December 1795* (K. ed. p. 790).

† Alexander Gilchrist, *Life of William Blake* (London 1942), pp. 37–47.

‡ David V. Erdman, 'Blake's Early Swedenborgianism', Comparative Literature, V, p. 3.

§ Blake's copy of Swedenborg's *Heaven and Hell*, 1784, is now in the Houghton Library, Harvard University. For details see *The Complete Writings of William Blake*. Edited by Geoffrey Keynes (Oxford University Press 1969), pp. 888, 927, 929.

‖ Desiree Hirst, *Hidden Riches* (London 1964), p. 213.

another world. Blake, who also worked with his hands, saw them as fellow workers. Blake delighted in honest toil and its natural rewards—as opposed to the exploitation and cunning which he obliquely censures in the proverb:

'All wholesome food is caught without a net or a trap.'*

'The question about Blake the man', says T. S. Eliot, 'is the question of the circumstances that concurred to permit . . . honesty in his work . . . The favouring conditions probably include these two: that, being early apprenticed to a manual occupation, he was not compelled to acquire any other education in literature than he wanted, or to acquire it for any other reason than that he wanted it; and that, being a humble engraver, he had no journalistic-social career open to him.

There was, that is to say, nothing to distract him from his interests or to corrupt these interests: neither the ambitions of parents or wife, nor the standards of society, nor the temptations of success. . . .'†

Blake had learned that he who depends on his own 'energy' of body or mind does not dwell on unhappiness, for 'The busy bee has no time for sorrow'.

* *Proverbs of Hell* (K. p. 151).
† T. S. Eliot, *The Sacred Wood* (London 1964), pp. 151–2.

Chapter Two

SONGS OF INNOCENCE AND OF EXPERIENCE

1. THE 'CONTRARY STATES'

Innocence and Experience, the Two Contrary States of the Human Soul, are opposite to each other. The state of Innocence is selfless and the state of Experience selfish, the one wants to please 'All' but the other has a devouring character which seeks to please only itself. But the dialectics of contrariety presented in *The Songs of Innocence* and *Experience* are complex. Innocence and Experience are contraries, but there are contrary states of Innocence and of Experience, manifested within the individual and within society, and exhibiting the contraries of 'Natural Man' and Imagination.*

To begin with, the identity of an individual is determined by the nature of his relationships with others, and in these relationships there are two contrary possibilities. One is that the individual sees another's woe but offers only abstract pity and mercy. The second possibility is that the individual sees another's woe and cannot bear not to be in sorrow too. He sacrifices selfhood by being a 'light' and guide for others. This contrast can be seen in the poem—'A Dream':

'Once a dream did weave a shade
O'er my Angel-guarded bed,
That an Emmet lost its way
Where on grass methought I lay.

Troubled, 'wilder'd, and fo[r]lorn,
Dark, benighted, travel-worn,
Over many a tangled spray,
All heart-broke I heard her say:

* The statement 'Without Contraries there is no progression' in *The Marriage of Heaven and Hell* was written specifically in criticism of Swedenborg's doctrine of 'contraries', and therefore has a different context to that of the *Songs* (see Chapter 3, section 3). It should therefore not be generalized to cover the message of the *Songs*, though they and *The Marriage* do share a basic principle in their social criticism.

"O, my children! do they cry?
"Do they hear their father sigh?
"Now they look abroad to see:
"Now return and weep for me."

Pitying, I drop'd a tear;
But I saw a glow-worm near,
Who replied: "What wailing wight
"Calls the watchman of the night?" '[1]

The passivity and hypocrisy of the father, with his abstract pity and empty sigh, is satirized and contrasted with the 'glow-worm', symbol of true innocence and selflessness who is:

' ". . . set to light the ground,
"While the beetle goes his round:
"Follow now the beetle's hum;
"Little wanderer, hie thee home." '[2]

In the poem the contraries are manifested by the empty sigh of the 'father' on one hand and by the selflessness and love of the 'glow-worm' on the other. These characters represent two contrary types or states of 'innocence'. One is dynamic and active, the other static and passive. The *Songs of Experience* represent the latter. The innocence of Tiriel (George III) and Thel (the priest or abstract religion) is opposed to that of the 'glow-worm' and the 'Clod of Clay'. One is based on selfishness and the other on selflessness. The innocence of King and Priest is contrary to that of Chimney Sweeper. These two opposite 'states' and mentalities are the product of two different social conditions. Because their states of 'innocence' are opposite to each other, their 'experience' is also opposite. The experience of the chimney sweeper is different from that of the child who has a nurse and enjoys comfortable living conditions. Thus *Songs of Innocence* and *Experience* each presents two contrasts, and true innocence is in revolt against the contrary innocence. Blake saw these contrasts within society and in his own imagination.

The innocence and experience of 'Natural Man' is different from that of Imagination. Blake in the *Songs of Innocence* satirizes the passive innocence, the kind of innocence that Swedenborg introduces in his *Heaven and Hell*,[3] or that Blake depicts in *Tiriel* and *Thel*. While satirizing passive innocence Blake introduces his creative and dynamic innocence. In the *Songs of Experience* he satirizes and attacks the experience of passive innocence by introducing the experience of creative innocence. One is the 'experience' of 'Natural Man' which is based on Locke's philosophy of 'experience' and is an outcrop of the existing social system; the other is the 'experience' of social reality by Poetic Genius—Imagination. Locke's philosophy of 'experience' attempts to establish and justify social relationships by stressing the importance of the five senses rather than that of the creative mind and the material conditions in which the five senses work. An experience based on Locke's theory, limited to the five senses and the natural impressions formed by them, sees only limited self. Blake's experience, on the contrary, is unlimited and social, based on human Imagination, the true innocence. His 'London' poem is an example of this experience:

> 'I wander thro each charter'd street,
> Near where the charter'd Thames does flow,
> And mark in every face I meet
> Marks of weakness, marks of woe.'[4]

The experience of true innocence opposes the abstract and limited philosophy of experience. The eyes that hold this social vision are not bound and limited by selfishness. For 'He who sees the Ratio only, sees himself only'.[5]

Blake in the *Songs of Innocence* satirizes the 'innocence' which is based on limited natural memories and which forms the garden and paradise of the reasoning mind. The mind formed by natural impressions is called a 'cave' or 'grave'.[6] Natural impressions enfold the creative mind as linen clothes and coffins enclose the dead. When the mind awakens, it elevates these natural impressions into mental deities. The reasoning mind calls this change the 'last judgment'[7] when 'Natural Man' returns into the 'cave' of his natural impressions. This cycle of generation is dramatized in the poems 'The Little Girl Lost' and 'The Little Girl Found' where the Virgin, like Thel, is surrounded by natural elements such as 'garden', 'desart wild', 'beasts of prey', 'lion', 'leopards' and 'tygers'. Blake, as

B*

true prophet, sees that in future the earth, the material world, will rise and see her 'maker meek', the creative man:

> 'In futurity
> I prophetic see
> That the earth from sleep
> (Grave the sentence deep)
>
> Shall arise and seek
> For her maker meek;
> And the desart wild
> Become a garden mild.'

But false prophecy and passive innocence are still repeating the cycle of their creation. The 'Little Girl' Lyca is lost in the 'desart wild', that is, in natural memories:

> 'In the southern clime,
> Where the summer's prime
> Never fades away,
> Lovely Lyca lay.
>
> Seven summers old
> Lovely Lyca told;
> She had wander'd long
> Hearing wild birds' song.'

The song is the song of natural man who lives under the tree of 'Good' and 'Evil'. The natural impressions, the mother, are the 'summer's prime' which, for the natural man, never 'fades away'. The 'wild birds' of self-pity sing the song of sleep:

> ' "Sweet sleep, come to me
> "Underneath this tree.
> "Do father, mother weep,
> "Where can Lyca sleep?
>
> "Lost in desart wild
> "Is your little child.
> "How can Lyca sleep
> "If her mother weep?
>
> "If her heart does ake
> "Then let Lyca wake;
> "If my mother sleep,
> "Lyca shall not weep.

> "Frowning, frowning night,
> "O'er this desart bright
> "Let thy moon arise
> "While I close my eyes." '

The mother, the symbol of natural and environmental impressions, has a will of her own and controls Lyca, the meek. The natural impressions and the parents have a deep influence on the mind. There is a conflict between this inherited background and individual identity, between Natural Man and Imagination, the false and true prophet. These influences cause guilt feelings and fear in the child and drive her into the sleep of natural impressions:

> 'Sleeping Lyca lay
> While the beasts of prey,
> Come from Caverns deep,
> View'd the maid asleep.'

The 'beasts of prey' are the 'natural' men who attempt to form the mind of a victim according to their bestial desire and limited outlook.

> 'The Kingly lion stood
> And the virgin view'd,
> Then he gambol'd round
> O'er the hallow'd ground.'

The 'Kingly lion', the symbol of individualism and false prophecy, possesses the virgin as its prey. There are also other 'beasts of prey', but the strongest will have the prey first:

> 'Leopards, tygers, play
> Round her as she lay,
> While the lion old
> Bow'd his mane of gold
>
> And her bosom lick,
> And upon her neck
> From his eyes of flame
> Ruby tears there came;

> While the lioness
> Loos'd her slender dress,
> And naked they convey'd
> To caves the sleeping maid.'

The Lion's energy and 'eyes of flame', like the King, springs from its social circumstances and material superiority. The 'lioness' is the priest. King and priest are male and female: 'Nature, Hermaphroditic Priest & King'.[8] The mind of innocent Lyca is enveloped by the natural memories of 'Kingly lion' and 'priestly care'. Thus the 'Little Girl' is lost in the 'wild' forest of natural memories and finally is found by her parents, that is by the regeneration of natural memories.

> 'All the night in woe
> Lyca's parents go
> Over vallies deep,
> While the desarts weep.
>
> Tired and woe-begone,
> Hoarse with making moan,
> Arm in arm seven days
> They trac'd the desert ways.
>
> Seven nights they sleep
> Among shadows deep,
> And dream they see their child
> Starv'd in desert wild.

The child is searching for its lost individuality. It lives in a 'desart wild', the insecure society, where 'shadows' are 'deep' and ways are misleading:

> 'Pale, thro' pathless ways
> The fancied image strays
> Famish'd, weeping, weak,
> With hollow piteous shriek.'

The 'hollow piteous shriek' is from 'Nature's wide womb' where the victim lives in 'unquenchable burnings'.[9] The weak part binds the creative part through self-pity until the weak part is weary and has lost its power of control:

'Rising from unrest,
The trembling woman prest
With feet of weary woe:
She could no further go.

In his arms he bore
Her, arm'd with sorrow sore;
Till before their way
A couching lion lay.'

The 'couching lion' is the ruling social interests and heavy power, which controls both the mind and body of his victims.

'Turning back was vain:
Soon his heavy mane
Bore them to the ground.
Then he stalk'd around,

Smelling to his prey;
But their fears allay
When he licks their hands,
And silent by them stands.'

The lion is a symbol of natural man whose strength springs from his natural existence, as the lion's power is the product of jungle life. His spirit is armed with the vision of the natural impressions which leads him to the 'cave' of self hood, a 'lonely dell', where Lyca, the true 'innocence', 'lies asleep':

'They look upon his eyes
Fill'd with deep surprise,
And wondering behold
A Spirit arm'd in gold.

On his head a crown,
On his shoulders down
Flow'd his golden hair.
Gone was all their care.

"Follow me", he said,
"Weep not for the maid;
"In my palace deep
"Lyca lies asleep."

> Then they followed
> Where the vision led,
> And saw their sleeping child
> Among tygers wild.
>
> To this day they dwell
> In a lonely dell;
> Nor fear the wolvish howl
> Nor the lions' growl.'[10]

Now the world of natural man has been restored and put in order and his last judgment completed. It is also this kind of last judgment and 'innocence' which Blake satirizes in Swedenborg.[11] Lyca loses her way in the chaos of her own natural memories and finally is found by the lion of the jungle. But the lion does not represent true 'innocence'. It is the symbol of individualism, a Tiriel-like character, who is 'an innocent old man' and 'the hypocrite that sometimes roars a dreadful lion'.[12] True 'innocence' sleeps. The parents:

> 'saw their sleeping child
> Among tygers wild.'

It is the jungle-like society which creates jungle beasts. The beast is lower than the human being and searches for its prey. Individualism and selfishness is beastly and non-human. Blake refutes this kind of bestial 'innocence' which is an outcrop of unjust social relationships. 'One Law for the Lion & Ox is Oppression.'[13]

Blake also traces this cycle of natural creation in his poems 'The Little Boy Lost' and 'The Little Boy Found'. Society is insecure where children are dependent only on their parents and the benevolence of God rather than on universal Imagination or energy within man. Man is subject to his own limited background and must cling to it or else be lost.

The 'Little Boy' is taught to look for his father lest he be lost.

> ' "Father! father! where are you going?
> "O do not walk so fast
> "Speak, father, speak to your little boy,
> "Or else I shall be lost." '

There is terror and a deep sense of insecurity in the poem and particularly in the 'natural' boy:

> 'The night was dark, no father was there;
> The child was wet with dew;
> The mire was deep, & the child did weep,
> And away the vapour flew.'[14]

The 'natural' boy is lost and found by his 'mother', that is, the natural background:

> 'The little boy lost in the lonely fen,
> Led by the wand'ring light,
> Began to cry; but God, ever nigh,
> Appear'd like his father in white.
>
> He Kissed the child & by the hand led
> And to his mother brought,
> Who in sorrow pale, thro' the lonely dale,
> Her little boy weeping sought.'[15]

The figure of 'God', like a 'father in white' who 'Kissed the child' satirizes the type of human salvation which the Church promises. The 'little boy' found is not innocent in the true sense of 'innocence'. His creative and true 'innocence' is bound by the limited, natural and passive innocence which is formed by the environment. It is again this kind of false innocence which Blake satirizes in 'Nurse's Song':

> 'When the voices of children are heard on the green
> And laughing is heard on the hill,
> My heart is at rest within my breast
> And everything else is still.'[16]

The satire is social. Blake's target is the social class whose literature is limited to recollection of their own childhood memories. Their 'heart is at rest' while the same memories are repeated. The satire is directed against the limited and exclusive nature of experience rather than against the children. The poet satirizes the exclusive innocence of the few who claim their intellectual superiority and innocence by the recreation of their memories. By this satire he in fact opposes the social condition itself; the gulf between the poor and the rich child.

The experience of the poor child and nurse in the *Songs of Experience* is different from that in the *Songs of Innocence*. In the poems discussed above the true 'innocence' is constricted by the natural memories based on the senses, and in the *Songs of Experience* the true 'innocence' is chained by poverty and the slavery of the Church. In the *Songs of Innocence* the 'little boy' and 'little girl' are lost and also found. But in the *Songs of Experience* a 'little boy' and a 'little girl' are simply lost. They are engulfed in a social condition where an authentic background, a genuine sense of purpose and place, do not exist. Little children are sold to the parish by the poor or employed by the Chimney Sweep. Blake satirizes the father and the priest:

> ' "Nought loves another as itself,
> "Nor venerates another so,
> "Nor is it possible to Thought
> "A greater than itself to know:
>
> "And Father, how can I love you
> "Or any of my brothers more?
> "I love you like the little bird
> "That picks up crumbs around the door."
>
> The Priest sat by and heard the child,
> In trembling zeal he siez'd his hair:
> He led him by his little coat,
> And all admir'd the Priestly care.
>
> And standing on the altar high,
> "Lo! what a fiend is here!" said he,
> "One who sets reason up for judge
> "Of our most holy Mystery."
>
> The weeping child could not be heard,
> The weeping parents wept in vain;
> They strip'd him to his little shirt,
> And bound him in an iron chain;
>
> And burn'd him in a holy place,
> Where many had been burn'd before:
> The weeping parents wept in vain.
> Are such things done on Albion's shore?'[17]

Albion, of course, is Britain. The poem is an image of vindictiveness and hypocrisy where the child, representing honesty, is crushed and condemned by the priest of a deceitful system. Individuality and creative imagination are destroyed. Bitter memories rule imagination rather than the sweet memories of inspiration. The difference between 'Nurse's Song' in *Songs of Innocence* and *of Experience* is the difference of social conditions. In *Innocence* the Nurse's 'heart is at rest' when she hears the voices of children on the green, but in *Experience* the Nurse's 'face turns green and pale' when she hears the voices of children:

> 'When the voices of children are heard on the green
>   And whisp'rings are in the dale,
>   The days of my youth rise fresh in my mind,
>   My face turns green and pale.'

The appearance of unpleasant memories of her own childhood makes the Nurse bitter and resentful towards other children:

> 'Then come home, my children, the sun is gone down,
>   And the dews of night arise;
>   Your spring & your day are wasted in play,
>   And your winter and night in disguise.'[18]

Neither of these two kinds of 'innocence' that we have discussed so far are true 'innocence'. One is founded on the basis of limited natural memories and individualism, the other is lost because of the absence of a genuine background. In other words, neither of them has achieved true freedom of Imagination. One is bound to sensuous existence and the other chained in bodily need. 'Tyger' and 'The Human Abstract' in the *Songs of Experience* are the product of this individualistic 'innocence' which in the end turns against true 'innocence'. 'The Divine Image' in the *Songs of Innocence* revolts against this individualism and selfhood.

'Lamb' and 'Tyger' are two opposing mentalities and social characters. The former is the symbol of humanity and the latter the symbol of bestial existence. The lamb represents selflessness but Tyger represents individualism and selfhood. Blake shows this selfhood in its bestial magnificence and power:

> 'Tyger! Tyger! burning bright
> In the forests of the night,
> What immortal hand or eye
> Could frame thy fearful symmetry?'

The 'forest' is also inhabited by natural man, like Tiriel whose 'fearful symmetry' is framed by mortal impressions which he assumes constitute an 'immortal' world. The poet satirizes the kind of 'immortality' that the natural man possesses. The answer to the question is that no 'immortal hand or eye' in the true sense of the word has framed the 'fearful symmetry' of natural man. The mortal hand and eye of the five senses, the environment, framed the 'fearful symmetry', where the 'unquenchable burnings' consume in a deep world:

> 'In what distant deeps or skies
> Burnt the fire of thine eyes?
> On what wings dare he aspire?
> What the hand dare seize the fire?'

Blake has answered these questions in his definition of Urizen, the 'Natural Man'. The 'fire' is within the selfhood of natural man:

> 'A void immense, wild, dark & deep,
> Where nothing was: Nature's wide womb;'[19]

In the first and second drafts of 'The Tyger' the 'fire' is 'cruel' and Urizenic:

> 'The cruel fire of thine eye?'[20]

The answers to the questions in 'The Tyger' are understood in the context of *Songs of Innocence* and *Experience*—the contrary states. The choice of words in the poem define the self-centred and destructive individualism which has an independent and separate mind and body from others:

> 'And what shoulder, & what art,
> Could twist the sinews of thy heart?
> And when thy heart began to beat,
> What dread hand? & what dread feet?

> What the hammer? what the chain?
> In what furnace was thy brain?
> What the anvil? what dread grasp
> Dare its deadly terrors clasp?'

In the first draft of 'The Tyger' we read the last stanza as follows:

> '[Could fetch it from the furnace deep
> And in thy horrid ribs dare steep
> In the well of sanguine woe?
> In what clay & in what mould
> Were thy eyes of fury roll'd? del.]'[21]

This is the Urizenic character whose dreadful hands, feet and whole organism are products of his binding selfhood, the 'well of sanguine woe' which is 'deadly' and terrifying to others because of its bestial and inhuman relationship. Blake asks similar satirical questions about the creation of Urizen:

> 'Lo, a shadow of horror is risen
> In Eternity! Unknown, unprolific,
> Self-closed, all-repelling: what Demon
> Hath form'd this abominable void,
> This soul-shudd'ring vacuum?'[22]

Urizen and Tyger are fallen men. Both are symbols of energy. Urizen has 'enormous forms of energy' and 'self-begotten armies' but he 'only takes portions of existence and fancies that the whole'.[23] To the eye of natural man this limited energy seems 'great' but to the eye of Imagination it is only a 'portion' of eternity:

> 'The roaring of lions, the howling of wolves, the raging of
> the stormy sea, and the destructive sword, are portions
> of eternity, too great for the eye of man.'[24]

The Tyger is a terrifying beast with the energy of the jungle. Urizen is a social tyrant with devouring power. Both are fallen characters because of their individualistic selfishness which has divided them from others. Thus the answer to the question: did 'he who made the Lamb' make Tyger is negative:

'When the stars threw down their spears,
And water'd heaven with their tears,
Did he smile his work to see?
Did he who made the Lamb make thee?'[25]

The 'Lamb' and 'Tyger' are social beings. Both are prophetic characters but one sacrifices his self-experience and selfhood for others and the other indulges his own limited and selfish interest by turning against others. The power of 'Lamb' springs from his relationship with others, that is, with 'all'. Lamb is making 'all the vales rejoice':

'Little lamb, who made thee?
Dost thou Know who made thee?
Gave thee life, & bid thee feed
By the stream & o'er the mead;
Gave thee clothing of delight,
Softest clothing, wooly, bright;
Gave thee such a tender voice,
Making all the vales rejoice?
    Little Lamb, who made thee?
    Dost thou Know who made thee?

Little Lamb, I'll tell thee,
Little Lamb, I'll tell thee:
He is called by thy name,
For he calls himself a Lamb.
He is meek, & he is mild;
He becomes a little child.
I a child, & thou a lamb,
We are called by his name.
    Little Lamb, God bless thee!
    Little Lamb, God bless thee!'

The Tyger is the product of a jungle-like society where the weak is the prey of the strong and the one who possesses bestial passion becomes the strongest by restraining others. But the Lamb represents a social and human unity, the selfless state of the 'Human Soul', where the 'Ox' does not live under the oppressive laws of the 'Lion'. The poem secularizes divinity and universalizes humanity. The divine and the human are one: 'He becomes a little child.' Man in his creative and selfless state is God. The 'child' in the poem represents true innocence which is selfless, free and universal humanity. Blake, as a true prophet—'I a child'—wants his song to be heard and shared by 'all', 'every child':

> 'Piping down the valleys wild,
> Piping songs of pleasant glee,
> On a cloud I saw a child,
> And he laughing said to me:
>
> "Pipe a song about a Lamb!"
> So I piped with merry chear.
> "Piper, pipe that song again;"
> So I piped: he wept to hear.
>
> "Drop thy pipe, thy happy pipe;
> "Sing thy songs of happy chear:"
> So I sung the same again,
> While he wept with joy to hear.
>
> "Piper, sit thee down and write
> "In a book that all may read."
> So he vanish'd from my sight,
> And I pluck'd a hollow reed,
>
> And I made a rural pen,
> And I stain'd the water clear,
> And I wrote my happy songs
> Every child may joy to hear.'[26]

Imagination which can see all children, and encompass humanity as a whole, is in revolt against limited innocence based on natural memories. The true prophetic voice is heard in the poem. It has a unifying force and universalizes humanity, the power which frightens his enemies and shakes Empires. Blake's characters are identified by means of their relationship with others. They change because their position and the nature of their relationship with others change. Rintrah, for example, is a dual character. One is the prophetic character: 'But Rintrah who is of the reprobate',[27] and another the Urizenic character or false prophet: ' "O Rintrah, furious King!" '[28] The Rintrah who starts 'The Argument' in *The Marriage of Heaven and Hell* is of the latter kind.

Blake saw the original social condition and relationship among men as similar to the one he depicts in 'The Lamb'; but the 'meek' and 'mild' are driven into the wilderness, social division, by selfhood and false prophecy:

> 'Once meek, and in a perilous path,
> The just man kept his course along
> The vale of death.
> Roses are planted where thorns grow,
> And on the barren heath
> Sing the honey bees.
>
> . . . .
>
> Till the villain left the paths of ease,
> To walk in perilous paths, and drive
> The just man into barren climes.'[29]

It is this false prophecy and social relationship which Blake opposes in the *Songs of Experience*. For Blake, poverty is created by man for man. His satire of 'Holy Thursday' in *Innocence* turns to a concise social criticism in *Experience*:

> 'Is this a holy thing to see
> In a rich and fruitful land,
> Babes reduce'd to misery,
> Fed with cold and usurous hand?
>
> Is that trembling cry a song?
> Can it be a song of joy?
> And so many children poor?
> It is a land of poverty!
>
> And their sun does never shine,
> And their fields are bleak & bare,
> And their ways are fill'd with thorns:
> It is eternal winter there.
>
> For where-e'er the sun does shine,
> And where-e'er the rain does fall,
> Babe can never hunger there,
> Nor poverty the mind appall.'

To Blake the sun shines and the rain falls, therefore the cause of poverty must be sought elsewhere. He finds the cause within society.

In 'The Human Abstract' Blake tells us that pity stems from poverty for which 'we' are responsible.

> 'Pity would be no more
> If we did not make somebody Poor;
> And Mercy no more could be
> If all were as happy as we.'[30]

Blake sees evil as existing within society and man. It is the seed of selfishness which is sown and grows in the 'Human Brain' rather than being an innate part of human nature:

> 'The Gods of the earth and sea
> Sought thro' Nature to find this Tree;
> But their search was all in vain:
> There grows one in the Human Brain.'

The 'Contrary States' in the *Songs of Innocence* and *of Experience* are understandable within their own social context. The innocence of Poetic Genius, the 'Human Soul', sees and experiences that those who teach love and regard themselves as guardians and fathers are, in practice, selfish and cruel. When Blake attacks the 'Father' he is attacking the social system and the cultural authority which teach abstract moral laws but in practice are immoral and inhuman in their relationship with others. The true innocence sees that Father, God, Priest and King who are set up as guardians and saviours are, in fact, the causes of evil and human misery. In the *Songs of Innocence* the chimney sweep child is sold by his father:

> 'When my mother died I was very young,
> And my father sold me. . . .'[31]

He cries when his head, 'like a lamb's back', is shaved. His friends quieten him by saying that

> ' "Hush, Tom! never mind it, for when your head's bare
> "You know that the soot cannot spoil your white hair." '

Tom dreams at night that he and all his friends were freed by an Angel:

> 'As Tom was a-sleeping, he had such a sight!
> That thousands of sweepers, Dick, Joe, Ned, & Jack,
> Were all of them lock'd up in coffins of black.
>
> And by came an Angel who had a bright key,
> And he open'd the coffins & set them all free;
> . . . .
> And the Angel told Tom, if he'd be a good boy,
> He'd have God for his father, & never want joy.'

The poet depicts this as typical of the abstract hope and vision that the Church and the ruling interests teach and paint in the mind of a hopeless and wretched people. But in *Songs of Experience*, the experience of Poetic Genius, the true innocence, unveils the deceit and accuses 'God & his Priest & King' for being responsible for this condition:

> 'A little black thing among the snow,
> Crying " 'weep! 'weep!' in notes of woe!
> "Where are thy father & mother? say?"
> "They are both gone up to the church to pray.
> . . . .
> "And because I am happy & dance & sing,
> "They think they have done me no injury,
> "And are gone to praise God & his Priest & King,
> "Who make up a heaven of our misery." '[32]

The difference between these two poems is the contrast between what the ruling interests preach and what they practice. These contrary states are living realities within society in which the poet, the 'Human Soul', exists. True 'innocence' sees that those who wish to lead others are themselves lost in their own passive memories which Blake calls 'bones of the dead'. In 'The Voice of the Ancient Bard' the true innocence revolts against this passive innocence and rationalism:

> 'Youth of delight, come hither,
> And see the opening morn,
> Image of truth new born.
> Doubt is fled & clouds of reason,
> Dark disputes & artful teazing.
> Folly is an endless maze,

Tangled roots perplex her ways.
How many have fallen there!
They stumble all night over bones of the dead,
And feel they know not what but care,
And wish to lead others, when they should be led.'[33]

Here Imagination and true innocence revolt against passive
memories and the selfish innocence of God, Father and King
who 'Know not what but care', which is binding and abstract.
Thus the contraries are within both the *Songs of Innocence* and
the *Songs of Experience*. True innocence revolts against selfish
and passive innocence, and the creative experience of true
innocence rejects the passive experience of rationalism.

Blake's innocence is free from both natural and socially-
imposed imprisonment and subjection. He saves his true
innocence by depending on his own energy and creative mind.
This 'innocence', like 'Imagination', can see clearly and speak
freely. Being conscious of the difference between Imagination
and natural memories, what is eternal and what is changeable,
gives birth to an 'Image of truth'. The vision of this truth
scatters the 'clouds of reason' and destroys 'doubt' and gives
creative energy for the poet. Holding the sight of this 'truth'
the poet attacks the selfish father whose wisdom is based on
'bones of the dead' and whose power is supported by fear and
restraint. In his 'Introduction' to the *Songs of Experience* Blake
calls upon 'Earth' to rise and free itself from the slavery of the
selfish father:

> 'Hear the voice of the Bard!
> Who Present, Past, & Future, sees;
> Whose ears have heard
> The Holy Word
> That walk'd among the ancient trees,
>
> Calling the lapsed Soul,
> . . . .
> O Earth, O Earth, return!
> Arise from out the dewy grass;'

To Blake, the vision of 'truth' is one and the same at 'Present,
Past, & Future'. For 'Error is created. Truth is Eternal.'[34] The
'Earth' rises from the 'slumberous mass' and man breaks the

chains of slavery. The poet's vision is being embodied in *The French Revolution* and his call receives positive response:

> 'Earth rais'd up her head
> From the darkness dread & drear.
> Her light fled,
> Stony dread!
> And her locks cover'd with grey despair,
>
> "Prison'd on wat'ry shore,
> "Starry Jealousy does keep my den:
> "Cold and hoar,
> "Weeping o'er,
> "I hear the Father of the ancient men.
>
> "Selfish father of men!
> "Cruel, jealous, selfish fear!
> "Can delight,
> "Chain'd in night,
> "The virgins of youth and morning bear?
>
> "Does spring hide its joy
> "When buds and blossoms grow?
> "Does the sower
> "Sow by night,
> "Or the plowman in darkness plow?
>
> "Break this heavy chain
> "That does freeze my bones around.
> "Selfish! vain!
> "Eternal bane!
> "That free Love with bondage bound." '[35]

The 'heavy chain' is created by the selfish father who lives at the expense of his children. The father binds the universal love of man by his selfish and limited love which can survive only by the cruelty of the tyrant and the fear of his victims.

The term 'love' in Blake must also be understood within its social context. In his poem 'The Clod & the Pebble' he clearly defines the word.

> ' "Love seeketh not Itself to please,
> "Nor for itself hath any care,
> "But for another gives its ease,
> "And builds a Heaven in Hell's despair."

> So sang a little Clod of Clay
> Trodden with the cattle's feet,
> But a Pebble of the brook
> Warbled out these metres meet:
>
> "Love seeketh only Self to please,
> "To bind another to Its delight,
> "Joys in another's loss of ease,
> "And builds a Hell in Heaven's despite." '

'Love' is identified through its social relationship. The 'love'
which lives as a parasite and reduces the rest of society to
poverty by building a 'Hell in Heaven's despite' is destructive
and inhuman. The limited and devouring nature of this love
is opposed to infinite and universal 'free love'. The selfish father
imprisons 'free Love with bondage bound' and makes the
whole society sick. Parasitic love is like a 'worm' which destroys
the tree of life and stops it from fruition. The poet shows this
kind of 'love' in 'The Sick Rose':

> 'O Rose, thou are sick!
> The invisible worm
> That flies in the night,
> In the howling storm,
>
> Has found out thy bed
> Of crimson joy:
> And his dark secret love
> Does thy life destroy.'[36]

The 'invisible worm' embodies the nature of selfish love which
teaches love and affection but in practice acts against love. It
hides its greed and selfishness under a veil of hypocritical
teaching about 'Pity, Mercy and Love', but in reality secretly
devours within society—'thy bed of crimson joy'—

> 'And the Catterpiller and Fly
> Feed on the Mystery.'[37]

Mystery is the teaching of the priest and the 'Catterpiller' and
'Fly' represent parasitic beings: 'As the catterpiller chooses
the fairest leaves to lay her eggs on, so the priest lays his curse
on the fairest joys.'[38] The Church lives amid material wealth

while teaching spirituality and self-denial. 'The Little Vaga-
bond' asks the Church to share her wealth instead of preaching
about God:

> 'Dear Mother, dear Mother, the Church is cold,
> But the Ale-house is healthy & pleasant & warm;
> Besides I can tell where I am used well,
> Such usage in heaven will never do well.
>
> But if at the Church they would give us some Ale,
> And a pleasant fire our souls to regale,
> We'd sing and we'd pray all the live-long day,
> Nor ever once wish from the Church to stray.'[39]

Blake speaks on behalf of the innocent and expresses their
desire. Thus the *Songs of Innocence* and *of Experience* show two
conflicting loves and interests in which the prophetic character,
Blake, sides with the innocent and meek against the selfish
ruling interests.

The true prophetic character is distinguished from the false
by the nature of his love and his relationship with others.
When Blake attacks God and his Priest and King he attacks
the nature of their relationship with humanity. It is thus a
mistake to interpret Blake's opposition to priest and Church as
opposition to religion. Blake attacks the priest and Church
because they separate religion from humanity and everyday
life on which religion was originally based. He criticizes the
perversion of religion, particularly Christianity, and its use for
limited ends. But true religion must not seek to fulfil its own
interest. For

> ' "Love seeketh not Itself to please,
> "Nor for itself hath any care,
> "But for another gives its ease,
> "And builds a Heaven in Hell's despair." '

This is Blake's religion. Blake opposes passivity and abstraction:
'He who desires but acts not, breeds pestilence.'[40] The one
who teaches love and brotherhood but does not practice them
creates a sick society, where words lose their original meaning
and abstraction takes the place of reality. Blake shows this
contrast in his poems: 'The Divine Image' in the *Songs of*

Innocence and 'The Human Abstract' in the *Songs of Experience*. In the latter poem the Church creates the 'Poor' on the one hand and offers 'Pity' and 'Mercy' on the other. But in the former poem: 'Mercy, Pity, Peace, and Love' are inseparable parts of human society, where

'. . . all must love the human form,
In heathen, turk, or jew;
Where Mercy, Love, & Pity dwell
There God is dwelling too.'

God must be recognized within a social context. In other words the nature of human relationships and conditions determines the existence of God. If the society is selfless, where 'Mercy, Love, & Pity dwell', there 'God is dwelling too'. Thus the abstract and 'heaven dwelling' God, who is out of human experience, is a false God and the negator of Man.

'For Mercy, Pity, Peace, and Love
Is God, our father dear,
And Mercy, Pity, Peace, and Love
Is Man, his child and care.

For Mercy has a human heart,
Pity a human face,
And Love, the human form divine,
And Peace, the human dress.

Then every man, of every clime,
That prays in his distress,
Prays to the human form divine,
Love, Mercy, Pity, Peace.'[41]

Blake universalizes the 'human form divine' and sees God in human unity and selflessness. All 'Religions &, as all similars, have one source. The true Man is the source, he being the Poetic Genius.'[42]

Poetic Genius, the creative energy in man, is the true God who 'only Acts & Is, in existing beings or Men'.[43] But man falls from this creative state when he uses his energy and Poetic Genius for selfish and limited ends, that is, against humanity. Man's individuality is beautiful and Poetic Genius is his strength, but individuality becomes ugly through the drives of individualism, and Poetic Genius loses its creativity and strength by separating itself from universal humanity. 'For let it be remember'd that creation is God descending according to the weakness of man. . . .'[44] The 'lion' and 'tyger' are symbols of energy and beauty but their beautiful individuality becomes ugly when they, like Tiriel, turn their energy against others:

> 'The pride of the peacock is the glory of God.
> The lust of the goat is the bounty of God.
> The wrath of the lion is the wisdom of God.'[45]

Blake, by his references to natural elements and animals, is in fact opposing such rationalist thinkers as Swedenborg who attempted to justify existing social relationships by comparing them with Nature; the animal kingdom, in this scheme, serving as a counterpart of the human. Natural elements and animals of the same or similar species, unlike Tiriel, do not misuse their power or exploit as man does man. 'The apple tree never asks the beech how he shall grow; nor the lion, the horse, how he shall take his prey.'[46]

Energy and material wealth are means, but it depends who and to what purpose the means are used. 'The fox condemns the trap, not himself.'[47] The error is with the user of the means. Greed and selfishness are man's trap. These proverbs are written against Swedenborg who put the blame on the material world, that is, on the means rather than on the users. Swedenborg also condemned the love of woman as sin. Opposing this travesty Blake writes: 'The nakedness of woman is the work of God' but the enslavement of woman by man and the treatment of her as a less intelligent and weak being is not the work of God. It is the work of a satanic system. Repudiating Swedenborg's idea that man is

> 'born to be intellectual, thus to think from intellect, but the woman is born to be voluntary'.[48]

Blake in this specific context satirically retorts, 'Let man wear the fell of the lion, woman the fleece of the sheep'.[49] Opposing the priest's passive life, Blake suggests that if man is born to be intellectual and has a stronger body, then he ought to be more active in practical life. The appreciation of the material world and the active life is better than passive and negative 'instructions'.[50] For 'The tygers of wrath are wiser than the horses of instruction'.[51] Blake repudiates both the negative attitude to the material world and subjection to it which lead to selfish individualism and division from others.

In the *Songs of Experience* the priest negates the love of self and of the world:

'I went to the Garden of Love,
And saw what I never had seen:
A Chapel was built in the midst,
Where I used to play on the green.

And the gates of this Chapel were shut,
And "Thou shalt not" writ over the door;
So I turn'd to the Garden of Love
That so many sweet flowers bore;

And I saw it was filled with graves,
And tomb-stones where flowers should be;
And Priests in black gowns were walking their rounds,
And binding with briars my joys & desires.'[52]

The priest by his negative instruction restrains joys and desires in others. By doing this he kills the soul and love, and turns human life into a graveyard where 'flowers should be'. By the negation of 'joys' and 'desires' the priest also negates Poetic Genius which without full use of the material world cannot develop into the 'Garden of Love': for 'Energy is the only life, and is from the Body; and Reason is the bound or outward circumference of Energy.'[53] Imagination falls either by subjection to the five senses or negation of them by poverty.

Blake discusses this in *Visions of the Daughters of Albion* and other Prophetical works. Freedom of the Imagination depends on the freedom of the five senses from 'slavery' and 'fear'. This slavery also characterizes the educational system of the time. The child in 'The School Boy' asks:

'How can the bird that is born for joy
Sit in a cage and sing?
How can a child, when fears annoy,
But drop his tender wing,
And forget his youthful spring?'[54]

The creative mind of the child, like 'The Fly', is 'brushed away' by 'some blind' and 'thoughtless hand', the natural man.[55] The voice of true 'innocence' is being heard all through the Prophetical works where Imagination is struggling for freedom.

2. IMAGINATION IN REVOLT

'Error is Created. Truth is Eternal', writes Blake in *A Vision of the Last Judgment*.[56] Error is a product of man in his social relationships with others. Truth and falsehood do not exist independently. 'There is not an Error but it has a Man for its . . . Agent, that is, it is a Man. There is not a Truth but it has also a Man. Good & Evil are Qualities in Every Man, . . .'[57] Truth and falsehood are qualities recognized through relationships with others. For they are human qualities and are opposite to each other. Though they act and counteract in complex ways, man is identified by one quality or the other: 'Man is a twofold being, one part capable of evil & the other capable of good; . . . both evil & good cannot exist in a simple being, for thus 2 contraries would spring from one essence, which is impossible. . . .'[58]

In order to understand the nature of the conflict between true man and false man we need to discover accurately what Blake means by the terms. Imagination, or true man, and false man are both within society. They represent two opposite mentalities, outlooks and interests. Imagination is creative man; false man is passive and negative. Passivity is the fallen state of man or mind which is limited and inhuman. Imagination is unlimited, social and humane. Blake's idea of Vision or Imagination, which is expressed in a wide variety of complex ways, is always rooted in his everyday experience of social life. He does not believe in a metaphysical source of Vision or Imagination. In Jerusalem he writes: 'My Streets are my Ideas of Imagination.'[59]

Imagination is creative power operating in a human and practical way. By this creative power man constructs and changes the surface of the earth. He removes obstacles, diverts rivers and harnesses Nature by his creativity. Opposing

Swedenborg's passivity and limited view of man, Blake writes in *The Marriage of Heaven and Hell*: 'All poets believe that . . . in ages of imagination . . . firm persuasion removed mountains'.[60] The term 'mountain' can be interpreted as a symbol of both a physical and a mental obstacle. As energetic men remove physical obstacles so creative minds remove mental bonds. In a fallen society Imagination is bound physically and spiritually. Law binds physically and religion binds spiritually. By the 'ages of imagination' Blake means the human societies which were not yet divided into classes; societies in which conventional systems were not yet created. Such systems and limiting laws were created to enslave Imagination or true Man:

> 'a system was formed, which some took advantage of, &
> enslav'd the vulgar by attempting to realize or abstract
> the mental deities from their objects: thus began Priest-
> hood;
> Choosing forms of worship from poetic tales.
> And at length they pronounc'd that the Gods had order'd
> such things.
> Thus men forgot that All deities reside in the human
> breast.'[61]

For Blake, creative power is a form of Godhead opposite to the passive and abstract God of priestcraft. 'Some will say: "Is not God alone the Prolific?" I answer: "God only Acts & Is, in Existing beings or Men." '[62] Passive man believes in an abstract God who is correspondingly passive and exterior to human experience. Blake terms this passive God Urizen who has built his own world on his limited impressions so that Imagination or true Man has been imprisoned by false man and his creative mind buried under abstract teachings through many centuries:

> ' ". . . Gods combine against Man, setting their dominion
> above
> "The human form Divine, Thrown down from their high
> station
> "In the Eternal heavens of Human [Thought del.]
> Imagination, buried beneath
> "In dark Oblivion, with incessant pangs, ages on
> ages, . . ." '[63]

Imagination is the 'Human form Divine'. Divinity should be sought in human relationships and unity, whereas the God of the priest divides man from man and divinity from humanity: 'Imagination is the Divine Body in Every Man.' 'The All in Man.'[64] Blake expresses it in his *Annotations to Berkeley's 'Siris'*. Imagination represents true Man or true God but Urizen represents false Man or false God. In Blake Imagination is in revolt against false Man and his systems. This opposition and revolt takes place within society where falsehood takes its existence. The struggle between true Man and false Man is both mental and social. The mental conflict is the articulation of social conflict.

This social and intellectual strife is manifested throughout Blake's writings. Blake was a rebel who kept to his Imagination and to the principle that: 'As all men are alike (tho' infinitely various), So all Religions &, as all similars, have one source. The true Man is the source, he being the Poetic Genius.'[65]

Further examination of how this conflict is portrayed in Blake's writings reveals his originality, honesty and greatness. It is perhaps the social vision of Blake and his honesty as a true poet which still attracts the imagination of younger generations all over the world. All men for Blake are potentially creative and have imaginative power. In opposition to Sir Joshua Reynolds he writes: 'The Man who says that the Genius is not born, but Taught—Is a Knave. . . Man is Born Like a Garden ready Planted & Sown. This World is too poor to produce one Seed.'[66] But the power of imagination in man is perverted by abstract teachings which see only the 'ratio':

'He who sees the Infinite in all things, sees God. He who sees the Ratio only, sees himself only.'[67]

Blake's greatness springs from his ability to see the infinite humanity as a whole against limited and fragmentary selfhood. 'One Power alone makes a Poet: Imagination, The Divine Vision'[68] he writes in his *Annotations to 'Poems' by William Wordsworth*. Selfhood, formed by natural impressions and limiting environment, which Blake calls 'Natural Man', is the negation of Imagination. 'There is no such Thing as Natural Piety Because The Natural Man is at Enmity with God.'[69] Self interest and natural impressions limit human

imagination and are at enmity with Imagination. 'Natural
Objects always did & now do weaken, deaden & obliterate
Imagination in Me. Wordsworth must Know that what he
Writes Valuable is Not to be found in Nature.'[70] Poetic Genius
gives life and meaning to Nature because 'Where man is not,
nature is barren'.[71] Natural objects as well as material wealth
should support Imagination so that man can be free and
creative. But when Nature and material wealth become ends
rather than means then Imagination becomes fragmented and
dies as a being subject to the non-human. 'The Natural Body
is an Obstruction to the Soul or Spiritual Body.'[72] Thus the
terms 'Infinite' and 'Ratio' or 'Imagination' and 'Natural Man'
in Blake must be studied in their human and social contexts.

'The wise man falleth 7 times in a day, and riseth again,'[73]

but 'Natural Man' is fallen man. He has fallen from Imagina-
tion, in Blake a condition of fatality, into his constricting
'Natural' memories which have encircled him like a shell and
divided him from society. Natural man is guided by a self-
interest opposed to organic community, the wider humanity
embraced by Blake's concept of 'Imagination'. Thus a miser
is conditioned by the perspectives of particular circumstances.
'I know', writes Blake in a letter to Dr. Trusler (August 23,
1799), 'that This World Is a World of imagination & Vision.
I see Every thing I paint In This World, but Every body does
not see alike. To the Eyes of a Miser a Guinea is more beautiful
than the Sun, & a bag worn with the use of Money has more
beautiful proportions than a Vine filled with Grapes. . . . As a
man is, So he Sees. As the Eye is formed, such are its Powers.'[74]
The miser has destroyed true Man in himself and is destroying
it in others.

Passivity and limited interest, then, are evil. Desire and will
also become evil when they turn against others. Opposing
Swedenborg's doctrine of free will maintained by the 'Angels'
in 'Heaven' to restrain the 'Devils' in 'Hell', Blake writes in
The Marriage of Heaven and Hell:

> 'Those who restrain desire, do so because theirs is weak
> enough to be restrained; and the restrainer or reason
> usurps its place & governs the unwilling.'[75]

False or weak men negate and restrain Imagination in them-
selves and others. They attempt to reduce the creativity of
mind by fragmentation and the establishing of systems. They
petrify 'all the Human Imagination into rock & sand',[76] the
fixed and the fragmentary. The 'cliffs of Memory and Reason-
ing; it is a barren Rock: it is also called The Barren Waste of
Locke and Newton'.[77] Thus Blake attacked Locke and Newton
because their ideas supported the existing established system.
Locke's concept of mind as *tabula rasa* and Newton's concept
of a mechanical universe served to suppress creative Imagina-
tion. Attacking Reynolds also on this principle Blake writes:

> 'Here is a Plain Confession that he Thinks Mind & Imagin-
> ation not to be above the Mortal & Perishing Nature.
> Such is the End of Epicurean or Newtonian Philosophy;
> it is Atheism.'[78]

Atheism here is the denial of human creative power, not the
denial of an abstract God.

Blake sees the same pattern of Imagination in all men—the
Human mind animating the objects of its environment. It is
attracted and attached to them. 'The ancient Poets animated
all sensible objects with Gods or Geniuses, calling them by the
names and adorning them with the properties of woods, rivers,
mountains, lakes, cities, nations, and whatever their enlarged
& numerous senses could perceive....'[79] It is, then, the creative
mind which informs all sensible objects by giving them names
and placing them under 'mental deity'. This creation is
peculiar to humanity regardless of their race and place. Blake,
we can see, uncompromisingly secularises deity and so uni-
versalises man. And by extending his own vision to *Paradise
Lost* he is able to write:

> 'The reason Milton wrote in fetters when he wrote of
> Angels & God, and at liberty when of Devils & Hell, is
> because he was a true Poet and of the Devil's party
> without knowing it.'[80]

Because Imagination puts human values above all abstract
moral laws it is regarded as a dangerous weapon against the
ruling interest. So 'The idiot Reasoner laughs at the Man of
Imagination'.[81]

Imagination is human identity, conceived of as an equalizing universality. Conversely, natural impressions formed by the five senses are like garments, cloaking and constricting human Imagination. When man is identified by his clothes, by natural impressions of a separable exterior rather than by his creative Imagination, then human identity becomes fetishized, and its wholeness of vision fragmentary. Thus true Man is identified by a false personality or individuality. False individualism is a fixed state whereas true individuality or Imagination is a dynamic combination. Blake consistently opposes in his poetry the social system which conditions and forms minds under the banner of 'individual freedom'. He writes:

> ' "We are not Individuals but States, Combinations of Individuals.
> "We were Angels of the Divine Presence, & were Druids in Annandale,
> "Compell'd to combine into Form by Satan, the Spectre of Albion,
> "Who made himself a God & destroyed the Human Form Divine.
> "But the Divine Humanity & Mercy gave us a Human Form
> "Because we were combin'd in Freedom & holy Brotherhood,
> "While those combin'd by Satan's Tyranny, first in the blood of War
> "And Sacrifice & next in Chains of imprisonment, are Shapeless Rocks
> "Retaining only Satan's Mathematic Holiness, Length, Bredth & Highth,
> "Calling the Human Imagination, which is the Divine Vision & Fruition
> "In which Man liveth eternally, madness & blasphemy against
> "Its own Qualities, which are Servants of Humanity, not Gods or Lords.
> "Distinguish therefore States from Individuals in those States.
> "States Change, but Individual Identities never change nor cease." '[82]

Individualism is different from individuality. Individualism is based on selfhood and division from others. For Blake, humanity, in ancient societies such as that of the Druids, were united in brotherhood and a freedom of Imagination. But Satan, the symbol of selfhood, divided humanity. Man was reduced from Imagination, the Combination of creative states, into a fixed state of fragmented 'individuals', the 'Shapeless Rocks'. Thus the 'Spectre of Albion', the 'Human abstract', has usurped the place of the 'Human Form Divine'.

Individual identity must be Imagination rather than a fragmented state. Satan as the symbol of selfhood and tyranny in society reduces Human Imagination to a limited and fixed state by fear of punishment, starvation and war. For 'Fear & Hope are—Vision'.[83] Satan has a fixed and limited mentality and attempts to form other minds accordingly. He has made himself a 'God & destroyed the Human Form Divine', which is brotherhood and true freedom. The individual freedom based on selfhood is not true freedom, it is self-imprisonment:

'If the many become the same as the few when possess'd,
More! More! is the cry of a mistaken soul; less than All
cannot satisfy Man.'[84]

Satan has a mistaken soul and possesses a kind of freedom which seeks only to please itself and bind the rest of society both economically, spiritually and intellectually. This is a devouring freedom, a devouring selfhood which creates war and tyranny, for 'More! More! is the cry of a mistaken soul'. Satan's slogan for individual freedom is in fact an excuse for his self-interest which divides him from the rest of humanity.

Imagination on the other hand seeks individual freedom within social and human freedom. One cannot be free if 'All' are not free: For 'less than All cannot satisfy Man'.[85] Freedom exists on a practical level within society. 'Liberality! we want not Liberality. We want a Fair Price & Proportionate Value & a General Demand for Art.'[86] Satirizing Satanic laws Blake writes:

'Lawful Bread, Bought with Lawful Money, & a Lawful Heaven, seen thro' a Lawful Telescope, by means of Lawful Window Light! The Holy Ghost, & whatever cannot be Taxed, is Unlawful & Witchcraft.

Spirits are Lawful, but not Ghosts; especially Royal Gin is Lawful Spirit [real del.] No Smuggling real British Spirit & Truth!

Give us the Bread that is our due & Right, by taking away Money, or a Price, or Tax upon what is Common to all in thy Kingdom. . . .

Leave us not in Parsimony, Satan's Kingdom . . . ; liberate us from the Natural Man.'[87]

It goes without saying that the Satan characterized above has nothing in common with Blake's use of Milton's Satan in *Paradise Lost* as a symbol of dynamic energy. Milton's God is Blake's Satan. In 'The Book of Job', writes Blake in *The Marriage of Heaven and Hell*, 'Milton's Messiah is call'd Satan.'[88] The drift of this freedom is selfless, prolific and fruitful. It seeks the interest of all human beings. Imagination revolts against the Satanic selfhood. It threatens Satan's limited interest. For this reason Satan suppresses Imagination, calling it 'madness'.

Blake believes that Imagination is dynamic, a creative energy which never changes. Environments and social conditions can change. It is, as we have seen, the social condition of a Miser which developes his miserliness, not some innate quality. 'Every Harlot was once a Virgin: every Criminal an Infant Love.'[89] The Human Condition compels him to be what he was not. This condition perverts his Imagination and cripples his humanity. Man, for Blake, is born to love and create but he is taught to hate and destroy. Crime is the result of perverted love, and such love, taught under the name of 'freedom', is not in fact free. Thus Blake locates evil within society and establishes his poetry within the same context.

Human nature, contrary to conventional teachings, is not evil for him. Evil is created and awakened by the exploiters of passivity and weakness in society. Human nature or Imagination is originally creative. Swedenborg states that

'. . . if he [the reader] be one of a sincere and humble Mind . . . his Humility and Sincerity will teach him, that Nothing doth in General so contradict Man's natural and favourite Opinions as Truth, . . .'

Blake comments: 'Lies & Priestcraft. Truth is Nature.'[90]

Imagination is the Human Nature which is destroyed by being reduced to a limited and selfish level. Blake calls this level 'Natural Man' whose mind is formed solely by his natural, sensuous impressions. But the human mind is originally prolific and dynamic: 'I always thought', writes Blake in his *Annotations to Reynolds*, 'that the Human Mind was the most Prolific of All Things & Inexhaustible.'[91] Blake is convinced that his philosophy of Imagination possesses a self-evident truth:

> "Judge then of thy Own Self: thy Eternal Lineaments explore,
> "What is Eternal & what Changeable, & what Anni-hilable.
> "The Imagination is not a State: it is the Human Existence itself.
> "Affection or Love becomes a State when divided from Imagination.
> "The Memory is a State always, & the Reason is a State
> "Created to be Annihilated & a new Ratio Created.
> "Whatever can be Created can be Annihilated: Forms cannot:
> "The Oak is cut down by the Ax, the Lamb falls by the Knife,
> "But their Forms Eternal Exist For-ever." '[92]

Here Blake shows the creative and dialectical nature of the Human Imagination. It is a dynamic energy which cannot be reduced to a fixed state. 'Memory is a State always'—but Imagination continually annihilates a state to recreate another. When the states of love, affection, memory and Reason are divided from Imagination they become negations of it. Imagination, as the eternal Human identity, never dies though temporarily suppressed.

The dynamic or revolutionary energy of Imagination is essentially derived from its selflessness and love of Man. It is this creative or selfless energy which rises continuously in Blake against selfhood or established systems:

> ' "To cast off the rotten rags of Memory by Inspiration,
> "To cast off Bacon, Locke & Newton from Albion's covering,

"To take off his filthy garments & clothe him with
    Imagination,
"To cast aside from Poetry all that is not Inspiration." '[93]

Blake turns against those who base their knowledge and
superiority on their own natural impressions formed by the
five senses. He terms these natural impressions 'filthy gar-
ments'. Although Blake recognizes the importance of the
material world, 'Energy is the only life, and is from the
Body',[94] yet he attacks and revolts against individualistic
materialism which enslaves and suppresses Imagination in
others. The material world is beautiful but must serve as a
means and be a servant of humanity. Once the artist treats
Nature as an end rather than a means for his art then he
becomes a mere copier or slave of something less than human.
Blake criticizes passive artists in his *Public Address*:

'Men think they can Copy Nature as Correctly as I copy
Imagination; this they will find Impossible, & all the
Copies or Pretended Copiers of Nature, from Rembrandt
to Reynolds, Prove that Nature becomes [tame del.] to its
Victim nothing but Blots & Blurs. Why are Copiers of
Nature Incorrect, while Copiers of Imagination are
Correct? this is manifest to all.'[95]

He continues:

'To Imitate I abhor. I obstinately adhere to the true Style
of Art such as Michael Angelo, Rafael, . . . not of Imita-
tion. Imagination is My World; this world of Dross is
beneath my Notice & beneath the Notice of the Public.'[96]

Blake's art was also linked with his social and human experience
since 'The Whole Business of Man Is The Arts, & All Things
Common. No Secrecy in Art.'[97]

'One power alone makes a Poet: Imagination.' This is, as I
have pointed out before, a concise definition of Blake's idea of
a poet. Description of personal or inherited memories which
cannot be shared by all are not the work of a true poet: 'A
work of Genius is a Work "Not to be obtain'd by the Invoca-
tion of Memory".'[98] The true poet stresses the importance of
human creativity rather than natural and limited memories.

c*

He inspires others by his freedom from subjection to what is limited and changeable or what is non-human. This inspiration is not a fiction or an abstract idea but practical and within the human experience of others.

> 'Vision or Imagination is a Representation of what Eternally Exists, Really & Unchangeably. Fable or Allegory is Form'd by the daughters of Memory. Imagination is surrounded by the daughters of Inspiration, who in the aggregate are call'd Jerusalem.'[99]

'Jerusalem' is a social symbol of human unity and freedom. It is 'called Liberty among the Children of Albion'.[100] The 'daughters of Memory', the limited natural impressions, divide man from his fellows but Imagination unites both body and mind:

> '. . . Albion fell down, a Rocky fragment from Eternity hurl'd
> By his own Spectre, who is the Reasoning Power in every Man,
> Into his own Chaos, which is the Memory between Man and Man.'[101]

A poet who is occupied with his own limited memory is not really free, that is, Imagination is being governed by his selfhood. In his *Annotations to 'Poems' by William Wordsworth* Blake writes:

> 'I see in Wordsworth the Natural Man rising up against the Spiritual Man Continually, & then he is No Poet but a Heathen Philosopher at Enmity against all true Poetry or Inspiration.'[102]

The greatness of a poet depends on how far he is able to see the whole by freeing his Imagination from personal and limited attachments to sources other than his own energy. Blake was able to keep his Imagination free by being dependent on his own energy, for he believed that 'Corporal Friends are Spiritual Enemies'.[103]

The Poet sees reality and what really exists. He derives his energy of Imagination from that reality. This reality can be Nature or society. He is conscious of two realities in society, one of which is limited and selfish and the other unlimited and selfless. Blake sees society as a whole. His *Songs of Innocence* and *of Experience* and, indeed, all of his works are the product of his conscious Imagination. He is deeply aware of what he writes and he is dedicated to that. Repudiating Plato's idea of poets and prophets Blake remarks: 'Plato has made Socrates say that Poets & Prophets do not know or Understand what they write or Utter; This is a most Pernicious Falsehood. If they do not, pray is an inferior kind to be call'd Knowing? Plato confutes himself.' The poet is aware of past, present and future. He sees the work of Imagination all through history, where 'Man Passes on, but States remain for Ever'.[104] The 'Artist', writes Blake in *A Descriptive Catalogue*, 'having been taken in vision into the ancient republics, monarchies, and patriarchates of Asia, has seen those wonderful originals called in the Sacred Scriptures'. The artist is Blake himself. His opposition to Greek art and poetry is based on his principle of Imagination. He recognized that most of the works of Greek artists were copies 'from greater works of the Asiatic Patriarchs. The Greek Muses are daughters of Mnemosyne, or Memory, and not of Inspiration or Imagination.'[105]

Man is the creator of Nature. He adorns the favourable elements and despises the unfavourable. Nature plays an important role in human life and is within its existence, it is part of Man. In *Poetical Sketches* Blake's poems 'To Spring', 'To Summer', 'To Autumn', 'To Winter', 'To the Evening Star' and 'To Morning', for example, are the work of Imagination. It is the creative Imagination which animates and gives identity to Nature:

> 'O Thou with dewy locks, who lookest down
> Thro' the clear windows of the morning, turn
> Thine angel eyes upon our western isle,
> Which in full choir hails thy approach, O Spring!'

Spring is made to look and turn her eyes upon the island. Hills tell each other the news of Spring:

> 'The hills tell each other, and the list'ning
> Vallies hear; all our longing eyes are turned
> Up to thy bright pavillions: issue forth,
> And let thy holy feet visit our clime.'[106]

Summer comes with 'ruddy limbs' and 'flourishing hair', and is invited to 'sit down . . . beside a river clear', throw his 'silk draperies off' and 'rush into the stream'. The sun is in the palm of the poet and he creates it according to his inspiration:

> 'O thou, who passest thro' our vallies in
> Thy strength, curb thy fierce steeds, allay the heat
> That flames from their large nostrils! thou, O Summer,
> Oft pitched'st here thy golden tent, and oft
> Beneath our oaks hast slept, while we beheld
> With joy thy ruddy limbs and flourishing hair.
> . . . .
> Sit down, and in our mossy vallies, on
> Some bank beside a river clear, throw thy
> Silk draperies off, and rush into the stream:
> Our vallies love the Summer in his pride.'[107]

Autumn is 'laden with fruits', which inspires the poet since 'to the Eyes of the Man of Imagination, Nature is Imagination itself'.[108] Blake can scarcely be said to have been a naturalistic poet at the beginning of his creative life, and to have changed into a social and prophetical one later. This assumption is erroneous and contrary to the poet's principle of 'Poetic Genius': 'Opinion is one Thing. Principle another', writes Blake in his *Annotation to Watson*: the 'Poetic Genius' is principle and 'No Man can change his Principles'. The poet who writes the Prophetical works is the same one who writes the *Poetical Sketches* though in different contexts. Blake's Imagination does not change but the states or circumstances in which he lived and wrote change and also alter his language. Studying his language and symbols independently or divorced from his Imagination is in fact setting fragmentary parts against the whole, the created against the creator—Blake. Thus his works must be seen and studied as a whole, as a work of Imagination—the 'Poetic Genius'.

The poet is inspired by his environment. He creates the fields that he roams and the people with whom he lives and loves. The material of Blake's poetry is derived from people, their joys and griefs. The mother who is feeding her young, the children who laugh and dance, the old villagers who meet and watch children, and the love of the 'black ey'd maid', all inspire Imagination:

> 'Love and harmony combine,
> And around our souls intwine,
> . . . .
> There she sits and feeds her young,
> Sweet I hear her mournful song;
> And thy lovely leaves among,
> There is love: I hear his tongue.'[109]

Inspired by the folk's love Blake writes:

> 'I love the jocund dance,
>   The softly-breathing song,
> Where innocent eyes do glance,
>   And where lisps the maiden's tongue.
> . . . .
> I love the oaken seat,
>   Beneath the oaken tree,
> Where all the old villagers meet,
>   And laugh our sports to see.
>
> I love our neighbours all,
>   But, Kitty, I better love thee;
> And love them I ever shall;
>   But thou art all to me.'[110]

Or the love of 'black-ey'd maid' inspires his song:

> 'Fresh from the dewy hill, the merry year
> Smiles on my head, and mounts his flaming car;
> Round my young brows the laurel wreathes a shade,
> And rising glories beam around my head.
>
> My feet are wing'd, while o'er the dewy lawn
> I meet my maiden, risen like the morn:
> Oh bless those holy feet, like angels' feet;
> Oh bless those limbs, beaming with heav'nly light!
>
> Like as an angel glitt'ring in the sky
> In times of innocence and holy joy;
> The joyful shepherd stops his grateful song
> To hear the music of an angel's tongue.

So when she speaks, the voice of Heaven I hear:
So when we walk, nothing impure comes near;
Each field seems Eden, and each calm retreat;
Each village seems the haunt of holy feet.

But that sweet village, where my black-ey'd maid
Closes her eyes in sleep beneath night's shade,
Whene'er I enter, more than mortal fire
Burns in my soul, and does my song inspire.'[111]

The poem is Vision or Imagination of what really exists. The
song is fresh and the sound is free. The inspiration of the poet
is derived from reality and his social experience. The poem is
real because the poet recreates what he sees, feels and reacts to,
which can be shared by all. His song is inspired while his
maiden is happy and joyful, and disappointed when she is
unhappy and full of tears:

'When early morn walks forth in sober grey,
Then to my black ey'd maid I haste away;
When evening sits beneath her dusky bow'r,
And gently sighs away the silent hour,
The village bell alarms, away I go,
And the vale darkens at my pensive woe.

To that sweet village, where my black ey'd maid
Doth drop a tear beneath the silent shade,
I turn my eyes; and, pensive as I go,
Curse my black stars, and bless my pleasing woe.'

The language of Imagination is dialectical. It is attracted to
love or joy and is repelled by woe and passivity. This conscious-
ness is indeed peculiar to 'Poetic Genius' in Man. It is this
power of consciousness which gives freedom of sound and
melody to the Muses. Once this creative power is limited and
abstracted from the reality of Imagination then sound becomes
forced and melody ceases. In *Poetical Sketches* Imagination is
in revolt against the established poetical and literary practice,
where the 'sound, is forc'd', the notes are few'. In his poem 'To
The Muses' Blake writes:

'Whether on Ida's shady brow,
    Or in the chambers of the East,
The chambers of the sun, that now
    From ancient melody have ceas'd;

Whether in Heav'n ye wander fair,
    Or the green corners of the earth,
Or the blue regions of the air,
    Where the melodious winds have birth;

Whether on chrystal rocks ye rove,
    Beneath the bosom of the sea
Wand'ring in many a coral grove,
    Fair Nine, forsaking Poetry!

How have you left the ancient love
    That bards of old enjoy'd in you!
The languid strings do scarcely move!
    The sound is forc'd, the notes are few!'[112]

In the age of imagination poets 'animated all sensible objects with God or Geniuses, calling them by the names . . . Till a system was formed' which abstracted the 'mental deities from their objects'. This happened in religion, philosophy, art and literary practice. The mental deities were divided and abstracted from their contexts. The Natural objects like woods, rivers, mountains, lakes, cities, sun, moon and stars inspired the poetic Imagination. But once Imagination is divorced from reality it loses its creative power and thus loses poetry. As the sun rises upon the earth with joy and melody so Imagination rises and is delighted by its environment. Imagination like the sun receives its energy and enjoyment from the world. But Imagination is divided from its context and poetry is reduced to deism and an abstract mental practice. Thus Imagination has lost its energy and inspiration, the main source of poetry.

'The chambers of the sun, that now
    From antient melody have ceas'd;
. . . .
The languished strings do scarcely move!
    The sound is forc'd, the notes are few!'

For Blake literary practice corresponds to the social system. In a society where the people are divided by poverty and riches, and governed by tyranny and enslaved, Imagination cannot exist freely. In Blake the imagination which revolts against abstract literary practices also opposes the social system which fosters these practices. In 'Gwin' he writes:

> 'Come, Kings, and listen to my song:
>   When Gwin, the son of Nore,
> Over the nations of the North
>   His cruel sceptre bore,
>
> The Nobles of the land did feed
>   Upon the hungry Poor;
> They tear the poor man's lamb, and drive
>   The needy from their door!
>
> "The land is desolate; our wives
> "And children cry for bread;
> "Arise, and pull the tyrant down!
> "Let Gwin be humbled!" '[113]

This poem offers a social history. The poetry has risen in defence of the 'Poetic Genius' in Man which is being destroyed by poverty and tyranny.

'The Arts & Sciences', writes Blake in his *Annotation to Reynolds*, 'are the Destruction of Tyrannies or Bad Governments. Why should A Good Government endeavour to Depress what is its Chief & only Support?'[114]

Blake considered that men share one common principle, the 'Poetic Genius', but do not have equal opportunities or favourable conditions in which to develop it. The dialectical creativity of Imagination is weakened by two strong social forces, one priestcraft and the other law. The priest and King complement each other. One teaches virginity and the other rapes. Religion forbids love of the world and instead teaches spirituality on the basis of self-denial, while the King devours and accumulates wealth. Tiriel and Thel represent two mentalities. Tiriel is the symbol of the King (George III) and Thel is the symbol of priestcraft. Tiriel has three characteristics, 'Hypocrisy, the idiot's wisdom & the wise man's folly'.[115]

Tiriel accuses his sons and lives on the punishment and death of others:

> ' "Accursed race of Tiriel! behold your [aged del.] father;
> "Come forth & look on her that bore you! come, you
>   accursed sons!
> "In my weak . . . arms I here have borne your dying
>   mother.
> Come forth, sons of the Curse, come forth! see the death
>   of Myratana!" '

But his sons revolt against their father. The eldest son of Tiriel raises his 'mighty voice':

> ' "Old man! unworthy to be call'd the father of Tiriel's
>   race!
> "For every one of those thy wrinkles, each of those grey
>   hairs
> "Are cruel as death & as obdurate as the devouring pit!
> "Why should thy sons care for thy curses, thou accursed
>   man?
> Were we not slaves till we rebel'd? Who cares for
>   Tiriel's curse?
> His blessing was a cruel curse. His curse may be a
>   blessing." '[116]

Tiriel is an aged man but Thel is a young virgin. Both have escaped into the 'forest' of passive natural memories. Thel refuses self-sacrifice. Although surrounded by natural beauties she cannot appreciate them nor has she any use for others. The 'Clod of Clay', the symbol of humility and selflessness, feeds the weak worm; but Thel, though teaching 'wisdom' and self-denial, considers only herself and lives amid 'gold' and 'silver'. For Blake wisdom cannot be found in selfish materialism:

> 'Does the Eagle know what is in the pit?
> Or wilt thou go ask the Mole?
> Can Wisdom be put in a silver rod?
> Or Love in a golden bowl?'[117]

Acquisitiveness blinds the eyes of Imagination. The King and priest justify their 'wisdom' and spiritual superiority by material wealth. But human experience and wisdom are above and distinct from passivity and selfhood:

> 'What is the price of Experience? do men buy it for a song?
> Or wisdom for a dance in the street? No, it is bought with
>   the price.
> Of all that a man hath, his house, his wife, his children.
> Wisdom is sold in the desolate market where none come
>   to buy,
> And in the wither'd field the farmer plows for bread in
>   vain.'[118]

Tiriel, *The Book of Thel*, *An Island In The Moon* and indeed *Poetical Sketches*, like Blake's later works, oppose and satirize the existing social and philosophical system. Blake's satire is powerful and complicated but the complication is created within society. Terms such as equality, freedom, love, innocence, etc. are perverted and have thus lost their original meaning. This perversion is, in fact, deliberate. Equality has become mechanical by adapting the Newtonian view of social relationships.

In *An Island In The Moon*, one of his great satirical works, Blake opposes abstract philosophical systems which are divorced from reality. 'The three Philosophers sat together thinking of nothing.'[119] Quid, the Cynic who is one of these three philosophers, asks the Obtuse Angle, who is perhaps Blake, for a song. The Angle, 'wiping his face & looking on the corner of the ceiling', sings:

> ' To be, or not to be
> "Of great capacity,
>   "Like Sir Isaac Newton,
> "Or Locke, or Doctor South,
> "Or Sherlock upon death?
>   "I'd rather be Sutton.
>
> "For he did build a house
> "For aged men & youth,
>   "With walls of brick & stone.
> "He furnish'd it within
> "With whatever he could win,
>   "And all his own.

"He drew out of the Stocks
"His money in a box,
     "And sent his servant
"To Green the Bricklayer
"And to the Carpenter:
"He was so fervent.

"The chimneys were three score,
"The windows many more,
     "And for convenience
"He sinks & gutters made,
"And all the way he pav'd
"To hinder pestilence.

"Was not this a good man,
"Whose life was but a span,
     "Whose name was Sutton,—
"As Locke, or Doctor South,
"Or Sherlock upon Death,
     "Or Sir Isaac Newton?" '[120]

The satire is turned against the abstract and mechanical philosophy of Newton and Locke. When Blake attacks Newton and Locke he is, in fact, attacking the social system that their philosophy was used to justify and support. Both the philosophers of Nature and the priest are Blake's targets in his social criticism. The philosophers of Nature subjected Imagination to visible Nature through 'deism', and the priest enslaved it by teaching belief in an invisible God.

We misunderstand Blake if we fail to appreciate his satire, and must distinguish between his use of words in a satirical and a literal sense. Once the poet realizes that truth is perverted by ruling interests and falsehood is used under the guise of truth then satire is an effective means to unveil the falsehood and show what lies within. Passivity and idleness are given the name of 'innocence', Tiriel 'is an innocent old man'. While Blake satirizes this kind of 'innocence' he offers his own definition of the word. In the *Songs of Innocence* we are, as I have tried to show, introduced to two opposing kinds of 'innocence'. One is based on passive natural memories and the other on creative Imagination. Thus it is erroneous to interpret

Blake's *Songs of Innocence* as a recollection of childhood memories.

In *An Island In The Moon* Blake also satirizes the Church which reduces innocent children to poverty by its worldly and selfish practice and then offers charity and pity:

> ' "Upon a holy Thursday, their innocent faces clean,
> "The children walking two & two in grey & blue & green,
> "Grey headed beadles walk'd before with wands as white
>   as snow,
> "Till into the high dome of Paul's they like thames'
>   waters flow.
>
> "O what a multitude they seem'd, these flowers of
>   London town!
> "Seated in companies, they sit with radiance all their
>   own.
> "The hum of multitudes were there, but multitudes of
>   lambs,
> '. . . . .
> "Thousands of little girls & boys raising their innocent
>   hands.
> . . . .
> "Beneath them sit the rev'rend men, the guardians of
>   the poor;
> "Then cherish pity lest you drive an angel from your
>   door." '[121]

Here 'innocence' is being defiled and perverted by poverty and abstraction.

> 'The child springs from the womb; the father ready stands
>   to form
> 'The infant head, . . .'[122]

The Child is innocent because its Imagination is creative and selfless. But once the child's mind is conditioned by the father then Imagination is kept undeveloped and passive. For Blake True Innocence is based on the creative Imagination and selflessness. 'Innocence dwells with Wisdom, but never with Ignorance.'[123] It is the Imagination of this 'innocence' which revolts against 'Experience', the selfish 'innocent old man', in the *Songs of Innocence* and *of Experience*.

Chapter Three

THE MARRIAGE OF HEAVEN AND HELL

I. 'THE ARGUMENT' AND 'RINTRAH'

My purpose here is twofold. Firstly, to demonstrate that 'The Argument' in *The Marriage of Heaven and Hell* refers throughout to Swedenborg's *Heaven and Hell*. Secondly, that the character of Rintrah in 'The Argument' represents the selfish or false prophet who is punishing not only the people in 'Hell' but also the 'just' man in himself. The interpretation of 'The Argument' and of 'Rintrah' is a matter of considerable social and literary importance, which has not as a rule been fully understood.[1]

The name 'Rintrah' is used by Blake in both his early and later writings, first appearing in *The Marriage of Heaven and Hell* (etched about 1790–93). Although David E. Erdman, later, rightly identifies Rintrah with William Pitt, yet both Erdman and N. K. Nurmi, for example, have tended to dismiss the possibility of identification in *The Marriage*, while Northrop Frye identifies Rintrah with prophetic anger:

> 'The prophet may flail his enemies with a haughty and arrogant contempt; this is the *saeva indignatio* of Rintrah which begins *The Marriage of Heaven and Hell*.'[2]

'Recent studies', writes Erdman in the Preface to his book *Blake, Prophet against Empire*, 'have related Blake's work to the Enlightenment and to the general context of the French Revolution and the Industrial Revolution. But "General knowledge is Remote Knowledge", as Blake was wont to insist, and we miss much of the vitality if not the sublimity of his "Sublime Allegory . . . addressed to the Intellectual powers" as long as we remain only remotely acquainted with the "acts" of his age which he considered it his poetic duty "to record and eternize".'[3] While Erdman is right in this suggestion, he fails to apply it in his study of *The Marriage of Heaven and Hell*.

Erdman does indeed point out that *The Marriage* is based on satirical and doctrinal opposition to Swedenborg's *Heaven and Hell,* but he does not discuss the precise textual relationship and doctrinal opposition between these works.[4] Instead he interprets *The Marriage* in the light of the French Revolution and counter-Revolution. For example he relates 'The Argument' to the counter-Revolution in France (1794), but his suggestion seems unconvincing. 'The Argument' is related to Swedenborg's *Heaven and Hell,* and Rintrah in 'The Argument' is the Urizenic character of Swedenborg.

My arguments against Erdman's interpretation of *The Marriage* are as follows:

Firstly he interprets 'The Argument', the 'Proverbs of Hell', and indeed *The Marriage* as a whole, in the general context of the French Revolution. Secondly he more or less dismisses the possibility of identifying Rintrah in 'The Argument'. And thirdly, to support his interpretation of 'The Argument', he suggests the addition of the word 'now' at the beginning of the fourth line of the first stanza in 'The Argument'.

The following proverbs from the 'Proverbs of Hell' commence Erdman's chapter on *The Marriage of Heaven and Hell*:

'Drive your cart and your plow over the bones of the
    dead.'
'The road of excess leads to the Palace of Wisdom.'
'Exuberance is beauty.'

The proverbs were, according to Erdman, written by Blake in support of the French Revolution. 'In *The French Revolution*', writes Erdman, 'we see what a deep and steady furrow Blake has determined to plow across the graveyard of old ideas and old allegiances. In *The Marriage of Heaven and Hell,* a collection of manifestos and proverbs and "Memorable Fancies" in parody of Swedenborg's "Memorable Relations", we see what a contrary and revolutionary step Blake has persuaded himself to take from an interest in the New Church to an enthusiasm for the New Society.'[5]

It is indeed true that Blake supported the French Revolution and this is clearly expressed in *The French Revolution.* The question whether or not the poet continued to support it after 1791 is outside the context of this study, although Jacob Bronowski has discussed the point in detail.[6] What we are concerned with at the moment is that *The Marriage of Heaven and Hell* and the 'Proverbs of Hell' are related to Swedenborg's *Heaven and Hell* and written in opposition to Swedenborg's social philosophy.

'The "Argument"', writes Erdman, 'serves to adapt the confidence of the prose text of *The Marriage* to a time of war or rumours of war.' We wonder how we can know this; Erdman suggests that the two following lines supply the 'proper atmosphere' of war:

'Rintrah roars & shakes his fires in the burden'd air;
Hungry clouds swag on the deep.'[7]

He supports his contention that these lines supply a warlike atmosphere, by pointing out that Blake had used a similar image in *Gwin*:

'The Heav'ns are shook with roaring war,
And dust ascends the skies.'[8]

It is indeed true that the lines share the common words 'roar' and 'shake'. But the key-words of these lines, 'fire', 'clouds', 'deep' and 'swag', are derived rather from Swedenborg's picture of 'Hell' or the coal-mines which the Angel Swedenborg so greatly abhors.

'The swagging (lowering) clouds', remarks Erdman, 'are doubtless war clouds hungry for blood. The roaring and the deep suggest the stormy roar and wintry seas of counter-revolution.' But in 'The Argument' it is Rintrah who 'roars and shakes his fires' not the 'stormy . . . seas of counter-revolution'. Is Rintrah then meant to represent 'the stormy roar and wintry seas of counter-revolution'? Rintrah has a definite role in 'The Argument', but Erdman states that he plays 'no further part after this roaring in the prologue and so must remain unidentified'.[9] Erdman's suggestion about images such as 'fire', 'cloud', and 'deep' and about the character of Rintrah seems implausible. We can see that the former come rather from Swedenborg's 'Hell' or the coal-mines. The 'burden'd air' is the suffocating air of this 'Hell' and Rintrah is the reasoning or Urizenic character of Swedenborg who rejects the 'burden'd air' of the coal mines in favour of the pleasant atmosphere of 'Heaven'.

The four stanzas which follow in 'The Argument' have also

been interpreted in the light of Blake's *French Revolution*. 'In his
French Revoluton,' writes Erdman, 'Blake had imagined the
commons planting "beauty in the desart craving abyss" and
had hoped that the priest would "No more in deadly black"
compel the millions to "howl in law blasted wastes!" '[10] 'In
the first prose page of *The Marriage*', Erdman further argues,
Blake 'had announced "the return of Adam into Paradise" ',
and, in accordance with Erdman's theory this announcement
heralded the return of the French peasant to freedom. The first
part of 'The Argument' after the Rintrah lines begins 'with a
recapitulation of the hopeful first stage of the revolution when
the meek peasant came out of the feudal shadow of death and
was free to . . . plant a fair harvest:

> 'Once meek and in a perilous path,
> The just man kept his course along
> The vale of death.
> [Now] Roses are planted where thorns grow,
> And on the barren heath
> Sing the honey bees'.

'As opposition gave way to peace, "the perilous path was
planted".'[11]

This interpretation again seems incorrect. If Blake meant by
'the return of Adam into Paradise' the return of the French
peasant into a state of freedom and peace, why did he place it
with the prophecy or the Last Judgement of Swedenborg?
Furthermore there is difficulty over the word 'once'. If 'once'
means the time after the peasant has 'come out of the feudal
shadow of death', we must, as Erdman suggests, add the word
'now' to the beginning of the fourth line in the first stanza, but
it seems wrong to do this because it breaks the dialectical
movement of the poem and because if an addition to the text
had been necessary, Blake would have added it.

The character of Rintrah depends on the context in which
he appears. In *Milton* Rintrah is prophetic, but in *Europe* and
the *Song of Los* he has a Urizenic character. Blake identifies
Rintrah, as he does his other characters, according to his
position and social relationships with other people. In other
words, Blake's characters are not abstract terms. If a character
is governed by his Poetic Genius then as true Man he is a

prophetic character, and if he is governed by his limited interest and impressions then he is Urizenic or Satanic in character. It is thus not helpful, for example, to interpret the Rintrah of *The Marriage of Heaven and Hell* in the light of information from later writings, because we cannot be sure to which character of Rintrah in the later works of Blake the Rintrah of *The Marriage of Heaven and Hell* corresponds. We must therefore examine the context and origins of *The Marriage* and that of 'The Argument' and consider Rintrah's social and human relationships. From the evidence thus obtained, we shall conclude that in *The Marriage* Rintrah has the Urizenic rather than prophetic character.

In *The Marriage* Blake criticizes the rigid class division implied by Swedenborg's doctrine of predestination. 'The Argument' is a concise statement of Blake's opposition to Swedenborg's metaphysical philosophy, the idea that the source of life is from the Lord or spiritual world and that evil is from the love of the material world and is within man. In *Heaven and Hell* he places the people who work in the mines and those who oppose him in his 'Hell', and the Church officials, the Royal family, the nobles and the mineowners in 'Heaven'. The 'hells' are ruled by a 'general influx of divine good and divine truth from the heavens'.[12] There are special angels whose duty is 'to restrain the insanities and disturbances which abound' in 'Hell'. This rule is one of fear. For some inhabitants of 'Hell', fear is 'implanted and ingrafted', but it must be supported by punishments which 'in hell are manifold';[13] the resulting fear of punishment is 'the only medium to restrain the violence and fury of those who are in the hells; there is no other'.[14] Thus Swedenborg restrains and punishes those who violate his 'granted' divine authority.

Many passages depict Swedenborg, who cast himself in the role of a divinely inspired prophet, walking amid fire and torment. He considers himself a righteous being, and his opponents devils. The evil ones in 'Hell' are suffering punishment. He exposes their weaknesses and sins, and depicts himself as a proud avenging warrior from 'Heaven'. Rintrah is this character of Swedenborg. Blake, after reading *Heaven and Hell*, identifies Swedenborg's prophecy with Urizen or Rintrah.

'Rintrah roars & shakes his fires in the burden'd air;
Hungry clouds swag on the deep.'[15]

Here Rintrah is Satan or a fallen hero. The 'burden'd air'
is the air of the coal mines. Swedenborg reasons between the
atmosphere of 'Heaven' and 'Hell' and his reasoning power
rejects 'Hell' in favour of his limited 'Heaven'. He supports his
case against those in 'Hell' by using arguments and exhortations
derived from the Bible, from the teachings of Jesus, from Old
Testament prophets such as Isaiah and Ezekiel and from what
he calls the Ancients.[16] For example, from his privileged
position amid the plenty of 'Heaven' he instructs the poor to
'resist the love of self and of the world' using the words of
Jesus:

'Learn of me, for I am *meek* and lowly of heart, and ye
shall find rest unto your souls; for my yoke is *easy*, and
my burden is light.'[17]

Defending the moral and human values of Jesus against the
self-interest of those in 'Heaven', Blake puts forward the
argument of those in 'Hell'. From their viewpoint, 'The
Argument' is that 'Heaven' and 'Hell' are the products of two
different social conditions: the 'paths of ease' and the 'perilous
path'.

'Once meek, and in a perilous path,
The just man kept his course along . . .
Till the villain left the paths of ease,
To walk in perilous paths, and drive
The just man into barren climes.'[18]

The terms 'meek' and 'the just' refer to an active or a working
class. Swedenborg's experience could be described in Blake's
terms as a change from the 'paths of ease' to the 'perilous
paths', from the passive to the active life; and his 'Heaven'
and 'Hell' are the product of two different social situations.

In his illustration of 'The Argument' Blake shows the passive
and active characters. The passive are lying on the ground of
ease and are bound to earth like vegetation, but their eyes are
wandering in the air or metaphysical world. The active are
represented by the tree of Life and by two people—one
standing at the root wearing gray (the colour of clay) and the

other on the branches of the tree in red colour. These figures illustrate the correspondence between the material and spiritual which, according to Blake, are inseparable parts of one being. The colours of gray and red represent the raw and the organic or mental forms of the material world. The organic form of matter is, apparently, identified by 'red clay' in 'The Argument'. It is the creative man who can turn 'bleached bones' or dead matter into 'red clay' or living form.

The terms 'Good' and 'Evil' do not then stand for eternally fixed moral values. They are conventional ideas which are created by the passive in 'Heaven' to oppose 'the just' or active people in 'Hell'. What Swedenborg calls 'Good', for example, is to Blake 'Evil'. Passivity is error or 'Evil'. For passivity is based on selfhood. It is selfhood which drives 'the just' into 'barren climes'. In other words 'Hell' or 'Evil' is within society and is created by the self-interest of the Angels in 'Heaven'. 'Error is Created. Truth is Eternal.'[19] If we take, as Swedenborg has described, 'Heaven' as a pleasant condition of living in wealth, and 'Hell' as a deprived condition of living in poverty, then to Blake the poverty of 'Hell' is created by the Angels who live passively.

In the first draft of 'The Human Abstract', contrary to Kathleen Raine's suggestion that this poem 'has a Swedenborgian framework'[20] Blake criticizes this Angelic hypocrisy:

> 'I heard an Angel singing
> When the day was springing,
> "Mercy, Pity, [& del.] Peace
> "Is the world's release."
>
> I heard a Devil curse
> Over the heath & the furze,
> "Mercy could be no more,
> "If there was nobody poor,
>
> And pity no more could be,
> "If all were as happy as we." '[21]

In the fair copy of 'The Human Abstract' (*Songs of Experience*) Blake writes:

> 'Pity would be no more
> If we did not make somebody Poor.'[22]

Poverty is, for Blake, a created condition.

Swedenborg reading the Bible with the Angels in 'Heaven' saw it as a kind of spiritual handbook. Blake, reading it with the working people in 'Hell', regarded it as a living story. The ancient prophets whom Blake mentions in *The Marriage of Heaven and Hell* were, to him, full of human feeling, of hope and inspiration; they praised work and creative energy.

> 'Roses are planted where thorns grow,
> And on the barren heath
> Sing the honey bees.
>
> Then the perilous path was planted,
> And a river and spring
> On every cliff and tomb,
> And on the bleached bones
> Red clay brought forth;'[23]

In this way Blake in *The Marriage of Heaven and Hell* (he ironically calls himself a Devil as opposed to the Swedenborgian Angel) teaches the Angel how to read the Bible and says: 'The worship of God is: Honouring his gifts in other men, each according to his genius, and loving the greatest men best: those who envy or calumniate great men hate God; for there is no other God.'[24] Here the Devil tells the Angel that having a respect for the creative energy in man is the true worship of God, rather than mere ceremonies. For, as Blake states in his *Annotations to Swedenborg's Divine Love*, 'the Whole of the New Church is in the Active Life & not in Ceremonies at all'.[25] Psychologically, Swedenborg is similar to Tiriel and Thel,[26] who refuse the self-sacrificing aspects of experience and flee back to their own natural memories of their own easy background or selfhood.

The hard active life of the people in the mines seemed a 'torment' and 'insanity' to Swedenborg. He now turns into a priest who moves like a 'sneaking serpent', which, perhaps, means to be bound to the earth or his selfhood, while punishing transgressors for their love of the self and of the world in 'mild humility'.

> 'Now the sneaking serpent walks
> In mild humility'[27]

He accuses those who apparently live in love of the world of being in 'Hell', while he himself lives in 'Heaven' and its 'paradisiacal scenes which exceed all idea of the imagination'.[28] Those in 'Hell', who delight in honest toil and its natural rewards rather than in the excess of things in Swedenborg's 'Heaven', live under punishment and are driven into the 'wilds':

> 'And the just man rages in the wilds
> Where lions roam.'[29]

Thus the prophet who is supposed to work and be a shepherd for his flock and a lover of the people has become a priest of evil by turning against the 'just man' in pernicious fury. The condition of hopelessness is perpetuated and Swedenborg, who had rebelled against priestcraft and worldliness, becomes the priest and mineowner instead.[30] The 'reasoning power' of 'natural man' is still heard in Rintrah or Swedenborg:

> 'Rintrah roars & shakes his fires in the burden'd air;
> Hungry clouds swag on the deep'.

'Hungry clouds' represent the selfish and devouring memories in the Angel. Thus 'The Argument' starts and ends with the Urizenic character of Rintrah. The would-be revolutionary prophet has fallen into his own selfhood and the cycle of error is repeated again.

The derivation of the word 'Rintrah' is another problem which confronts Blake scholars. It is, however, probably derived from the word 'Indra', the God of thunder in Hindu mythology. The name 'Indra' seems first to have made its appearance in a western work in Sir William Jones' translation of *Sakuntala* or *The Fatal Ring*, an Indian drama by Kalidas. This was first published in 1789 and was widely read in Britain. The translation of *Sakuntala* was first published in Calcutta in 1789. Second and third editions were published in 1790 and 1792 in London. The fourth edition was published in Edinburgh in 1796. Blake perhaps read the second or third edition (1790 or 1792). The word 'Rintrah' is probably the combination of 'Reason' (dynamic personality or mind peculiar to the just man) and 'Indra' (the limited and static reason peculiar to Urizen, your reason).[31] The 'ah' at the end of 'Rintrah' is an

English transliteration of the vowel sound 'a' as in 'Jehovah'. By this combination Rintrah serves as a twofold character: one is the would-be prophetic character: 'But Rintrah who is of the reprobate';[32] and another the Urizenic character: 'O Rintrah, furious King'.[33] All this means that Rintrah, as a human character, is a twofold being: 'Man is a twofold being, one part capable of evil & the other capable of good'.[34] Evil is passive and good is active, and 'Man is bad or good as he unites himself with bad or good spirits'.[35]

There are two pieces of evidence which might support my assumption of the Indian origin of the word 'Rintrah'. One is the date (1790–92) of the publication of *Sakuntala* which coincides with the date of *The Marriage of Heaven and Hell* (1790–93). The second piece of evidence is the appearance of 'Rintrah', 'Brama' and 'East' together in *The Song of Los* (1795): 'When Rintrah gave Abstract Philosophy to Brama in the East.' I would suggest that this line relates to the British occupation of India. 'Abstract Philosophy' suggests the mechanistic philosophy of Newton and Locke, which was a reflection of the eighteenth century Urizenic system similar to that of Swedenborg's *Heaven and Hell*.

'. . . a Philosophy of the Five Senses was complete.
Urizen wept & gave it into the hands of Newton and Locke.'[36]

Rintrah, here, is the Urizenic character or the false prophet and Brama represents priestcraft. It is Rintrah in this same Urizenic form who appears at the outset of 'The Argument' in *The Marriage of Heaven and Hell*.

2. SWEDENBORG'S 'LAST JUDGMENT'

Plate 3 of *The Marriage of Heaven and Hell*.

'As a new heaven is begun, and it is now thirty-three years since its advent, the Eternal Hell revives. And lo! Swedenborg is the Angel sitting at the tomb: his writings are the linen clothes folded up . . .'[37]

This passage refers to Swedenborg's Last Judgment or

prophecy. In his book of *The Last Judgment* Swedenborg states
that he has been 'granted' divine authority:

'. . . it was granted me to see with my eyes, that the last
judgment is now accomplished, and that the evil are cast
into the hells, and the good elevated into heaven, and
thus that all things are reduced to order, and thereby the
spiritual equilibrium restored, which subsists between
good and evil, or between heaven and hell. . . . This last
judgment commenced in the beginning of the preceeding
year 1757, and was fully accomplished at the end of the
same year.'[38]

Swedenborg rejected the orthodox view that the Last Judgment
would take place in the next world. The churchman 'should
from ignorance continue in such faith . . . concerning the last
judgment. . . . The belief of what is said about it in the literal
sense of the Word. . . .'[39] He also repudiated the view that the
Last Judgment would occur on earth at some future date.
Swedenborg's Last Judgment is based only on the idealism of
his own limited background and memories which he sets up
against the rest of society. While sitting in 'Heaven' and
dividing himself from the people, he prophetically declares
that 'the last judgment is accomplished, and that the evil are
cast into the hells . . .' He is in 'Heaven' but his children suffer
in 'Hell'. In other words 'Hell' already exists in society and
the condemned are already relegated there when Swedenborg
announces his last judgment.

In her large and scholarly work Kathleen Raine discusses
the relationship between Blake and Swedenborg in detail and
attempts to identify Blake with Swedenborg. Blake 'was not
casting doubt on Swedenborg's prophecy of a New Age', writes
Miss Raine, 'but assuming both the prophecy and Swedenborg's
authenticity as the Angel; . . . In *Milton* Blake describes
Swedenborg as the "strongest of men, the Samson shorn by
the Churches". Conventional religious ideas were the bonds
that curbed his natural genius. This we may suppose to be
Blake's final judgment upon him'.[40]

It is true that 'conventional religious ideas' were the bonds
that curbed Swedenborg's 'genius' and Blake indeed criticizes
and rejects this false character in Swedenborg in favour of his

'genius' or true man. Blake similarly rejects Swedenborg's false prophecy which is based on his passive memories formed by these 'conventional religious ideas'. Blake opposed the Urizenic or punishing God of Swedenborg in 'Heaven', and sympathized instead with the people in 'Hell'. This seems to be Blake's criticism of Swedenborg's prophecy in *The Marriage of Heaven and Hell* and also in *Milton*.

It is true that, as Miss Raine says, Blake describes Swedenborg as '. . . strongest of men, the Samson shorn by the Churches . . .' But she misses the point of the rest of the passage where Swedenborg's strong part has apparently given way to his weak and vindictive character, who

> ' "Shewing the Transgressors in Hell, the proud Warriors
>   in Heaven,
> "Heaven as a Punisher, & Hell as One under Punish-
>   ment,
> "With Laws from Plato & his Greeks to renew the
>   Trojan Gods . . ." '41

The Trojan or Urizenic God (natural man) rises in Swedenborg over his true God or spiritual man. Blake casts doubt on this passive and Urizenic prophecy of Swedenborg who is sitting like a proud 'Warrior' in 'Heaven' while the innocent suffer punishment in 'Hell'.

In Plate 3 of *The Marriage of Heaven and Hell* Blake satirizes Swedenborg's prophecy which for ever divided society into 'Heaven' and 'Hell'; 'As a new heaven is begun . . . it is now thirty-three years . . . The Eternal Hell revives.'

The 'new heaven' is the last judgment of Swedenborg which, as we have noted, began in 1757. Blake was also born in this year. Thirty-three years after Swedenborg's last judgment Blake wrote *The Marriage of Heaven and Hell*. *The Marriage* is undated but the date is deduced (1790) by the addition of 33 years on to 1757. Swedenborg had ascended to 'Heaven' but 'Eternal Hell' was still reviving in society. The word 'Eternal' is an ironical criticism of Swedenborg's rigid class system and philosophy of predestination in which men are 'enrolled' in 'Heaven' or 'Hell' after 'Departure from the World'. In other words those in 'Heaven' and 'Hell' are assigned to their places by 'Divine Providence':

'But the Man who doth not suffer himself to be led to, and enrolled in Heaven, is prepared for his place in Hell; . . . This is the Intimum of the Divine Providence concerning Hell.'[42]

Blake wrote underneath the passage: 'What is Enrolling but Predestination? . . .'[43] In another passage Swedenborg said:

'Since every Man . . . lives after Death to Eternity, and according to his Life here hath his Place assigned to him either in Heaven or in Hell, . . . it follows, that the human Race throughout the whole World is under the Auspices of the Lord, and that everyone, from his Infancy even to the End of his Life, is led of Him in the most minute Particulars, and his *Place foreseen,* and at the same *Time provided.*'[44]

All this means that according to Swedenborg the social positions of those in 'Heaven' and 'Hell' are predestined and thus the social system or relationship is established and fixed. Blake, while underscoring the phrases 'Place forseen' and 'Time provided', wrote underneath the passage: 'Devils & Angels are Predestinated'.[45] Thus the 'law', 'order' and 'equilibrium', which Swedenborg writes of in his *Last Judgment,* are based on rigid and inhuman class relationships.

The irony of 'Eternal Hell' in Plate 3 of *The Marriage of Heaven and Hell* is also relevant to the economic condition of England at the time. In 1757, when Swedenborg set himself up as an appointed prophet, it 'was a year of dearth' in England. 'So scarce was corn that Parliament forbade its use in the making of spirits . . . from 1757, throughout Blake's life, the years of dearth grew common.'[46] And when Blake was writing *The Marriage of Heaven and Hell* the 'Eternal Hell' was still 'reviving'. In other words it was, as we have seen in the first chapter, again a 'year of dearth'. The economic condition of Sweden, due to her engagement in war and crop failure, was perhaps worse.[47] But the prophet Swedenborg, instead of being a shepherd to his wretched flock, retires back to his own passive memories while writing about the 'numbers', 'weight' and 'measure' of things and a place in the church of 'Heaven'.

D

Blake commenting on this writes in 'Proverbs of Hell': 'Bring out number, weight and measure in a year of dearth.'

Since Swedenborg's knowledge of 'Heaven' and 'Hell' as Last Judgment is based on the impressions formed by his limited upbringing and the passive principle of the senses, 'his writings are the linen clothes folded up'. The 'linen clothes' represent the passive memories or 'material' in which the creative personality or mind is wrapped up. The passive rationalist, at his Last Judgment, sees the passive memories or linen clothes rather than the man. In his *Heaven and Hell* Swedenborg has collected only his passive memories or 'linen clothes'.

Swedenborg explains and describes his impressions of everything belonging to those who are in 'Heaven'. In support of his belief he quotes from the Bible, stating how the angels appeared to the prophets and Jesus:

> 'Inasmuch as the angels are clothed with garments in heaven, they have . . . also appeared clothed with garments when they have been seen in the world, as when they were seen by the prophets, and likewise at the Lord's sepulchre; on which latter occasion it is said that "*Their appearance was like lightning*", and "*their raiment glittering and white*", Matt. xxviii. 3; Mark xvi. 5; Luke xxii. 4; John xx. 12, 13; and they who were seen in heaven by John had "*garments of fine linen and white*", Rev. iv. 4; xix. 11, 13".'[48]

For Swedenborg the garments signify truths and intelligence, or that the Angels' external appearance corresponds to their internal qualities.

Swedenborg formed these impressions from his upbringing in a clerical environment. Since the Church and its officials belong to the 'Heaven' or the Lord, therefore whatever they have is from the Lord: Angels

> 'are clothed with various garments hath been seen by me a thousand times: I have enquired whence they had them, and they have told me that they had them from the Lord, and that they are given to them, and that they are occasionally clothed without knowing . . .'[49]

Thus Swedenborg reproduces his impressions of the garments

and clothes of church officials in his prophetical writing or Last Judgment, which Blake satirizes in the Plate 3 as 'the linen clothes folded up' or as the collection of impressions formed from Swedenborg's limited environment.

Then 'linen clothes' also correspond to the 'Female Garment', as we shall see later in *The Gates of Paradise*. The creative or prophetic mind is hidden in the 'Female Garment'.

The symbol of 'linen clothes' is essentially derived from the Bible. Jesus after rising leaves his 'linen clothes' behind.

'. . . The linen clothes lying; yet went he not . . . the linen clothes lie.' (John xx. 4–7.)

Jesus as a creative personality leaves the 'linen clothes' or the natural memories behind and rises with the 'Immortal Man', whereas the priest leaves the 'Saviour' or creative personality behind and instead picks up his 'linen clothes' or his limited natural memories.

Swedenborg thus escapes from social reality and his true life experience. He is now 'sitting at the tomb' or at the 'Grave' of his natural memories describing 'the linen clothes' or the impressions as his 'paradise'.

'Now is the dominion of Edom, & the return of Adam into Paradise; see Isaiah xxxiv & xxxv, Chap. . . .'[50]

Edom represents the false prophecy. The 'return of Adam into Paradise' suggests the return of Swedenborg as the false prophet into his paradisiacal memories instead of returning to the earth or society and active life.

Isaiah xxxiv and xxxv apparently convey two opposite ways or paths. One path leads to 'Death's Door' or limited natural memories: 'Nature's wide womb', inside which are 'unquenchable burnings'—'A void immense, wild, dark & deep, . . .'[51] Isaiah xxxiv shows us the place to which the false prophet or Urizenic character returns (after his last judgment). We hear the voice of false prophet or Urizenic character in Isaiah xxxiv:

'. . . my sword shall be based in heaven: behold, it shall come down upon . . . the people of my curse, to judgment. The sword of the Lord is filled with blood, it is made fat with fatness, and with the blood of lambs and goats . . .'

In the dominion of the false prophet and his punisher God

'. . . the streams . . . shall be turned into pitch . . . and
the land . . . shall become burning pitch. It shall not be
quenched night nor day'.

The 'burning pitch' in Isaiah xxxiv corresponds to the
'unquenchable burnings' in the wide womb of Urizen.

Isaiah xxxv shows the other path which leads to Zion or the
land of joy and freedom from social sorrow. Zion corresponds
to Edom as its opposite. Zion, opposite of Edom, is the
dominion of true prophecy. Chapter xxxv starts like the first
part, after the Rintrah lines in 'The Argument':

'The wilderness and the solitary place shall be glad for
them; and the desert shall rejoice, and blossom as the
rose.'

The society here, contrary to the one we have seen in the
beginning of this chapter, is not divided into 'Heaven' and
'Hell':

'No lion shall be there, nor any ravenous beast shall go up
thereon, it shall not be found there; but the redeemed
shall walk there: And the ransomed of the Lord shall
return, and come to Zion with songs and everlasting joy
upon their heads: they shall obtain joy and gladness, and
sorrow and sighing shall flee away' (Verses 9–10).

Blake's purpose in putting chapters xxxiv and xxxv together
is, in fact, to show the two opposite states of the human soul
after the Last Judgment. Everybody reads the Bible according
to his state of mind or soul, which is mainly formed by social
circumstances. Some, like Swedenborg, arrive at a sort of
'innocence' which is based on their passive social background.
Tiriel is an example of this innocence: 'He is an innocent old
man & hungry with his travel'.[52] Blake's Last Judgment is
based on Imagination or Vision, which is opposed to passive
memories and rationalism. In *A Vision of The Last Judgment*
(1810) he writes: 'The Last Judgment [will be] when all
those are Cast away who trouble Religion with Questions
Good & Evil or Eating of the Tree of Knowledges of Rea-
sonings which hinder the Vision of God, turning all into a

Consuming Fire . . . the Last Judgment . . . & its Vision is seen by the [Imaginative Eye del.] of Every one according to the situation he holds.'[53] Since the Last Judgment is based on Imagination or Vision, we should understand it in the light of Blake's idea of 'Imagination'. Imagination or Vision, from Blake's viewpoint, is based on human experience of the material world, and the poet's understanding of the Last Judgment is derived from his deeper life experience. Repudiating Plato's view of art, contrary to Kathleen Raine's identification of Blake's idea of Imagination and Art with the 'Platonic view of art',[54] Blake writes:

> 'Plato has made Socrates say that Poets & Prophets do not know or Understand what they write or Utter; this is a most Pernicious Falsehood . . . Plato confutes himself'.[55]

Blake does not believe in a metaphysical source of Vision and Imagination. His idea of Vision or Imagination is the vision of his everyday experience of social life. 'My Streets are my Ideas of Imagination . . .'[56] The Last Judgment is based on this Imagination: 'The Last Judgment is not Fable or Allegory, but Vision' (K. p. 604). Imagination or Vision is not something separate from the material world. Indeed, Blake explicitly says so in a letter to Dr. Trusler (August 23, 1799): '. . . I know that This World Is a World of imagination & Vision. I see Every thing I paint In This World, but Every body does not see alike' (K. p. 793). The reason why 'Every body does not see alike' and to different People the Last Judgment 'appears differently' lies in differences in their social situation. The source of social and private ills according to Blake, contrary to what Miss Raine tells us,[57] is within society and man: 'As a man is, So he Sees. As the Eye is formed, such are its Powers.' The miser is not born a miser but he is born into a social situation which awakens his narrow self-interest against society and Imagination.

The Last Judgment takes place within society and man. Swedenborg's Last Judgment has a fundamental difference from Blake's. Swedenborg's Last Judgment attempts to support and justify the position of the Angels in 'Heaven' against those in 'Hell'. But Blake's Last Judgment is against social injustice and evil:

> 'Last Judgment is not for the purpose of making Bad Men better, but for the Purpose of hindering them from oppressing the Good with Poverty & Pain by means of . . . Vile Arguments & Insinuations.'[58]

After his Last Judgment Swedenborg returns to the paradise of his limited memories which he regarded as opposite or contrary to 'Hell'. But Blake's Last Judgment expresses the Imagination which has overcome limitations and comprehends 'the Infinite', and which can see the whole of society rather than only the limited self:

> 'He who sees the Infinite in all things, sees God.
> He who sees the Ratio only, sees himself only.'

Swedenborg's Last Judgment and idea of 'contrary progression' is based on ratio and negation.

3. THE IDEA OF 'CONTRARY PROGRESSION'

The idea of 'contraries' follows Blake's ironic reading of Swedenborg's prophecy in Plate 3 of *The Marriage of Heaven and Hell*:

> 'Without Contraries is no progression. Attraction and Repulsion, Reason and Energy, Love and Hate are necessary to Human existence.
> From these contraries spring what the religious call Good & Evil. Good is the passive that obeys Reason. Evil is the active springing from Energy.
> Good is Heaven. Evil is Hell.'[59]

The passage seems to provide a summary reading of *Heaven and Hell* and, like 'The Argument', is a concise statement of Blake's opposition to Swedenborg's philosophy.

The following is an attempt to examine both the word itself and the idea of 'contrary' in Swedenborg's *Heaven and Hell*, which will lead to the conclusions that, firstly, Blake's ideas of 'contraries' and 'progression' in *The Marriage of Heaven and Hell* are directly related to *Heaven and Hell*—a view somewhat at variance with that put forward by Martin K. Nurmi and Kathleen Raine, who relate them to Jacob Boehme;[60] and secondly, that Blake opposed Swedenborg's doctrine of the 'contrary state' on the grounds that it was based only on 'negation' and was thus the outcome of a system of merely passive rationalism.

Nurmi agrees with Erdman's interpretation of Rintrah,[61] but his approach to *The Marriage* as a whole differs from Erdman's. Nurmi admits that *The Marriage* is written in opposition to Swedenborg's doctrine of predestination, but he nevertheless interprets Blake's idea of 'contraries' in the context of Boehme's doctrine.[62]

Nurmi discusses the idea of 'contraries' in detail, and indeed his work *Blake's Marriage of Heaven and Hell* is, perhaps, the first detailed critical study of the work. He rightly argues that *The Marriage* does not teach diabolism. Blake 'merely adopts the terms "Heaven" and "Hell" and uses them ironically to show that they are meaningless as the orthodox intend them'.[63] But as a whole his study, though rich in information, seems hardly helpful towards gaining an overall understanding of *The Marriage of Heaven and Hell* and particularly of the idea of 'contraries' in this work.

Nurmi attempts to elucidate the work and the idea of 'contraries' in the light of information gleaned from Blake's later writings, more specifically from *Milton* and *Jerusalem*.[64] It is true that Blake never altered his basic principles, but he believed, as Nurmi himself has pointed out in his Preface, that every work must be studied and understood in its 'minute particulars'.[65] In other words, every work of art must be studied in its particular context.

Nurmi, then, examines the idea of 'contraries' in the context of Boehme. ' "Attraction" and "repulsion" as contraries' in Blake, he writes, 'possibly suggests a relatively recent spiritual crisis involving both Swedenborg and Boehme, a crisis in which intellectual affinity shifted from Swedenborg to Boehme.'[66]

There are in fact two hypotheses in Nurmi's suggestion: firstly that there was an affinity between Blake and Swedenborg, and secondly that the idea of 'contraries' in *The Marriage of Heaven and Hell* represents the divergence of Blake from Swedenborg to Boehme. Even if, contrary to what Erdman suggests in his article *Blake's Early Swedenborgianism: A Twentieth Century Legend*, with which Nurmi apparently agrees, we assume that the first hypothesis is true,[67] the second still seems unconvincing. The idea of 'contraries' in *The Marriage* is directly related to Swedenborg's *Heaven and Hell* and was written in opposition to Swedenborg's system.

Blake nowhere announced his intellectual shift from Swedenborg in favour of Boehme, nor does the latter have any special prominence in *The Marriage of Heaven and Hell*. If the mere mention of Boehme's name in *The Marriage* is to be considered evidence for Blake's taking up Boehme's doctrines, then one might as well attribute his assumed intellectual shift from Swedenborg to the influence of Shakespeare who is mentioned in *The Marriage* in the same passage with Boehme and Paracelsus and Dante.

There is an essential contradiction in Nurmi's argument. On the one hand he says that 'to look at *The Marriage* as in part a triumphant rejection of Swedenborg in favour of Boehme is helpful to an understanding of the spirit of its ideas . . .'. On the other hand he advises us not to take Blake as a Boehmeist.[68]

Even if we were to accept such an assumption it is difficult to see how it would help our understanding of Blake. After quoting the key statement: 'Without Contraries is no progression. Attraction and Repulsion, Reason and Energy, Love and Hate', Nurmi says,

> 'Not all of the paired terms of this first statement are equally relevant to Blake's essential doctrine of contraries. "Reason" and "Energy" are the key terms . . . But the other pairs can hardly be taken at face value or elevated to the status of metaphysical principles. "Love and Hate" do not constitute the basis of Blake's cosmos . . . In response to the gleam of satire in the author's eye, we may take "Love and Hate" as ironic designations of the pious mildness and the wrathful intransigence of the religious orthodox and the visionary unorthodox, respectively. Yet if we apply such an assumption to the other pair, "Attraction and Repulsion", the only ironic meanings that emerge seem too blurry to be Blake's. Here it is safer to suppose that we are confronted with an unassimilated pair of contraries derived from Jacob Boehme.'[69]

If Blake rejected Swedenborg in favour of Boehme, why

should he derive an 'unassimilated pair of contraries' from him which might disturb the unity of the work and create more difficulty in its understanding?

Nurmi adds in the following paragraph that:

'an examination of Boehme's use of such contraries as attraction and repulsion will yield the conclusion that Blake's and Boehme's ideas about "contraries" differ in important respects'.[70]

If Blake's 'contraries' differ in important respects from Boehme's, then what other aspects made Blake reject Swedenborg in favour of Boehme? This has not been explained. It seems apparent that Nurmi has failed to realize the source of 'unassimilation' among the paired terms of 'contraries'. But this 'unassimilation' is more due to the investigation of the remoter Boehme in order to understand *The Marriage of Heaven and Hell*, than to the possibility of inconsistency in Blake's own usage. If one looks at the paired terms of 'contraries' in relation to Swedenborg, however, there are no inconsistencies to be accounted for.

Swedenborg and Blake have opposing ideas of the meaning of the word 'contrary'. This opposition stems from their different social backgrounds. Blake views the 'contrary' states of life and mind as alike necessary elements for progression or creation. 'Human existence' or Imagination is based on these contrary states. We appreciate warmth by the ratio of cold, leisure by the ratio of work or, to use Swedenborg's terms, 'Heaven' by the ratio of 'Hell'. But Swedenborg regards any thing or state of feeling which is 'contrary' or 'opposite' to 'Heaven' as unnecessary or 'evil'. He loves 'Heaven' because his 'driving love' and 'internal state' agrees with what exists there. He rejects and negates 'Hell' and its inhabitants because he feels his 'driving love' is opposed to them.

But Swedenborg's ideas of 'love', 'joy', 'delight', 'truth' and 'good' are derived only from his own limited experiences. Whatever agrees with his personal 'driving love' or his memories and views is 'good' and whatever disagrees with them is 'evil':

'. . . *love* is the receptacle of all things of heaven, which are peace, intelligence, wisdom, and happiness: for *love*
D*

> receives all and singular the things which are in agreement
> with itself; it desires them, enquires after them, imbues
> them as of its own accord, . . . this . . . known to man, . . .
> the *love* in which he is principled . . . *draws* from the things
> of his *memory* all things which are in agreement with it, . . .
> but all other things, which are not in *agreement*, it rejects
> and exterminates.'[71]

In other words, man has two opposing principles. One is
attracted to and agrees with all things that he loves, and the
other rejects or disagrees with the things that he does not love.
Man's being in 'Heaven' or 'Hell' depends upon his 'internal
driving love'. The reason that the Angels are in 'Heaven', for
example, is that they 'have *loved* what is *good* and true for the
sake of what is *good* and true, and implanted those principles
in their lives. . . .'[72]

It is from these opposite principles of personal 'agreement'
and 'disagreement' or 'love' and 'rejection' that Swedenborg
develops his doctrine of 'contrary states' which are based on
'negation'. The spiritual or subjective world negates the
material or objective world. 'Heaven' negates those who are
in 'Hell'. The people in 'Hell' love the self and the world, but
those in 'Heaven' love the Lord. Since all love, truth, wisdom,
intelligence and delight stem from the Lord and He is the
Lord of 'Heaven' and the Angels, therefore the people in 'Hell'
are 'contrary' to divine 'love', 'truth', 'wisdom', 'intelligence'
and heavenly 'delight'. In other words, those in 'Hell', who
are not similar in thought and appearance to those in 'Heaven',
are in an opposite or 'contrary' state to 'divine order':

> 'As all things which are according to divine order corre-
> spond to heaven, so all things which are *contrary* to divine
> order correspond to hell.'[73]

Swedenborg explains that the light and heat in 'Heaven'
are different from the light and heat in 'Hell'. The light of
'Heaven' is divine truth, divine wisdom and intelligence. In
the light of 'Heaven' those in 'Hell' seem as 'monsters with
horrible countenances and horrible bodies'.[74] The heat in
'Heaven' is 'Celestial fire', the love of the Lord, while that of
'Hell' is 'infernal fire', the love of self and of the world.

The heat and light of 'Heaven' or 'energy' springs from divine sources; thus to believe that worldly things excite love and heat in 'Heaven' is 'contrary' to divine order:

> 'They are very greatly deceived, who believe that the influx of the heat of the world excites loves, for natural influx into what is spiritual does not exist, but spiritual into what is natural; the latter influx from divine order, but the former *contrary* to divine order.'[75]

The spiritual world operates independently from the external or material world. The material world is being rejected as opposed to the mental forms or ideas which, according to Swedenborg, are the source of the external world.

Swedenborg frequently uses the phrase 'contrary to divine order'. In his chapter 'Concerning the Form of Heaven' he wrote:

> 'There is no influx given from the inferior heavens into the superior, because it is contrary to order.'[76]

And in the chapter 'Concerning the Power of the Angels of Heaven' he writes:

> '. . . The power of the angels in the spiritual world is so great, that . . . if any thing in that world makes resistance,' . . . it is . . . 'to be removed because it is *contrary* to divine order. . . .'[77]

or again:

> 'If men could be saved by immediate mercy, all would be saved, even they who are in hell, . . . neither would there be a hell, because the Lord is Mercy Itself, Love Itself, and Good Itself; wherefore it is *contrary* to His Divine (Principle) to say, that he is able to save all immediately; and doth not save them. . . .'[78]

The word 'contrary' is used in many and varied contexts in *Heaven and Hell*. There frequently occur statements such as:

> Those 'who are in hell are altogether *contrary* to innocence'.[79]

or

> 'Those things which are *contrary* to the things of heaven and of the Church.'[80]

The idea of 'contraries' in *The Marriage of Heaven and Hell*, however, specifically refers to the chapters 'Concerning the Changes of State of the Angels in Heaven', 'Concerning Time in Heaven' and 'Concerning Space in Heaven'.

Swedenborg discusses his 'love' and 'progression' towards good or the superior state of life or 'Heaven' and his rejection or negation of disagreeable states or 'Hell'. Blake by over-turning Swedenborg's 'Heaven' on earth retorts by saying that 'love', 'affection' and 'attraction' to the good of life and hate or repulsion of undesirable life is necessary for human existence, but 'Energy is the only life, and is from the Body; . . .' Swedenborg's love, affection and attraction have material bases for Blake.

Kathleen Raine has also related the idea of 'contraries' in *The Marriage of Heaven and Hell* to Boehme. 'Blake derived', writes Miss Raine, 'such thought as: "Without Contraries is no progression" ', from passages like the following:

> ' "God is also an *Angry Zealous* or *Jealous God, and a con-suming Fire*; and in that source standeth the Abyss of Hell, the anger and malice of all the Devils, as also the poison of all creatures: and it is found that without poison and eagerness there is no Life; and from thence ariseth all contrariety and strife; and it is found that the strongest and most eager, is the most useful and profitable: for it *maketh* all things, and is the *only cause* of all mobility and life!" '[81]

The term 'contrariety' does indeed appear in the passage and there is conflict and strife between the Angry or Jealous God and the useful or profitable God. Nevertheless this quotation hardly seems a sufficient basis for Blake's statement:

> 'Without Contraries is no progression. Attraction and Repulsion, Reason and Energy, Love and Hate, are necessary to Human existence.'

If this hypothesis arises from the use of the term 'contrariety' then there are numerous passages in all the works of Swedenborg which contain the word 'contrary' or 'contrariety'. Let us, for example, take his *Arcana Caelestia* where the words 'contrary' or 'contrariety' occur frequently:

They 'are with difficulty, brought to receive Truths which are *contrary* to their falses!'[82]

'The ends regarded are what alone cause either *contrariety* between the internal and external man. . . .'[83]

'Therefore in the word of those things are treated of which are *contrary* to the Divine (Principle).'[84]

'The evils and falsities with which goods and truths cannot be mixed, are such as are *contrary* to love to God and to Love towards neighbour.'[85]

'If there is *contrariety* the exterior man altogether perverts or extinguishes what flows in through the interior!'[86]

'The cause of abomination is, that they are *contrary* to received principles and loves, ...'[87]

'By desolations and temptations also, states *contrary* to heavenly life are perceived, ...'[88]

'. . . those things which are of the light of heaven become darkness, when they fall into those things which are of the world's lumen, for in themselves they are *contraries*, ...'[89]

'There are . . . spirits who infuse *contrary* persuasions, . . . they speak things *contrary* to those which the instructor spirit from the angels said, ...'[90]

'every perception of a thing is according to reflection relative to discrimination arising from *contraries* in various modes and degrees'.[91]

These are just random examples taken from different volumes of *Arcana*. Beside the term 'contrariety' or 'contraries' other key words, such as 'progression' also occur.

For example, Swedenborg writes:

'These words signify *Progression* to things Divine, ...'[92]

'. . . The *Progression* of the celestial thing of love.'[93]

'. . . if this *Progression* be made from Scientific and rational truths. . . .'[94]

'*Progression* is from Scientific to things rational, ...'[95]

'. . . There are *progressive* motions (Progression) amongst the inhabitants in another life, ...'[96]

'. . . hereby is signified the Lord's *progression* in the goodness and truths of faith . . . .'[97]

'. . . by which is signified a further and more interior *progression*, ...'[98]

'. . . it was a continual *progression* of the human (Principle) to the Divine, . . .'[99]

'It was shown me what is the manner of the *progress* of the delights arising from conjugial love, this way towards heaven, and that way towards hell: . . . The *progression* was more interior . . . .'[100]

'. . . in the present verse are signified those who are in *progression*, ...'[101]

'. . . in respect to growing up, and increasing in age even to the last, this appertains to the state of *progress*; the state of *progress* succeeds from nativity . . . .'[102]

'. . . *progression* to further things, ...'[103]

'. . . by the journeys . . . of Abraham and Jacob were represented *Progression* into the truths of faith . . . .'[104]

'. . . such *progressions* and derivations are perceptual with the man who is regenerated . . . .'[105]

Although we can record similar examples from other works of Swedenborg, nevertheless Blake's statement 'Without Contraries . . .' is certainly related especially to Swedenborg's *Heaven and Hell* and written in opposition to his philosophical system.

The passage from Boehme, if we take it as it stands, is quite opposed to Blake's idea of 'contraries'. The 'Angry' or 'Jealous God' in Boehme is, according to Blake, the symbol of 'negation' and tyranny. Negation is not contrariety in the creative sense of the term. Negation is a fallen state of man or society. It is true that the 'Angry' or 'Jealous God' is opposed to the useful and profitable God, but they are hardly contraries. Blake when discussing the difference between 'negation' and 'contraries' in *Milton* wrote:

' "There is a Negation, & there is a Contrary:
"The Negation must be destroy'd to redeem the Contra-
    ries.
"The Negation is the Spectre, the Reasoning Power in
    Man:
"This is a false Body, an Incrustation over my Immortal
"Spirit, a Selfhood which must be put off & annihilated
    alway.
"To cleanse the Face of my Spirit by Self-examina-
    tion." '106

The 'Selfhood' or 'Reasoning Power' in *The Gates of Paradise*
is called 'Serpent Reasoning' which negates the 'Eternal Man'
by its poisonous laws of 'Good' and 'Evil':

> 'Serpent Reasonings us entice
> Of Good & Evil, Virtue & Vice.
> Doubt Self Jealous, Wat'ry folly,
> Struggling thro' Earth's Melancholy.'107

The 'Serpent Reasoning' is not contrary to creative or
'Eternal Man' but is a 'negation' of it. Thus Boehme's statement
that 'without poison and eagerness there is no Life' is utterly
alien to Blake's thought. Swedenborg wrote in his *Divine Love*:

> 'It follows that the one Sun is living and that the other
> Sun is dead, also that the dead Sun itself was created by
> the living Sun from the Lord.'

Blake remarks: 'How could Life create death?'108

The 'Contraries' in *The Marriage of Heaven and Hell* are
written in criticism of Swedenborg who sees all that he loves as
attributes of 'Heaven' and the Angels, and all that he hates as
attributes of 'Hell' and the Devil. He, for example, regards the
passive life as 'Heavenly' and the active life as 'Hell'. Blake
says that it is natural to love a favourable condition, and that
this love must be based on one's own energy. Blake, then, uses
the terms 'Heaven' and 'Hell' to oppose Swedenborg by his
own terms.

> 'From these contraries spring what the religious Call
> Good and Evil. Good is the passive that obeys Reason.
> Evil is the active Springing from Energy. Good is Heaven.
> Evil is Hell.'

This is an ironic summary of Swedenborg's *Heaven and Hell*.

Closer examination of Blake's early writings can also show that the 'thought' of contraries in *The Marriage* was not derived from Boehme. Blake had acquired knowledge through his own experience. In his *Annotations to Swedenborg's Wisdom of Angels Concerning Divine Love and Divine Wisdom* (1788) Blake seems to have formed his philosophy of 'contraries'. Swedenborg writes:

> 'Man is only a Recipient of Life. From this Cause it is, that Man, from his own hereditary Evil, reacts against God; but so far as he believes that all his Life is from God, and every Good of Life from the Action of God, and every Evil of Life from the Reaction of Man; Reaction thus becomes correspondent with Action, and Man acts with God as from himself.'

Blake wrote underneath:

> 'Good & Evil are here both Good & the two contraries Married.'

In other words 'Good' and 'Evil' are the product of passive reasoning. Good is the passive force that obeys Reason and Evil the active force springing from Energy. The marriage between 'Good' and 'Evil' is, in fact, the marriage of the active and passive, the subjective and objective, the spiritual and material world. In the same book Blake has displayed the dialectical form of thought. Swedenborg writes:

> 'Moreover it was shown in the light of Heaven . . . that the interior Compages of this little Brain was . . . in the Order and Form of Heaven; and that its exterior Compages was in Opposition to that Order and Form.'

Blake, using Swedenborg's terms 'Heaven' and 'Hell', sums up his dialectic very briefly as follows:

> 'Heaven & Hell are born together.'[109]

In other words 'exterior' and 'interior' or matter and spirit (object and subject) are born together, but the material world or (as Swedenborg here puts it) 'Hell' is, from Blake's viewpoint, prior to spirit or 'Heaven'. It is also the same mind in Blake that opposes and satirizes Swedenborg's static system of 'Heaven' and 'Hell' in *The Marriage*.

In the chapter 'concerning the change of State of the Angels in Heaven' Swedenborg explains the mental states of the Angels at different times of the day. The angelic life consists of 'love' and 'faith' or 'wisdom' and 'intelligence'. Since all wisdom and intelligence stem from the Lord, those who are in love with the Lord and have faith in His divine principle possess wisdom and intelligence. In other words the states of wisdom and intelligence are based on love and faith. The Angels live in this state because they are in love with the Lord. They do not depend on the world or active life, but live in the 'state' of love. The delight of the Angels depends on the 'state' of their love'.

Although the Angels live only in the 'state' of love, argues Swedenborg, nonetheless the degree of their love varies: 'angels are not constantly in a similar state as to love . . . sometimes they are in a state of interior; it decreases by degrees from its greatest or its least'.[110] When the Angels are in the greatest degree of love they are then 'in the light and heat of their life, or in their brightness and *delight* . . .'.[111] In other words the delight of Angels increases or decreases by the change of their 'love'. They change like 'the variations of the state of light and shade, of heat and of cold, or like morning, mid-day, evening and night . . . morning the first and highest degree of love; mid-day wisdom in its light; evening wisdom in its shade . . .' All these changes occur in the abstract thought of Swedenborg who has divorced himself from the active life. Blake brings them down to earth by writing in the 'Proverbs of Hell':

'Think in the morning. Act in the noon. Eat in the evening. Sleep in the night.'[112]

All this means that for Swedenborg 'love' and the 'delight' of life in the 'Heavens' are derived from divine sources as opposed to the love and delight which are derived from the material world and the creative energy of man. And the change of 'state' in 'Heaven' is the change of 'love' and 'delight' which are the 'life' and 'progression' of the Angels.

In the chapters 'Concerning Time in Heaven' and 'Space in Heaven' which follow the chapter on 'The Changes of State . . .', Swedenborg discusses the idea of 'progression'.

Progression means a change from one 'state' to another. In the world this progression takes place in 'time' and 'space' but in 'heaven' time and space do not exist.

> 'The reason why there are times in the world, is, because the sun of the world to appearance is in successive *progression* from one degree to another, and makes the times. . . . It is otherwise with the sun of heaven; this doth not, by successive *progressions* and circumgyrations, make years and days, but, to appearance, changes of state . . . hence the angels cannot have any idea of time, but in its place they have an idea of state. . . .'[113]

Because the angels have no idea of time, their concept of 'eternity' differs from the earthly meaning of the word:

> 'The angels by eternity perceive infinite state, but not infinite time. . . .'[114]

To the passive personality or mind 'eternity' or creation is based on abstract memories and is therefore independent of the realities of 'time' and 'space'. For the creative personality it is based on an active life within time and space. In his 'Proverbs of Hell' Blake criticizes Swedenborg's idea of 'time' by stating that:

> 'Eternity is in love with the productions of time.'

In other words, 'eternity' depends on time which represents creativity and activity or the beginning and end of an act of creation on earth. Since the end of one act of creation is the beginning of another cycle of creation therefore 'eternity' is in love with the production of 'time'. The new is born out of the old and the present out of the past. This is demonstrated both in nature, in society and in the daily life of an active person like Blake. The words 'eternity' and 'time' in the proverb are taken from the chapter 'Concerning Time in Heaven'.[115]

By the idea of 'time' Swedenborg means 'state'. Even in the Bible: 'times, in the Word, signify states'.[116] The concepts of progression' and of 'contraries' in *Heaven and Hell* depend on the idea of 'state':

'All *progressions* in the spiritual world are affected by changes of the state of the interiors, so that *progressions* are nothing else but changes of state.'[117]

The word 'state' means the interior quality of every man: '*States* are predicated of *life*, and of those things which relate to life'.[118] The interior state of every man determines his external life. It is the interior 'state' of the Angels which makes 'Heaven' and similarly with the interior 'state' of the inhabitants of 'Hell'. 'Heaven' and 'Hell' are opposite to each other because their interior states are opposite. The interior 'state' of the Angels in 'Heaven' is 'good' but the interior 'state' of the people in 'Hell' is 'evil' because:

'. . . the state of heaven . . . is the conjunction of good and of truth . . . , and the state of hell is the conjunction of what is evil. . . .'[119]

In other words, the interior of those who do active or manual work is 'evil', and the interior of Angels who with their passive memories belong to 'Heaven' is 'good'.

A closer examination of *Heaven and Hell* reveals that to Swedenborg, 'state' meant the memories formed by sense impressions. In other words these memories form the 'state' of the interiors of the inhabitants of 'Heaven' and 'Hell'. The motivating love of every man is based on his interior state or memories. Those who have good interiors are attracted to the 'good' or 'Heaven' whereas those with 'evil' interiors are attracted to 'Hell'. The 'progressions' are also based on the changes of interior states:

'progressions are nothing else but changes of state;'[120]

From the ideas of 'interior state' and 'progression' Swedenborg forms his idea of 'contrary state'. The 'progression' is based on the 'interior state' or memory. Man progresses towards 'similitudes' or what agrees with the 'state of the interior'. He rejects or removes 'dissimilitudes'. Therefore those who are in a similar 'state' are near to each other and at a distance or divided from those who are in a 'contrary state'. All the Angels progress towards 'similitudes' according to their 'state of the interiors' and separate themselves from what is in a 'contrary state':

> 'This being the case with *progressions*, it is evident that approximations are similitudes as to the state of the interiors, and that removals are dissimilitudes; hence it is that they are near to each other who are in a similar state, and at a distance, who are in a dissimilar state, . . . hence likewise it is that the heavens, as being in a *contrary* state.'[121]

What agrees with the driving 'love' or memories of Swedenborg is for him 'good' and whatever disagrees is 'evil'. Blake's 'contraries' contain more than simply a 'Mental Fight' between the 'radical and conservative imagination', as Northrop Frye has suggested; they point a particular criticism of the self-centred material interests of Swedenborg, the conservative. From Blake's viewpoint 'Without Contraries is no progression. Attraction and Repulsion, Reason and Energy, Love and Hate, are necessary to Human existence', but attraction, reason and love have material origins. The 'state of the interior' which Swedenborg loves and to which he is attracted, is thus given a material source which is formed by Swedenborg's social environment:

> 'Energy is the only life, and is from the Body.'

Blake who worked throughout his whole life and depended on the rewards of his own energy speaks out, as the 'Devil' from 'Hell', against the abstract religion of Swedenborg, who is sitting amid the plenty of 'Heaven' and condemning the less fortunate for their love of the world or 'Body'.

4. PLATE 4: 'THE VOICE OF THE DEVIL'

At this point Blake explicitly shows how his 'contraries' or dialectic are based on the material world.

> 'All Bibles or sacred codes have been the causes of the following errors:
>
> 1. That a man has two real existing principles: Viz.: a Body & a Soul.
> 2. That Energy, call'd Evil, is alone from the Body; & that Reason, call'd Good, is alone from the Soul.

3. That God will torment Man in Eternity for follow-
ing his energies.

But the following Contraries to these are True:

1. Man has no Body distinct from his Soul; for that
call'd Body is a portion of Soul discern'd by the five
senses, the chief inlets of Soul in this age.
2. Energy is the only life, and is from the Body; and
Reason is the bound or outward circumference of
Energy.
3. Energy is Eternal Delight.'[122]

This plate is one of the most important parts of *The Marriage*
where two opposing theories of the source of life are juxtaposed.
One theory is that man's thought, delight, joy and energy
spring from the 'soul', or a metaphysical source, and the other
theory is that they spring from the 'Body' or the material
world.

Swedenborg assumed that all things in life, including all the
good things of 'Heaven', flow, like a fountain, from the Lord.
Those who are showered with divine good and truth from this
fountain are in 'Heaven', and those who reject this divine good
and truth are in 'Hell'. The Angels' life stems from one single
source, the Lord. He insists that 'there is only one single
fountain of *life* and that the *life* of man is a stream thence
derived, which would instantly cease to flow, if it did not
subsist continually from its fountain'. Those who receive
divine good and divine truth '. . . in faith and *life* have heaven
in them, but those who reject them . . . turn them into hell.'[123]
Discussing the 'life of love' and the 'life of the will of man',
Swedenborg writes in the same passage:

'. . . all of *life* is from the Lord, they also confirm by this
consideration, that all things in the universe have reference
to the good and truth, the *life* of the will of man, which is
the *life* of his love, to good, and the *life* of the under-
standing of man, which is the *life* of his faith, to truth;
wherefore since every thing good and true comes from
above, it follows that all of *life* is likewise from the same
source.'[124]

This is the orthodox religious interpretation, which despises the material world. Human energy comes from the 'Body' and is anyway inferior to 'Reason'. But again, for Blake 'Energy is the only life, and is from the Body; . . .' Man's ability to work depends on food and drink from the material world, and his thoughts correspond to the objects of his particular interest in the world.

'Energy is the Only Life' is the title of Chapter 15 in Volume I of Kathleen Raine's *Blake and Tradition*. 'Miss Raine', writes John Wren-Lewis in his review of the work, 'devotes a whole chapter to Blake's "Energy is Eternal Delight", but she somehow to me never conveys the feel of it, and I think the clue to this failure is to be found in Blake's recognition that "Energy . . . is of the body." Miss Raine's vision seems dominated by her belief that Blake draws again and again on mystical traditions whereby the body is seen as a tomb of the soul, a "wreath of moist cloud", a "fibrous polypus" in which man's divine imagination has somehow become ensnared.'[125]

Miss Raine has attempted to interpret and relate the statement 'Energy is the only Life' in *The Marriage of Heaven and Hell* to Boehme and Swedenborg. It should be clear by now that Blake's idea that 'Energy is Eternal Delight' is not derived from the mysticism of Boehme. Nor can it be assumed, as Miss Raine asserts, to exist 'within the structure of Swedenborgian thought'.[126] We have shown that Blake's thought is based on his own originality and experience rather than on a passive borrowing from Boehme or from other sources, and that Blake's thought not only was not within the structure of Swedenborgian thought but rather was written against Swedenborg's philosophical system.

Miss Raine argues that Blake's philosophy of energy was not the product of his own acquired knowledge or 'invention'.

> 'This philosophy of energy as "the only life" that is "from the Body",' writes Miss Raine, 'was certainly no invention of Blake's. Boehme's Father and his seven nature-spirits is nothing less than the energy of nature and of the body:

> "For here you must understand, that there are two Wills in one Being, and they cause *two Principles*: One is love and the other is the Anger or the Source of Wrath. The

first Will is not called God, but Nature; the second Will is called A and O, the beginning and the End, from Eternity to Eternity: and in the first Will, Nature could not be manifest, the second Will, makes Nature manifest. . . . and the one would be *nothing* without the other." '[127]

I do not see how Blake could possibly have derived his philosophy of 'Energy' from the above-mentioned passage or similar passages: Boehme's passage does relate indeed to the contrary nature of man, but does not refer to Energy, but to Will. And, moreover, Blake, long before writing *The Marriage of Heaven and Hell*, had formed a clear vision of the contrary capacities of man. In his *Annotations to Lavater's Aphorisms on Man* (1788) Blake writes, for example:

'Man is a twofold being, one part capable of evil & the other capable of good; that which is capable of good is not also capable of evil, but that which is capable of evil is also capable of good. . . .'[128]

Again:

'. . . man is either the ark of God or a phantom of the earth & of the water; . . .'[129]

But Blake would not agree with Boehme's idea that 'there are two Wills in one Being'. According to Blake when man is informed by one Will or driving love he cannot be so by another at the same time.

'. . . both evil & good cannot exist in a simple being, for thus 2 contraries would spring from one essence, which is impossible; . . .'[130]

Blake furthermore suspected that 'Will' was 'Evil'. In his *Annotations to Swedenborg's Divine Love* he wrote:

'There can be no Good Will. Will is always Evil; it is pernicious to others or suffering.'[131]

Even if we accept one of Boehme's Wills as meaning 'Love' and the other as meaning 'Wrath', we are still dealing only with a passive 'Love' and 'Hate', or with something like Swedenborg's 'Heaven' and 'Hell'. For:

'Understanding or Thought is not natural to Man; it is acquir'd by means of Suffering & Distress, i.e. Experience, Will, Desire, Love, Pain, Envy, & all other affections are Natural, but Understanding is Acquir'd. . . .'[132]

This acquired 'Understanding' tells us that 'Without Contraries there is no progression': in other words, man by his genius or reason distinguishes good from bad, but this recognition of reason and its 'love' and 'attraction' to the good things in life and 'hate' and 'repulsion' from the undesirable has its basis in the material world. If 'Will', measuring 'Love', is not based on the active life or 'Energy' then it is passive and thus 'Evil'. For Blake, 'Energy' does not consist in passive states of either love or wrath, but it is rather the active and creative personality of man. In his *Annotations to Lavater* Blake gives some idea of what he meant by 'Energy'. Lavater wrote:

'He alone is good, who, though possessed of energy, prefers virtue, with the appearance of weakness, to the invitation of acting brilliantly ill.'

Blake wrote underneath:

'Noble! But Mark! Active Evil is better than Passive Good.'[133]

Energy, then, is the true man, and the active personality of Blake is opposed to abstract and passive memories.

Even if we assume that Boehme held an idea of 'Energy' similar to that of Blake there is still a sharp contradiction in Miss Raine's argument that the 'philosophy of energy . . . was certainly no invention of Blake's.' The contradiction lies between Blake's experimental method of acquiring knowledge and Miss Raine's attributing to him a derivative method.

The true method of Knowledge, according to Blake, leads to Knowledge which is experienced practically by man himself. In *All Religions are One* (1788) Blake has clearly and precisely defined his philosophy of Knowledge:

'The Argument. As the true method of knowledge is experiment, the true faculty of knowing must be the faculty which experiences. This faculty I treat of.'

This method of knowledge is opposed to memory or the passive knowledge which Blake describes as follows:

'The Argument. Man has no notion of moral fitness but from Education. Naturally he is only a natural organ subject to Sense.'

Blake's own knowledge was certainly not based on this principle, and he fought against this mechanistic philosophy all through his writings. In his *Annotations to Berkeley's 'Siris'* (1820), for example, he wrote:

'Knowledge is not by deduction, but Immediate by Perception or Sense at once. Christ addresses himself to the Man, not to his Reason. . . .'[134]

Thus if we accept Miss Raine's statement that the 'philosophy of energy . . . was certainly no invention of Blake's' then we indeed turn against Blake's principle. But the term 'invention' is wholly inappropriate as applied to Blake, who did not want to invent but rather to discover or create through his practical experience; it is hardly accurate, moreover, to say that the poet whose living depended on his daily work or energy throughout his life borrowed his idea of 'energy' from sources other than his own experiences of life.

' "Energy is Eternal Delight" ', writes Miss Raine, 'is still also within the structure of Swedenborgian thought . . .' and she goes on to quote from Swedenborg's *True Christian Religion*:

' "Delight is the All of Life to every one in Heaven, and the All of Life to everyone in Hell: they who are in Heaven perceive the Delight of what is good and true, but they who are in Hell, the Delight of what is evil and false: for all delight is of Love, and Love is the *Esse* of the Life of Man; wherefore Man is Man according to the Quality of his Love, so he is Man also according to the Quality of his Delight. The activity of Love is what causeth a Sense of Delight which Activity in Heaven is attended with Wisdom, and in Hell with Insanity, each whereof in their respective Subjects exciteth Delight; but the Heavens and the Hells are in opposite Delights." '

Blake 'takes for his own', argues Miss Raine, 'the essence of this wisdom of hell . . .'.[135]

It is true that Swedenborg uses the term 'Delight' extensively in his writings, and particularly in *Heaven and Hell* in the chapter entitled 'The Delights of the Life of Every One after Death are turned into correspondent ones'. There occur many passages similar to that which Miss Raine quotes, as for example:

> '. . . The ruling affection or predominant love remains to *eternity* with everyone, . . . the *delights* of that affection or love are turned into correspondent ones, . . . by being turned into correspondent ones, is meant into spiritual *delights* which are correspondent to natural: that they are turned into spiritual *delights*, may be manifest from this consideration, that man, so long as he is in his terrestial body, is in the natural world, but when he leaves that body, he comes into the spiritual world, and puts on a spiritual body. That angels are in a perfect human form, and likewise men after death, and that their bodies, with which they are clothed, are spiritual. . . .'[136]

> 'All the *delights* appertaining to man are of his ruling love, for man is not sensible of any other *delight* that of when he loves, . . . these specific *delights* with everyone have reference to his one love, which is the ruling love, for they compose it, and thus make one with it: in like manner all delights in general have reference to one universally ruling love, in heaven to love to the Lord, and in hell to the love of self.'[137]

> '. . . the *delights* of everyone's *life* are turned after death into corresponding *delights* . . . All they who are principled in evil, and have confirmed themselves in falses against the truths of the church, especially they who have rejected the Word, shun the light of heaven, and plunge themselves into hiding places, which in the apertures appear extremely dark, and into clefts of rocks, . . . because they have falses and have hated truths.'[138]

To Swedenborg, as has been indicated earlier, the active life of those in 'Hell' or the mines is based on falsehood and the passive life of those in 'Heaven' is based on truth. Although the ruling affection or predominant love 'remains to eternity

with everyone', and turns into 'correspondent' ones, neverthe-
less the driving love and delights of the Angels in 'Heaven' are
good because they come from 'above', or from the spiritual
world as opposed to the earth or material world. In the chapter
'Concerning Heavenly Joy and Happiness' Swedenborg writes:

> 'All *delights* flow forth from love, for what a man loves,
> this he feels as *delightful*, nor hath he any one *delight* from
> any other source, hence it follows, that such as the love is,
> such is the *delight*: the *delight* of the *body* or of the flesh all
> flow forth from the love of self and from the love of the
> *world*, hence also they are concupiscences and the pleasures
> attending them, but the *delight* of the *soul* or spirit all flow
> forth from love to the Lord and from love towards the
> neighbour, . . .'[139]

The Angels in 'Heaven' look upwards to the Lord but those
in 'Hell' look to the world.

> 'The *delights* of heaven are ineffable, and likewise are
> innumerable, but of those innumerable *delights* not one
> can be known nor credited by him who is in the mere
> *delight* of the body or of the flesh, since, . . . his interiors
> look from heaven to the world, . . . for he who is immersed
> in the *delight* of the *body*.'[140]

Those who are in the world or 'body' live in opposition to
the delight of 'Heaven'. They 'desire' to be admitted into
'Heaven' but when they approach the portals they begin to
be tortured and 'tormented':

> '. . . the *delight* in which they are who are principles in the
> loves of self and of the *world*, when they approach to any
> heavenly society, is the *delight* of their concupiscence, thus
> likewise altogether opposite to the *delight* of heaven; . . .
> they who are principled in the love of self and of the
> world approach to the first threshold of that heaven, they
> begin to be tortured and so interiorly *tormented*, . . .'[141]

These passages show in what a wide sense the term 'delight' is
used by Swedenborg. Nevertheless it cannot be asserted that
Blake's statement 'Energy is Eternal Delight' is 'within the
structure of Swedenborgian thought', when Blake's statement

is patently written against and in repudiation of Swedenborg's philosophy.

Blake would agree that the natural spontaneous 'delights' of affection or love are turned into 'correspondent ones'; and 'by being turned into correspondent ones, is meant into spiritual delights which are correspondent to natural'. But Blake believed that 'delight' is from the 'Body'. Herein lies the philosophical difference between the two writers. Another difference is moral. Swedenborg, as we have shown above, regarded the 'delights' of those in 'Heaven' as good and based on truth but the 'delights' of those in 'Hell' or coal mines as evil because they were based on love of self and of the 'delights' of the world.

> '. . . the delight of the *body* or of the flesh all flow forth from the love of self and from the love of the *world*, . . . but the *delight* of the *soul* or spirit all flow forth from the love to the Lord . . . hence they are the affections of good and truth, and interior satisfactions: These latter loves with their *delights* flow in from the Lord, and out of heaven, by an internal way, which is from above, and they affect the interiors; but the former loves with their *delights* flow in from the flesh and from the world by an external way, which is from beneath, and they affect the exteriors.'[142]

The delight of those in 'Heaven' turns to good and truth or heavenly delight because when they lived in the world they lived a life full of the love of God. But those who live in 'Hell' amid 'infernal fire' do so because of their love of the world. 'Hell' is separated from 'Heaven' because of 'driving' delight. The people in 'Hell' are in mere delight of the 'Body' but those in 'Heaven' are in the delight of the 'soul' and of the 'spirit'.[143]

> '. . . the *delights* of the love of self and of the *world* are then turned into what is painful and direful, because into such things as are called *infernal* fire, and by turns into things defiled and filthy, corresponding to their unclean pleasures, which, what is wonderful, are in such case *delightful* to them; but the obscure *delight* and almost imperceptible blessedness, which appertained to those in the *world* who

were principled in love to God and in love towards their neighbour, is then turned into the *delight* of heaven, which is in every way perceptible and sensible. . . .'[144]

Blake, defending the 'delight' of the active life in 'Hell' against the passive 'delight' of life in 'Heaven' wrote:

1. Man has no Body distinct from his Soul; for that call'd Body is a portion of Soul discern'd by the five Senses, the chief inlets of Soul in this age.

2. Energy is the only life, and is from the Body; and Reason is the bound or outward circumference of Energy.

3. Energy is Eternal Delight.'[145]

Blake indeed believed in the spiritual being of man, but not in the kind of spiritualism which is based on selfishness. It is ironical that Swedenborg believed in the spiritual origin of 'delight' while living amid worldly wealth and writing about precious stones in 'Heaven', whereas Blake, while working for the daily bread of his wife and himself, believed in the worldly origin of 'delight'. This irony also affects the theme and the colour of language of the poet in *The Marriage*. Blake recognized that the superior position of the Angels in 'Heaven' stems mainly from their economic superiority rather than from an innate goodness. His central viewpoint that 'Energy is the only life, and is from the Body' formed the social vision and philosophy of his later writings. In *Visions of the Daughters of Albion* (1793) he denounces conventional laws and asks:

' "are there other wars beside the wars of sword and fires?
"And are there other sorrows beside the sorrows of poverty?
"And are there other joys besides the joys of riches and ease?
"And is there not one law for both the lion and the ox?
"And is there not eternal fire and eternal chains
"To bind the phantoms of existence from eternal life?" '[146]

The child in 'The Little Vagabond' from the *Songs of Experience* points the same idea. He represents those who live in 'Hell' and who reject 'Heaven' as represented by the Church because, instead of pouring out sustenance 'gratis', it is barren and 'cold'. The child says that if the Church would share its material wealth and let the people in 'Hell' be as happy as those in 'Heaven', then the two separate classes would join, and good and evil marry:

> 'Dear Mother, dear Mother, the Church is cold,
> But the Ale-house is healthy & pleasant & warm;
> Besides I can tell where I am used well,
> Such usage in heaven will never do well.

> But if at the Church they would give us some Ale,
> And a pleasant fire our souls to regale,
> We'd sing and we'd pray all the live-long day,
> Nor ever once wish from the Church to stray.'[147]

Blake criticizes the selfish greed for possessions of the Church and its Christian Charity all through his works. In *The Laocoön* (1820), for example, he writes:

> 'The True Christian Charity is not dependent on Money (the life's blood of Poor Families), that is, on Caesar or Empire or Natural Religion: Money, which is The Great Satan or Reason, the Root of Good & Evil In The Accusation of Sin.'

Thus the war between 'Heaven' and 'Hell' arises from material conflict.

The word 'Reason' in the passage from *Laocoön* is the symbol of selfhood and therefore Blake identifies it with Satan. Blake also criticizes the same kind of 'Reason' in *The Marriage*, thus offering further evidence of his inversion of Swedenborg's system. Swedenborg, for example, in *Heaven and Hell* writes:

> Man ... 'is capable of being elevated, as to all the interiors of his mind ... by ... discoursing from reason ...',[148]

and those Angels who are in love, wisdom and intelligence are in the centre of 'Heaven' where the Lord is, and those who are less excellent are round about 'comparatively as light in its decrease from the centre to the circumferences'.[149] The words 'reason' and 'circumference' appear in close conjunction in *Heaven and Hell*. They also occur together in Swedenborg's

Divine Providence where he uses the word 'Reason' frequently while discussing his idea of 'free will' or 'Rationality':

> 'Man hath Reason and Free-will, or Rationality and Liberty; and . . . these two Faculties are from the Lord in Man'.[150]

The word 'Reason' in Swedenborg conveys the rational mind which binds or is the 'outward circumference' of 'Energy'. It is the material wealth of 'Heaven' which attracts Swedenborg's reason. But his reason, according to Blake, is passive and thus has no moral value. Reason is passive when it is based on the limited memories of a passive personality which Blake calls Urizen (your reason). 'Urizen', writes Dorothy Plowman, 'is derived from the Greek word οὑρίζειν, meaning "to bound" or "limit", with the cognate form "Uranus" the Lord of the Firmament, or that first self-imposed setter of bounds whose rule became a tyranny that his own sons were impelled to break and supplant. . . .'[151] Reason is creative and a necessary part of 'progression' and Imagination when it is not limited to selfhood. It is only the limited or passive 'Reason' in 'Heaven' which negates and restrains the people in 'Hell'. The 'ruling love' and will of the Angels are based on passive 'Reason'. Man acts from 'Liberty according to Reason' says Swedenborg.[152] The Angels in 'Heaven' are attracted to the things appropriate to them according to their passive 'Reason'. Thus 'Reason' distinguishes 'good' from 'evil'. Those who are 'good' form the centre which is 'Heaven' and the evil-doers live on the 'circumference'.

> 'Goods . . . make the center, and remove the Evils towards the circumference . . .'[153]

Swedenborg here again reflects his social background. In 'Heaven' the Angels live in dwellings which correspond to the 'good' of Angels. The Angels and governors dwell in the middle of society: 'They dwell in the midst of society, in situations elevated above others, and likewise in magnificent palaces. . . .'[154] Thus the inhabitants of 'Heaven' are in the centre of society but the inhabitants of 'Hell' are at the circumference. Swedenborg's mind is attracted to the centre where the Lord is:

'It was principally given to perceive, and likewise to be sensible, that there was an *attraction* and as it were a plucking away of the interiors of my mind, thus of my spirit, from the body, and it was said that this was from the Lord.'[155]

But Swedenborg's rational mind or reason is attracted only to his own passive and limited memories. By this passive reason he negates and restrains the desire and love of those in 'Hell'.

5. SWEDENBORG'S GOD IS BLAKE'S SATAN

Plates 5–6: 'Those who *restrain desire*, do so because theirs is weak enough to be *restrained*, and the restrainer or reason usurps its place & governs the unwilling.

And being *restrained*, it by degrees becomes passive, till it is only the shadow of desire.'[156] This is one of the most difficult passages in *The Marriage of Heaven and Hell*. It is difficult to discover what kind of 'desire' is 'restrained' and who is the 'restrainer'. But it nevertheless becomes understandable in the context of Swedenborg's *Heaven and Hell*, where the word 'restraint' is used in various ways where its contexts are crucial to its meaning. There frequently occur statements such as:

'. . . unless there were governments the infernals could not be kept under any *restraint*.'[157]

'. . . cannot be *restrained* nor broken except by punishments.'[158]

'. . . they . . . act without being *restrained* by external bonds. . . .'[159]

'. . . unless civil laws . . . *restrained* him. . . .'[160]

'. . . Lord *restrained* the insults from the hells. . . .'[161]

'. . . the attempt ascending from hell was *restrained* . . .'[162]

'. . . the general tendency . . . issuing forth from the hells is checked and *restrained*. . . .'[163]

'. . . to *restrain* the insanities and disturbances. . . .'[164]

'The fear of punishment is the only medium to *restrain*....'[165]

'. . . torments in the hells are permitted by the Lord, . . .
evils cannot otherwise be *restrained* . . . the only medium
of *restraining* . . . keeping the infernal crew in bonds, is the
fear of punishment. . . .'[166]

'. . . if good did not re-act against evil, and continually
restrain its insurrection, . . . unless the Divine (Being or
Principle) alone affected such *restraint*:'[167]

'. . . outrages in the hells are subdued, and cruelties are
restrained, . . .'[168]

A sense of clarity begins to emerge. The word 'desire',
contrary to Kathleen Raine's assertion that it was taken from
Boehme as one of the 'attributes of Hell',[169] seems rather to
refer to Swedenborg's *Heaven and Hell*, as the following illu-
strations will show:

'. . . love receives all . . . things which are in agreement
with itself; it *desires* them.'[170]

'. . . he comes there sooner when he *desires* it, and later
when he doth not *desire* it, . . .'[171]

'. . . the way itself being lengthened and shortened
according to *desire*, . . .'[172]

'. . . they who have had little of . . . *desire*, receive little, . . .
but they who have had much . . . *desire* receive much. . . .'[173]

They '. . . *desire* truth, and from *desire* seek it. . . .'[174]

They '*desire* heaven with greater ardour than others, . . .'[175]

By the poor is meant 'those who are wanting in those
knowledges, and yet *desire* them, . . .'[176]

'. . . the poor man who lay at his gate, and *desired* to be
filled with the crumbs which fell from the rich man's
table. . . .'[177]

'Spirits who come from the world into the other life,
desire nothing more. than to be admitted into heaven,...'[178]

'. . . they are called poor who are not in the knowledge of
E

good and truth, and still *desire* them, in consequence of which *desire* they are likewise called hungry.'[179]

Examples are legion; this selection shows their general tendency. Those in 'Hell' who attempt to ascend and 'desire' to know about heavenly joy and delight are being restrained. In the book of *Hell* the word 'lust' corresponds to the word 'desire': The '*lust* of doing evils . . . originate in the love of self and of the world . . .'.[180]

Blake has picked out these words as of great significance and importance. To Blake the word 'restraint' means 'negation', and 'negation' is evil. The Angels who fulfil their own desires but restrain the desire of those in 'Hell' by calling them lust are committing the act of 'negation'. Blake associates the laws of restraint with reasoning and passivity. Northrop Frye, while discussing Blake's theory of evil, writes: '. . . all evil consists either in self-restraint or restraint of others',[181] and 'evil . . . arises only from passivity, the negative refusal to perform a creative act which results in frustrating either one's own development or that of others'.[182]

The poet seems to have great insight into the psychological mechanism of the passive being. By the passive being is meant the personality or mind which is not based on an active and practical life. The priest is a passive being, having power only to restrain and negate desire and energy in others. He is too passive to work creatively and his natural life depends on other people's work. Thus Swedenborg restrains the desire and energy of those in 'Hell' because he himself is not active. The restrainer is passive and weak. He escapes from reality and builds a protective circle around himself by the reasoning power of good and evil. This negative attitude builds up until the personality becomes wholly passive and ruled by 'Reason'. 'Urizen' is based on this passive 'Reason'. It is limited and essentially formed by sense perception or natural memories, which are based on selfhood.

'The history of this is written in Paradise Lost, & the Governor or Reason is call'd Messiah.
And the original Archangel, or possessor of the command of the heavenly host, is call'd the Devil or Satan, and his children are call'd Sin & Death.

But in the Book of Job, Milton's Messiah is call'd Satan.
For this history has been adopted by both parties.

It indeed appear'd to Reason as if Desire was cast out;
but the Devil's account is, that the Messiah fell, & formed
a heaven of what he stole from the Abyss.

This is shewn in the Gospel, where he prays to the Father
to send the comforter, or Desire, that Reason may have
Ideas to build on; the Jehovah of the Bible being no other
than (the Devil del.) he who dwells in flaming fire.'[183]

This passage is a brief interpretation of *Paradise Lost*. I am
more interested at the moment, however, to illustrate how the
words 'restraint' and 'Satan' refer to *Heaven and Hell*. Blake,
while commenting on Swedenborg's doctrine of 'restraint' and
fear of punishment, wanted to point out the similarity of
subject matter in Swedenborg, Milton and the *Book of Job*,
though each work has a different perspective.

In *Paradise Lost* the 'Governor or Reason is called the
Messiah', in *Heaven and Hell* the Governor and restrainer is
called the Lord; but in the *Book of Job*, Milton's Messiah is
called Satan. Blake implies that Swedenborg's restraining or
punishing character, who sees the world only through the
'abyss of five senses' or selfhood, is Satan. This 'abyss of five
senses' is the limited natural memories on which the Angel's
knowledge is based.

Swedenborg's God is rather Blake's Satan and Blake's God
is Swedenborg's Satan. Swedenborg's God is the passive
character who has but one desire, one love and one law. His
desire is passive and limited to what he has already perceived;
therefore his reason is also limited.

Reason can be creative and unlimited only when desire is
creative and active. 'Reason is the horizon', writes Erdman,
'kept constantly on the move by man's infinite desire. The
moment it exerts a will of its own and attempts to restrain
desire, it turns into that negative and unnecessary Reason
which enforces obedience with dungeons, armies and priest-
craft, and which Blake refers to as "the restrainer" which
usurps the place of desire and "governs the unwilling".'[184]
The passive and negative reason is Satan who accuses and
punishes man.

Discussing the identity of Satan, Frye writes: 'In the human mind he is the death-impulse or Selfhood which reduces men to becoming either death-dealing tyrants or torpid and inert victims of them. He is the "accuser" or principle of unbelief which makes tyrants revengeful and victims terrified, this mutual interaction of revenge and terror being the basis of fallen society. In this world Satan is therefore the objective counterpart of the death-impulse. . . .'[185]

Frye's interpretation is apt and correct, but in his study of *The Marriage* he has not examined Swedenborg's God and Satan.

Swedenborg's God seems to have the characteristics of Satan. He is selfish and cruel; he accuses his children of indulging themselves in love of the self and of the world while he himself lives amid material wealth, or, in other words, he is imprisoned in his own selfhood both in mind and body. The people in 'Hell' are restrained from their desire and are thus victims of the priest's negative selfhood. The priest justifies himself by committing all his negative actions in the name of the Lord. Thus Blake writes: 'Know that after Christ's death, he became Jehovah.' The priest alters the original teachings of Jesus after his death, and accuses and punishes the people in the name of Christ. In *A Vision of The Last Judgment* (1810) Blake is explicit:

> 'The Modern Church Crucifies Christ with the Head Downwards. . . . Thinking as I do that the Creator of this World is a very Cruel Being, & being a Worshipper of Christ, I cannot help saying: "The Son, O how unlike the Father!" First God Almighty comes with a Thump on the Head. Then Jesus Christ comes with a balm to heal it.'[186]

Thus the Christ who came to bring love becomes Jehovah, the God of punishment.

The death-impulse is created in the priest because he has divided himself from the people. He first becomes himself the victim of his own selfhood. Then his passive reason or selfhood leads him to rule the unwilling part in himself and in others. He is divided from others both in mind and body; in mind because he considers himself superior to and wiser than the simple people and uses his wisdom as a means for his own ends;

in body or society because he considers his material wealth as proof of his moral superiority over others.

This outlook, in Blake's view, springs from the priest's passive upbringing and 'systematic reasoning':

> 'I have always found that the Angels have the vanity to speak of themselves as the only wise; this they do with a confident insolence sprouting from systematic reasoning.'[187]

Swedenborg's Satan, unlike his God, seems an active and creative being. Swedenborg, in general, calls the energetic or active people who work in 'Hell' Satan and devil. He repudiates the orthodox view of there being one Satan in 'Hell', saying 'in the Word mention is made of the devil and Satan, and also of Lucifer'. The devil is 'That hell which is to the back and where the worst dwell'; Satan is 'That hell which is in front, the inhabitants of which are not so malignant . . .'; and Lucifer is 'Babel or Babylon'. All 'who are in the hells, like all who are in the heavens, are from the human race'.[188]

Since by Satan and the devil, Swedenborg means those who work in 'Hell' or coal mines, it follows that Blake's Satan and devil are the active and creative characters in 'Hell' who oppose the selfish and passive God of the priests and mine-owners. They are ruled over by the unjust laws of the Church whose votaries 'steal the labor of others to support'[189] their God. God represents law; and Satan, like Milton's Satan, is struggling to be free. R. W. Harris in his recent book, *Romanticism and Social Order* has pointed out that in

> '. . . Blake's pregnant criticism of Milton's *Paradise Lost*, which was very similar to Shelley's: . . . God stood for the law, whereas Satan appeared as the individual struggling to be free, and Blake's sympathy like that of Shelley, was on the side of Satan.'[190]

Swedenborg's Satan or devil seems to Blake more prolific and moral than his devouring God. It is also, perhaps, this moral superiority of the devil character in Swedenborg which makes Blake side with him and speak for the Devil against the Angel. The energetic beings in 'Hell' or the coal mines are

morally more acceptable and attractive than the passive
Angels and their God in 'Heaven':

> 'Messiah or Satan or Tempter was formerly thought to be
> one of the Antedeluvians who are our Energies.'[191]

Blake puts 'Messiah' or 'Satan' or 'Tempter' on an equal
footing because, although people look at the active life and at
energy differently and give them different names, they are
basically the same thing. Swedenborg regards energy as
infernal and calls it Satan; Blake sees it as creative and calls it
'Messiah'; for the history of the Messiah and Satan 'has been
adopted by both parties'.[192] One party looks at energy and
active life through the 'abyss of the five senses' and sees it as
finite and infernal. The fallen man is drowned in the flood of
sense-perception which closes him up 'till he sees all things
thro' narrow chinks of his cavern'.[193] Another party looks at
energy and active life through transparent windows of per-
ception and sees it infinite and holy. Energy is holy because it
is the prolific part of man, and the natural life and individuality
or dignity of man depends on his creative energy. Ante-
diluvian, perhaps, are the energies which have not yet closed
themselves up in the abyss of the five senses or selfhood who is
Satan and Accuser. Blake in his 'Epilogue' to *The Gates of
Paradise* (1818) wrote:

> 'To The Accuser who is
> The God of This World
>
> Truly, My Satan, thou art but a Dunce,
> And dost not know the Garment from the Man.
> . . . .
>
> Tho' thou art Worship'd by the Names Divine
> Of Jesus & Jehovah, thou art still
> The Son of Morn in weary Night's decline,
> The lost Traveller's Dream under the Hill.'[194]

6. 'PROVERBS OF HELL'

The proverbs are a concise expression of the conflicts between
'Heaven' and 'Hell' and are related to the text of Swedenborg's

Heaven and Hell. Blake takes the words from *Heaven and Hell* and gives them his own meaning. The Last Judgment of Swedenborg led him to the wonders of 'Heaven', but Blake's Last Judgment led him to the active life in Hell. The 'Proverbs of Hell' are written in defence of 'Energy' or active life against 'Heaven' or passive life.

'As I was walking among the fires of hell, delighted with the enjoyments of Genius, which to Angels look like torment and insanity, I collected some of their Proverbs; thinking that as the sayings used in a nation mark its character, so the proverbs of Hell show the nature of Infernal wisdom better than any description of buildings or garments.

When I came home: On the abyss of the five senses, where a flat sided steep frowns over the present world, I saw a mighty Devil folded in black clouds, hovering on the sides of the rock: with corroding-fires he wrote the following sentence now perceived by the minds of men, & read by them on earth:

How do you know but ev'ry Bird that cuts the airy way, Is an immense world of delight, clos'd by your senses five?'[195]

Swedenborg walks among the people in 'Hell' or the 'infernal inhabitants' and records all his uneasy feelings. The coal mines or 'Hell' seem to him 'torment' and 'insanity' and the people there seem as 'monsters with horrible countenances and horrible bodies'. But Blake's experience of walking in 'Hell' is different. What seems 'torment' and 'insanity' to Swedenborg, a representative of the Angels, does not appear so to Blake. Instead he is 'delighted with the enjoyment of Genius' which is the creative and working 'Energy' in man.

Plates 6–7 are based on ironical criticism of Swedenborg who puts his passive memories before and against practical life. We have seen that the words 'fire', 'joy', 'torment', 'insanity', 'infernal', 'wisdom', 'building' and 'garment' occur frequently in *Heaven and Hell*, and Blake's own use of them in Plates 6–7 was almost certainly suggested by Swedenborg. It will be helpful to list some examples of these words in *Heaven and Hell* and show how Blake inverts Swedenborg's usage.

Fire:

'The heat in heaven is what is meant by sacred and celestial *fire* and the heat of hell is what is meant by profane and *infernal fire*, . . .'[196]

'. . . some spurious *fire*, kindled by the love of self and of the world, ...'[197]

'. . . a dense *fiery* appearance exhaling from the hells where self love prevails, and a flaming appearance from the hells where the love of the world prevails.'[198]

'Such torments are the torments of hell, which are called infernal *fire*.'[199]

Joy:

'. . . it is not known what heavenly *joy* is. . . .'[200]

'. . . external *joys* which are of the natural man'.[201]

'. . . from those principles heavenly *joys* proceed.'[202]

Those in hell 'desired to know what heavenly *joy* is. . . .'[203]

'. . . worldly *joys* are of no account respectively. . . .'[204]

'. . . granted me by the Lord to perceive the delights of heavenly *joys* . . . .'[205]

Torment:

'. . . an infernal ardour *torments* those who do not worship . . . .'[206]

'. . . they begin to be tortured and *tormented*, . . . they feel in themselves rather hell than heaven, . . .'[207]

'. . . they apperceive in themselves infernal *torment* instead of heavenly joy . . . .'[208]

'. . . they are likewise inwardly *tormented* . . . .'[209]

Those who 'do not submit themselves, and yield implicit obedience, are again *tormented* by various methods; . . . such *torments* are the *torments* of hell . . . .'[210]

Insanity:

'They are tattered, dirty and hideous, everyone according to his *insanity* . . .'[211]

'. . . their delight dwells in *insanity* . . . .'[212]

'. . . concerning their *insanities*, and concerning their lot . . . .'[213]

'. . . Lord restrained the insults from the hells, and checked the *insanities*. . . .'[214]

'. . . excites in him lusts . . . with the sick *insanities*. . . .'[215]

Infernal:

'. . . the Angels cannot endure *infernal* discourse: . . .'[216]

They 'should induce *infernal* darkness . . . .'[217]

'. . . their *infernal* fire is the lust of glory . . . .'[218]

'. . . either heavenly or *infernal* . . . .'[219]

'. . . the things done from the Lord are all of them good; but the deeds and works of moral and civil life are *infernal*, . . . they are done from *infernal* love, . . . are done from the man himself . . . .'[220]

'every man . . . is conjoined to some society either *infernal* or heavenly . . . .'[221]

'. . . the *infernal* society which is in similar love: . . . whereas that love is *infernal* . . . .'[222]

'Hence . . . all *infernal* spirits turn . . . backward from the Lord . . . .'[223]

Wisdom:

'What is the quality of the *Wisdom* of angels of heaven . . . .'[224]

'. . . it was made evident to me how great is their *wisdom*, . . .'[225]

The 'palace of *wisdom*, . . .'[226]

E*

'. . . in the light of *wisdom* . . . .'[227]

'They wonder how anyone can believe that he is *wise* from himself, . . .'[228]

'. . . he who descends from a superior heaven is deprived of his *wisdom*, . . .'[229]

'. . . the celestial angels discourse from . . . interior thought . . . they speak from *wisdom* . . . .'[230]

'. . . the speech of the *wise* is more interior . . . .'[231]

'. . . they are in a superior place, who, . . . excel others in *wisdom*.'[232]

'. . . the light of heaven is divine wisdom . . . .'[233]

'In the same degree in which *wisdom* and intelligence prevail among angels, wickedness and cunning prevail also amongst infernal spirits . . . .'[234]

'. . . angels are perfected in intelligence and *wisdom* . . . .'[235]

'Building' or 'Habitation' and 'mansion':

Angels 'have *habitations* . . . according to every one's state of life.'[236]

They 'are more magnificent than earthly *habitations* . . . .'[237]

'I have seen the *palaces* of heaven, . . .'[238]

'. . . their *habitations* are given gratis . . . .'[239]

'. . . some of them *dwelling* in *palaces* . . . .'[240]

'The hells are everywhere, . . . there is an exhalation . . . of fire with smoke, such as appears in the air from *buildings* on fire . . . .'[241]

'In some hells there is an appearance as of the ruins of *houses* and cities after fires, in which ruins the infernal spirits dwell. . . .'[242]

'Garment':

'. . . the *garments* with which, the angels appear clothed . . . .'[243]

'. . . the *garments* of the angels correspond to their intelligence . . . .'[244]

'. . . one hath more excellent *garments* than another . . . .'[245]

'. . . less intelligent have *garments* of different colours . . . .'[246]

'. . . the most intelligent have *garments* glittering as from flame . . . .'[247]

'. . . *garments*, in the Word, signify truths and intelligence.'[248]

'. . . they have more *garments* than one, . . .'[249]

It should be clear that the satirical force of *The Marriage* comes partly from the way Blake appropriates Swedenborg's vocabulary.

When Swedenborg returns to 'Heaven' or home from his visit to 'Hell' or the coal mines he feels peace and 'heavenly joy'; then he reasons from this that those who are in 'Hell' must also begin to be tortured inwardly when they approach near any heavenly society:

'. . . they who are principled in the love of self and of the world approach to the first threshold of heaven, they begin to be tortured and so interiorly *tormented*, that they feel in themselves rather hell than heaven, wherefore they cast themselves down headlong thence, nor are they at rest until they come into the hells amongst those of their quality. It hath also very frequently been the case, that such spirits have desired to know what heavenly joy is, and when they have been told that it is in the interiors of the angels, they have wished to have it communicated to themselves, wherefore this also was granted, for what a spirit desires, who is not yet in heaven or in hell, is given him, if it conduces to any good purpose; but when the communication was made, they began to be tortured, insomuch that, by reason of their pain, they did not know in what posture to place their bodies; they were seen to thrust down their head even to the feet, and cast themselves to the earth, and there to writhe themselves into folding in the manner of a serpent, and this by reason of interior torture: such was the effect which heavenly delight produced with those who were in delights derived from the love of self and of the world.'[250]

But when Blake returns home from visiting 'Hell' he does not see the gulf between 'Heaven' and 'Hell', or riches and poverty, as so wide and terrifying as Swedenborg did. Seen from 'the abyss of the five senses' of the Angel there seems a wide gulf between work and home, as between two conditions: 'where a flat sided steep frowns over the present world'. To Swedenborg the people in 'Hell' are being tormented because of their 'infernal delight' or love of self and of the world. He sees how they are 'folding in the manner of a serpent'.

When Blake returns home from visiting 'Hell' he does not see the people in 'Hell' as Swedenborg does. Instead he sees a 'mighty Devil folded' (alluding to Swedenborg's 'folding . . . serpent') who asks the Angel:

'How do you know but ev'ry Bird that cuts the airy way,
Is an immense world of delight, clos'd by your senses five?'

Blake implies that Swedenborg sees the world through his own limited outlook. In other words he is projecting his own feeling on those who work in 'Hell'. For a person who is accustomed to receiving all needs of life 'gratis' from the Lord, it is possible to look at active and practical life as infernal and its delight as not heavenly. Consequently, those who have to provide the necessities of life by their own labour, seem engulfed in the love of self and of the world. Their work seems infernal. Swedenborg wants everything around him similar to himself, even in appearance, reflecting his own condition, and assumes that he is the one who is morally superior to those who work and live in 'Hell'.

'the crow wish'd every thing was black, the owl that everything was white'.[251]

The following proverbs from the 'Proverbs of Hell', for example, will serve to illustrate how they oppose Swedenborg's rationale and how Blake sets his active or true Man against Swedenborg's passive memories.

'Drive your cart and your plow over the bones of the dead.'

'The road of excess leads to the palace of wisdom.'

'Exuberance is Beauty.'

'Bring out number, weight & measure in a year of dearth.'

'The most sublime act is to set another before you.'

The first three proverbs are used by D. V. Erdman in his *Prophet against Empire* as a heading for his chapter on *The Marriage of Heaven and Hell*. I shall examine and discuss four of these proverbs in the context of Swedenborg's *Heaven and Hell*. I have chosen the proverb: 'The most sublime act is to set another before you' to define Blake's meaning of the word 'act', which in turn leads to the definition of the word 'negation'.

Let us begin with the first proverb:

'Drive your cart and your plow over the bones of the dead.'

This proverb is directly related to *Heaven and Hell* rather than inspired by the French Revolution as David V. Erdman has implied.[252]

The proverb refers to the chapter on 'The state of man after Death'. Swedenborg relates his memories of when he was in the natural body. 'Natural memory' means all that man has 'heard, seen, read, learned and thought, in the world, from earliest infancy even to the conclusion of life'.[253] All the things which have entered the memory 'remain, and are never obliterated';[254] the impressions one receives stay fixed in the mind. Consequently, man can have an idea only of those things that he has seen.[255]

There are some who appear beautiful, but are ruled by an evil memory. 'A wicked person, who in externals assumes the semblance of a good man' . . . but within whom 'is concealed filth of every kind'.[256] Swedenborg quotes the Bible:

Ye are like to whitened sepulchres, which outwardly appear beautiful, but within are full of *the bones of the dead*, and of all uncleanness.' (Matt. xxiii. 27.)[257]

By using the phrase '*bones of the dead*' from the St. Matthew quotation, Blake tells the Angel that if he desires to cleanse himself from 'uncleanness' and from 'the bones of the dead' he should honour and uphold the active and creative life. Reading the Bible differently Blake advises the Angel to drive his 'cart' and 'plow' over 'the bones of the dead'. In Blake's reading 'the bones of the dead' represent the passive memories upon which Swedenborg depends. In order to free the creative personality or Imagination we must not base our values and human relationship upon our limited sense-perceptions and memories.

The words 'drive', 'cart' and 'plow' are also derived from the whole context of 'the state of Man after Death'. Swedenborg uses many symbols derived either from his environment or from nature. To explain the idea of 'memory' he represents life as a road along which man 'passes' from one world into another.[258] As man 'carries'[259] along with him his possessions he likewise carries along with him his natural memories. The 'memory' or the rational principle is also similar to 'ground newly ploughed; . . .'[260] The vehicle used for carrying was the carriage or 'cart'. In the proverb Blake uses the words 'cart' and 'plow' as the symbol of active life against Swedenborgian passivity. We hear the same creative intelligence in 'The Voice of the Ancient Bard' (*Songs of Innocence*) rejecting the abstract memories—'the bones of the dead'—of 'Experience':

'. . . They stumble all night over bones of the dead,
   And feel they Know not what but care,
   And wish to lead others, when they should be led.'
(K. p. 126).

The second proverb, 'The *road* of *excess* leads to the *palace of wisdom*', is again related to Swedenborg's *Heaven and Hell* rather than inspired solely by the French Revolution. Swedenborg illustrates at great length the '*excess*' of all goods of life and joy which the Angels possess—garments, house, delights, knowledge, will, power, wisdom and so on. The Angels' 'possessions' are like those on earth but 'as to form more perfect',[261] their 'delights' are 'innumerable'[262] and their light '*exceeds*'[263] that of the world. The things in 'Heaven' are 'stupendous, all shining as of gold, silver and precious stones'.[264] There are furthermore 'innumerable things which could not be expressed in human language'.[265] Those who enter 'Heaven' are first shown paradisaical scenes which '*exceed*' all idea of the imagination.[266] Everything is more perfect in 'Heaven' in so far as 'angelic *wisdom exceeds* human *wisdom*'.[267]

Swedenborg then discusses the *'wisdom'* of the Angels which is difficult to comprehend as it so far *'transcends'* human wisdom.[268] They do not, however, have all the same degree of wisdom. The Angels are divided into classes according to their degree of wisdom, and only those who learn it to the highest degree can enter into the third, or innermost 'Heaven'. This 'Heaven' contains 'a magnificent palace full of all things designed for use, encompassed with paradises on all sides, and with magnificent objects of various kinds'.[269] Those lesser Angels who reason and 'dispute' about 'Truths'[270] cannot enter into this paradise. They 'cannot approach to the first threshold of the palace of wisdom'.[271] They are not able 'to enter into the palace and walk about in the paradise, since they step at the beginning of the *way* that *leads* to it'.[272]

Thus the Angels in 'Heaven' exceed the inhabitants of 'Hell' in everything. But only the Angels of the third 'Heaven' can enter the *'palace of wisdom'*. While recounting the degrees of Angels, Swedenborg compares the wisdom of these third degree Angels with a *'Palace full of all Things'*. Since only the highest Angels can enter the 'palace of wisdom' it follows that the *'palace full of all things'* or *'excess'* corresponds to the *'palace of wisdom'*.

In opposition to all this, Blake writes that it is a road, or active life, not a palace of excess, that leads to the 'palace of wisdom'. We perhaps hear the same voice in 'Thel's motto':

'Does the Eagle know what is in the pit?
Or wilt thou go ask the Mole?
Can Wisdom be put in a silver rod?
Or Love in a golden bowl?'[273]

By the 'road of excess' Blake means the road of the excess of work and experience in life. 'Understanding or Thought', he wrote in his *Annotations to Swedenborg's Wisdom of Angels,* 'is acquired by means of Suffering and Distress, i.e. Experience. Will, Desire, Love, Pain, Envy . . . are Natural, but Understanding is Acquired . . .'[274]

In other words, work or creation is peculiar to the genius of man. Those who depend on their own creative energy are closer to true Man, who is the 'Poetic Genius' or creative part in everybody. This also corresponds to 'The Argument' that:

> 'Once meek, and in a perilous path,
> The just man kept his course along . . .'

Human civilization originated from perilous paths and is based on human creative work. Passivity came later.

Swedenborg attempts to find the origin of abundance in 'Heaven'. He relates it to the interior or spiritual 'state' of the Angels and, justifying the church officials and mineowners, he gives a Biblical interpretation to their existing position:

> 'In the Word, by places and spaces, and by all things which derive anything from space, are signified such things as relate to state . . . by *measure* of various kinds, by *length*, *breadth*, *height* and *depth* and by innumerable other things . . . in heaven . . . by length is meant a state of good, by breadth a state of truth, and by height their discrimination according to degrees . . . as in Ezekiel . . . by *measure*, as to length, breadth, and height, is described the new temple and new earth . . . therefore by these *measures* are signified the things which are of the Church.'[275]

'Bring out *number, weight & measure* in a year of dearth', remarks Blake.[276]

Blake was not against variety in material life. On the contrary he believed that 'Exuberance is Beauty'. But he opposed the self-interest and idealized materialism of the Angels in a society which exploits man's productive works. Swedenborg on the one hand repeatedly mentions the 'excess' of everything in Heaven: Things are so 'numerous'[277] they 'could not be expressed in human language . . . .'[278] On the other hand he is horrified by the appearance of the people in 'Hell', who are to Blake the source of 'Heaven' and its 'sensual existence'.[279]

'Exuberance is Beauty',[280] is also related to *Heaven and Hell*. In this brief statement lies a deep criticism of Swedenborg who tries to rectify everything according to his own image and taste. Those in 'Hell' seem like men to each other, but in 'the light of heaven' they are 'as monsters with horrible countenances and horrible bodies. . . . In like manner man appears as to his spirit, when he is viewed by the angels; if he be a good man, he appears *beautiful* . . . if an evil man, as a monster . . .'.[281]

To Swedenborg all the various beauties of the external world are vastly inferior to the one beauty of the heavenly world. In the perfect spiritual world all appearances stem from the one source; in man, the material world produces differences and variety. And those faces that differ from Swedenborg's image of the greatest and his ideas of what is good and wholesome appear in the spirit as deformed, black and monstrous;

> 'It hath been occasionally shewn me what was the spirit of man in its form and it was seen that in some who had beautiful and handsome faces, it was deformed, black and monstrous, so that it might be called and image of hell, not of heaven.'[282]

The '*beautiful and handsome faces*' are deformed from within because their beauty is derived from the various beauties of the world and not from 'Heaven'. In 'Heaven', everyone's quality is 'manifest in the face' and thus 'all are known as to their quality in the light of heaven'.[283]

Blake, on the other hand, regards variety of faces, colour, opinions and professions not as a possible deformity,[284] but rather as exuberant and beautiful: 'Exuberance is Beauty.' Blake has discussed this in more detail in his *Annotations to Lavater*.

> 'Variety does not necessarily suppose deformity, for a rose & a lily are various & both beautiful. Beauty is exuberant . . . etc.'

The body of man is beautiful in the variety of its members, and people are beautiful in their variety of faces, desires, opinions and professions. 'The apple tree never asks the beech how he shall grow; nor the lion, the horse, how he shall take his prey.'[285] The differences of body and energy in the horse and the lion are indeed beautiful. For 'Some See Nature all Ridicule & Deformity, . . . But to the Eyes of the Man of Imagination, Nature is Imagination itself.'[286] The God of the priest is based on his passive memories, but the God of the poet is the creative energy. Thus

'The pride of the peacock is the glory of God.
The lust of the goat is the bounty of God.
The wrath of the lion is the wisdom of God
The nakedness of woman is the work of God.'[287]

The 'pride of peacock', the 'lust of goat', the 'wrath of the lion' and the 'nakedness of woman' are manifestations of energy and genius. The image of reality is beautiful. The lion in Nature is the symbol of Imagination or energy but the Angels' lion is a passive grass-eating cave animal represented by Nebuchadnazzar in *The Marriage*. Nebuchadnazzar is the symbol of natural man who feeds on the ground of his natural memories. The 'Exuberance' of 'Energy' is beautiful but selfishness is not. The priest, instead of blaming his own selfishness, blames the material world as evil. 'The fox condemns the trap, not himself' writes Blake.

7. 'THE MOST SUBLIME ACT IS TO SET ANOTHER BEFORE YOU'

In this proverb the key word is 'act'. Blake and Swedenborg have opposing views on the meaning of this word. Blake looks at an 'act' from a practical viewpoint and its values are based on whether the action is creative or negative. But for Swedenborg an 'act' is based on the 'will' of every man. Its values depend on the 'will' and 'affection': 'To act is to will.'[288] Swedenborg does not, however, seem to consider the moral side of the argument, that is to say, whether we can be sure that our 'will' or 'act' is not evil or pernicious to others. This 'will', like his 'desire', is selfish 'will'. The priest does not work but only wills and receives.

Swedenborg believes that a man's 'act' is derived from his 'will' and 'understanding', and thus those in 'Heaven' and 'Hell' act according to their will and understanding. Men act well or badly by conjunction with 'Heaven' or conjunction with 'Hell'. These conjunctions are related to his 'will' and 'understanding', for from those principles the body acts. The driving love and affection of men determines their 'act' and place in 'Heaven' or 'Hell'. The Angels are in 'Heaven' because they desire, love and 'will' to be in 'Heaven'. They act according to their own 'will' and affection because man

'. . . is of such a quality as his affection and thought are, or of such a quality as his love and faith are; hence all his external acts drive their life, for to act is to will, and to speak is to think. . . .'[289]

Swedenborg has even given his own interpretation to what is said about 'deed' in the Bible. He believed that what is meant by the word 'deed' in the Bible is action derived from thought and affection.

'. . . since everyone acts from will and speaks from thought; therefore by what is said in the Word, that man shall be judged according to his deeds, and that he shall be recompensed according to his works, is understood that he shall be judged and recompensed according to his thought and affection, which give birth to his deeds. . . .'[290]

When we examine *Heaven and Hell* closely we learn that what Swedenborg means by the words 'thought' and 'affection', on which man's 'will' and 'acts' are based, is in fact produced by his own conditioning. In other words he can think and 'will' only from his own limited standpoint. He desires and wills only what he has already seen or what is fixed in his mind. Since the priest's 'affection' and 'will' are based solely on his abstract memories rather than on active life his 'will' and 'act' are consequently harmful to others. By his abstract memories and teachings the priest restrains and negates life in others. The harm comes from his passive and selfish action. He lives upon his children. He puts his desire and 'will' before others and thus his 'act' is pernicious and his 'will' evil.

Blake opposes Swedenborg's doctrine of 'Will' and writes in his Annotation to Swedenborg's *Divine Love and Divine Wisdom*: 'There can be no Good Will. Will is always Evil; it is pernicious to others or selfishness.'[291] It is evil because it is an imposition on others based on selfishness.

Blake, on the contrary, looks at action from a practical and moral viewpoint. There is a difference between creation and destruction. To create is an 'act' but to destroy is merely the 'negation' of an 'act'. The priest who restrains his children bodily and mentally is not performing an 'act' but negating the action of others. Blake in his annotations to Lavater has defined the word 'act':

'. . . all Act . . . is Virtue.'

But

> 'To hinder another is not an act; it is the contrary; it is a
> restraint on action both in ourselves & in the person
> hinder'd, for he who hinders another omits his own duty
> at the same time.
>> Murder is Hindering Another.
>> Theft is Hindering Another.
>> Backbiting, Undermining, Circumventing, & what-
>> ever is Negative is Vice.'[292]

By the definition of the word 'act', Blake, however, has also
defined the idea of 'negation'. To hinder another is not an
'act'; it is the 'negation' of an act. In other words the 'negation'
is the restraint of creation in others and omitting one's own
duty at the same time. Thus 'negation' is hindering the 'act' of
creation.

In the proverb, Blake is opposing the negative and selfish
'act' of Swedenborg when he writes:

> 'The most sublime act is to set another before you.'

Chapter Four

'ALL DEITIES RESIDE IN THE HUMAN BREAST'

I. THE IDEA OF CORRESPONDENCE

My purpose in this chapter is twofold. Firstly, to discuss Swedenborg's idea of 'correspondence' and Blake's opposing viewpoint. Secondly, by the evidence thus obtained I shall show how Swedenborg divides the subject from its object or the spirit from the body and thus abstracts mental deities from their material contexts. This discussion will finally lead us to Blake's idea of 'animism' and 'imagination', his theory of mind. Plate II of *The Marriage of Heaven and Hell* follows the 'Proverbs of Hell':

'The ancient Poets animated all sensible objects with Gods or Geniuses, calling them by the names and adorning them with the properties of woods, rivers, mountains, lakes, cities, nations, and whatever their enlarged & numerous senses could perceive.

And particularly they studied the genius of each city & country, placing it under its mental deity;

Till a system was formed, which some took advantage of, & enslav'd the vulgar by attempting to realize or abstract the mental deities from their objects: thus began Priesthood;

Choosing forms of worship from poetic tales.

And at length they pronounc'd that the Gods had order'd such things.

Thus men forgot that All deities reside in the human breast.'[1]

This Plate is, in fact, the poet's view of how organized religion or priesthood was created and used to enslave others. By this enslavement man forgot that he possessed Poetic Genius or a creative mind. He started worshipping what was created by man himself. Thus the creator of true art became enslaved by

false art or established forms of worship. To justify the corre-
spondence between his God and the Angels in 'Heaven'
Swedenborg appeals to the ancients, as the following examples
show:

> 'Such being the perception concerning The Divine (Being
> or Principle) in the heavens, it is accordingly implanted
> in every man who receives any influx from heaven, to
> think of God under a human shape: this was the case
> with the *ancients*. . . .'[2]

> '. . . the *Ancients* had an idea of a Human (Principle) in
> regard to the Divine, . . .'[3]

> 'It was otherwise with the *ancients*, to whom the science of
> correspondence was the chief of all sciences:'[4]

> 'The most *ancient* people, who were celestial men, by virtue
> of correspondence thought as the angels, . . .'[5]

> '. . . wherefore the *ancients*, who were in the science of
> correspondences, celebrated their holy worship in
> groves; . . .'[6]

> '. . . inasmuch as gold from correspondence signifies
> celestial good, in which the most *ancient* people were
> principled . . .'[7]

> 'Hence it was that the *ancients*, with whom the church was
> representative, . . .'[8]

> 'Hence some of the *ancients*, had an opinion, that after
> some thousands of years they should return into their
> former life, . . .'[9]

More specifically, however, Plate II refers to passages in the
chapters of *Heaven and Hell* entitled: 'That it results from the
Divine Human Principle of the Lord, that Heaven in the
whole and in part resembles a Man' and 'That there is a
correspondence of all Things of Heaven and Hell with all
things of man'.

In one chapter, while defining his idea of God, Swedenborg
wrote that:

> '. . . the *ancients* had an idea of a Human [Principle] in

regard to the Divine, is manifest from the appearances of the Divine before Abraham, Lot, Joshua, Gideon, Manoah, his wife, and others, who, although they saw God as a Man, still *adored* Him as the God of the universe, *calling* Him the God of heaven and earth, and Jehovah: . . .'[10]

Blake's use of the terms 'ancient', 'adorning' and 'calling' in Plate II was almost certainly suggested by Swedenborg's passage.

Elsewhere, while discussing his idea of 'correspondence' Swedenborg wrote:

'I have been instructed from heaven, that the most *ancient* people on our earth, who were celestial men, thought from correspondences themselves, and that the natural things of the world, which were before their eyes, served them as means of so thinking, and that in consequence of their being of such a quality, they had consociation with the angels, and discoursed with them, and that thus by them heaven was conjoined to the world: it was for this reason that that time was called the golden age, of which also it is said by *ancient* writers, that the inhabitants of heaven dwelt with men, and held converse with them as friends with friends. But after that period other men succeeded, who did not think from correspondences themselves, but from the science of correspondences. . . .'[11]

Blake would agree with Swedenborg's idea that

'ancient people . . . thought from correspondences . . . and that the natural things of the world, which were before their eyes, served them as means of so thinking . . .'

But Blake does not agree with Swedenborg's contradictory idea that the natural world owes its existence to the spiritual world. The contradiction in Swedenborg's outlook is obvious. On the one hand he says the 'natural things of the world . . . served . . . as means of thinking . . .' On the other hand he says that the 'natural world exists and subsists from the spiritual world'.

By the word 'correspondence' Swedenborg means that the

'whole natural world corresponds to the spiritual world . . .

whatever exists in the natural world from the spiritual, this is said to be correspondent'.

In his philosophy of 'correspondence' Swedenborg essentially attempts to establish the 'Heaven' and 'Hell' relationship by saying that

'the natural world exists and subsists from the spiritual world, altogether as an effect from its efficient cause'.[12]

In other words the natural world is created from the spiritual world, the material world is a reflection of the spiritual or intellectual. Everything in society and nature corresponds to the spiritual world. The whole doctrine of correspondence in *Heaven and Hell* might be put briefly as follows:

Firstly, the universal Heaven or Angels resemble one man, and is called the 'Grand Man', and the Angelic societies correspond to the members of the 'Grand Man'.

Secondly, there is correspondence between heaven and the three kingdoms of 'animal', 'vegetable' and 'mineral'.

Thirdly, there is correspondence between Heaven and the sun and light in the natural world.

The 'Grand Man' apparently represents the whole of 'Heaven'. The Angelic societies of which 'Heaven' is composed form the different parts of the man—the head, the breast, the arms, the loins. Those in the head excel the others, for they are wholly principled in wisdom and intelligence. All things in the world have a meaning through correspondence: apart from the head, by which intelligence and wisdom are signified, charity is signified by the breast.[13]

'by the *loins*, conjugal *love*; by the *arms* and *hands*, the power of truth, by the *feet*, the natural principle'.[14]

Blake comments on this in the proverb:

'The head Sublime, the heart Pathos, the genitals Beauty, the hands & feet Proportion.'[15]

The words, '*head*', '*heart*' (love), '*genitals*' (loins), '*feet*' and '*hands*' in the proverb are taken from the relevant chapter.

Swedenborg gives a character to every part of the body. As those in the 'Heaven' excel all others, so those in the feet are lower than others. Those in the 'ears', for example, are mainly principled in hearkening and obedience, those in the 'nostrils' in perception and those in the 'mouth' in discourse.[16] Blake satirizing this 'Grand Man', which is the reflection of the existing social system, writes in the proverb:

> 'The eyes of fire, the nostrils of air, the mouth of water, the beard of earth.'[17]

He would add that, if the head excels all others, then:

> 'When thou seest an Eagle, thou seest a portion of Genius; lift up thy head!'[18]

Blake, by using the words from the material world or reality turns Swedenborg's philosophical system upside down.

> 'It is to be noted', writes Swedenborg, 'that the natural world exists and subsists from the spiritual world, . . .'[19]

Swedenborg in fact takes his passive memories of the material world as the source of origin of the existing material world. He also applies this theory to animals, vegetables and minerals.

There is correspondence between 'Heaven' and these three kingdoms. Swedenborg draws similarities between the intellectual progression of the Angels and the processes that take place in a tree starting from its 'seed', with its growth, putting forth leaves, then flowers and finally bearing fruit or seeds. According to their different species trees 'correspond' to the perception and knowledge of good and truth, from which come intelligence and wisdom; wherefore 'the *ancients*, who were in the science of correspondences, celebrated their holy worship in groves'.[20] The Church and man are compared to different trees according to the extent of their use. Food is also derived from trees:

> '. . . specially that which is produced from the *seeds* of *harvest*, corresponding to the affections of good and of truth'.[21]

> '. . . to know the spiritual things in heaven, to which the natural things in the world correspond, is impossible for any one at this day except from heaven . . .'[22]

Swedenborg attempts to justify his 'Heavenly' position by the objects in nature. In other words, as the seed is to a tree so is wisdom to the Angels, and their natural or material life springs from their spiritual world. The inverted trees in Blake's illustrations image this philosophical system. Demonstrating the practical side of life, Blake writes in the proverb:

'In seed time learn, in harvest teach, in winter enjoy.'

Peasants, farmers and those whose life is directly dependent on the earth look forward to the harvest day, and are necessarily interested in the rate of production. Swedenborg's joy in winter comes from his spiritual or intellectual heat but the peasants' joy comes from a good harvest.

Swedenborg lists the animals which, like all things in the world, correspond to the 'Heaven'. He discusses, for example, how the bees 'make provision' for themselves and their young for the future, and have a form of government, discarding the useless. The

'bees know how to collect honey from flowers, to build cells of wax in which to store up their honey'.[23]

Blake takes the word 'bee' from the passage and uses it in the proverb:

'The busy bee has no time for sorrow.'

In other words, an active being like the 'bee' is so busy in its productive work that it has no time for needless worry about its correspondence to the abstract spiritual world or 'Heaven'.

All this means that Swedenborg attempts to demonstrate that all objects correspond to the spiritual world. They exist and subsist in nature from divine order.

'Divine order is the result of the divine good, which proceeds from the Lord; . . .'[24]

The Angels in 'Heaven' receive divine good and thus are able to see the corresponding order in mundane nature. Divine order

'proceeds from Him through the heavens successively into the world, and there terminates in ultimates: those things, which are according to order there, are correspondences; . . .'[25]

Thus Swedenborg's philosophy is the opposite extreme of the

philosophy of nature which Newton and Locke propagated. Swedenborg derives the divine order of nature from invisible spiritual sources but Newton and Locke derive our ideas of order solely from ever-present nature.

Blake accepted neither Locke's theory of mind[26] nor Swedenborg's metaphysic. Both Locke and Swedenborg make man subject to external objects by underrating the importance of human creativity. Locke regarded the human mind as passive, the 'tabula rasa', and, by doing so, made man subject to the senses: 'None could have other than natural or organic thoughts', writes Blake, 'if he had none but organic perceptions.'[27] Locke indeed recognizes the existence of the material world. But he denies the creativity of mind by regarding it as a passive and unwilling being subject to external impressions.

Swedenborg denies the individuality and creativity of man by going to the other extreme in his metaphysical system. He not only failed to recognize man's creative energy but even regarded man as an unimportant being by saying that:

'Still without man as a medium, divine influx into the world continues, . . .'[28]

The proverb 'Where man is not, nature is barren' is a concise criticism of this idea.

A closer examination of *Heaven and Hell* reveals the basic contradiction in Swedenborg. On the one hand he lists the numerous objects, material possessions, garments and buildings in 'Heaven'. In other words, he recognizes the existence and importance of the material world. But on the other hand he denies the existence of the material world by dividing his memories or 'mental deities' from objects. He calls his memories 'wisdom' and 'intelligence', then makes his memories the source of the material world. Thus the Angels possess glory and eminence in 'Heaven' because they have heavenly intelligence and wisdom. Their degree in 'Heaven' depends on the degree of their intelligence and wisdom.

By the possession of this wisdom and intelligence the Angels register their superiority:

'It is believed that the wise will possess glory and eminence in heaven above the simple.'[29]

Those who are superior in intelligence can also walk in beautiful gardens and gather flowers.

> 'To those who are principled in intelligence, there appear gardens and paradises, full of trees and flowers of every kind: the trees are there planted in the most beautiful order, so combined as to form arbors, through which are arched entrances, and around which are shady walks, all in such beauty as it is impossible to describe: they who are principled in intelligence also walk there, and gather flowers, and form garlands, with which they adorn little children: there are also species of trees and flowers there, which were never seen nor given in the world: on the trees also there are fruits, according to the good of love, in which the intelligent are principled: . . .'[30]

In other words, according to Swedenborg, the joy and beauty of the gardens and all material objects arise from the 'intelligence' of the Angels. But to Blake, intellectual delight and energy rise from the 'Body'. 'Energy is . . . from Body' or the objective world. Mental deities derive from man in the real world. Swedenborg postulates divine intervention in order to justify the existence of things in 'Heaven'.

> '. . . the things which are in the heavens cannot be seen by the eyes of man's body, but by the eyes of his spirit; . . . when it pleases the Lord. . . .'[31]

Blake criticises Swedenborg for separating the mental deities or energy from their objects.

Deities are the imaginative or mental forms of material objects. Man created 'mental forms' of the objects of his environment and can imagine, think over, compare and choose his pleasant and delightful impressions. The mind of man has this unchangeable power which he applies to his particular environment. But Swedenborg sets his limited vision against unlimited and universal man, whereas Blake stresses the developing and creative mind, believing:

> 'The true Man is the source, he being the Poetic Genius.'

The 'Poetic Genius' is the source because it is unchangeable. It applies its unchangeable power of imagination to changeable objects or environments.

2. ANIMISM OR THEORY OF OBJECT-SOUL

Man as poet animates reality or real objects, in contrast to the priest who animates his passive memories.

Swedenborg uses the term 'animate' when he is discussing the naturalists' point of view that the Universe is like an animal body and all things in it are actuated by the principle of life and motion. Swedenborg in denouncing such ideas in favour of faith in the Lord wrote:

'. . . they who profess to believe in an invisible Divine (being or principle), which they call the *animating* principle . . . of the universe, from which all things existed, and reject faith in the Lord, have been taught by experience that they believe in no God, because an invisible Divine (being or principle) is to them like nature in its first principles, which ... is no object of thought: these have their lot amongst those who are called naturalists. . . .'[32]

The philosophers of nature, as we saw earlier, regarded the universe either as the Great Machine working by rigidly determined laws or as a great living being in which every part had an organized and proper function. The living being was regarded as the Deity or the Soul of the world.

For instance, in Hume's *Dialogues concerning Natural Religion,* one of the characters, Philo, expresses what Swedenborg would call a naturalist philosophy:

'. . . if we survey the universe, so far as it falls under our knowledge, it bears a great resemblance to an animal or organized body, and seems actuated with a like principle of life and motion. A continual circulation of matter in it produces no disorder: a continual waste in every part is incessantly repaired: the closest sympathy is perceived throughout the entire system and each part or member, in performing its proper offices, operates both to its own preservation and to that of the whole. The world, there-fore, I infer, is an animal, and the Deity is the Soul of the world, actuating it, and actuated by it.'[33]

Hume continues to suggest various other theories about the

origin of the world. His character Cleanthes contesting the previous theory says:

'. . . it seems to me, that, though the world does, in many circumstances, resemble an animal body; yet is the analogy also defective in many circumstances, the most material: no organs of sense; no seat of thought or reason; no one precise origin of motion and action. In short, it seems to bear a stronger resemblance to a vegetable than to an animal, . . .'[34]

But Philo, whose position Richard Wollheim believes to be identical with that of Hume,[35] suggests that:

'The world plainly resembles more an animal or a vegetable, than it does a watch or a knitting loom. Its cause, therefore, it is more probable, resembles the cause of the former. The cause of the former is generation or vegetation. The cause, therefore, of the world, we may infer to be something similar or analogous to generation or vegetation.'[36]

Swedenborg denounces Deism, yet he himself, as we have seen before, deifies his own passive memories.

Blake objected to 'Natural Religion' or Deism for reasons different from those of Swedenborg. Swedenborg rejected deism in favour of the established Church whereas Blake rejected it because of its mechanistic philosophy which regarded the mind of man as passive and his ideas as derived only from the senses. The deists saw the deity in nature but Blake said that deity existed in man. In other words, for Blake it is man who creates and gives meaning to nature. His interpretation of the word 'animate' is similar to that of the romantic poets.

Blake uses the word 'animate' in *The Marriage of Heaven and Hell* in a different sense from that of Swedenborg and the philosophers of nature. To Blake the act of animation by the ancient people was based on creative life. This was not merely a fanciful act or illusion but closely related to practical life and its needs. The action was a creative and unifying power, therefore hopeful and inspiring. This creative animism counteracts passive and static memories. The animism or deism which Blake criticizes in his writings is based on passive memories.

Passive animism has three main characteristics. Firstly, as I have pointed out before, it abstracts or separates the mental images or spirit from their objects or body. Secondly it interprets its mental images as being granted by divine providence and as the sign of its excellence or superiority. Thirdly, it calls the enjoyment of mental images or passive memories 'Heaven' as opposed to 'Hell'.

Blake uses the word 'animated' in his early writings too. It first appears in *She Bore Pale Desire* (written before 1777). He explains how 'conscience' was sent as a 'guard to reason'. Reason was once fairer than light till it 'foul'd in Knowledge's dark Prison house, For knowledge drove sweet Innocence away'. This knowledge is based on abstraction. It animates only its limited and static memories. Natural man is proud only of his own memories and calls them god and goddess;

> 'Pride made a Goddess fair, or Image rather, till knowledge
> animated it; 'twas call'd Self love.'[37]

'Self love' and selfhood are the same thing and are based on limited natural memories. The passive personality animates its own limited memories and calls them knowledge, which process operates within a cave or 'dark prison house'. This passive and limited knowledge negates 'innocence' or creative imagination. The difference between animism in *Then She Bore Pale Desire* and in *The Marriage of Heaven and Hell* is that in the first the knowledge of good and evil animates the passive memories which exist only in the passive mind of the reasoner. But in *The Marriage* the poet-man or creative man animates sensible objects. The creative mind or imagination does not passively subject itself to external objects and external nature by only passively remembering sense-impressions, but neither does it separate from their external objects the mental images it creates. The passive personality, on the other hand, separates or divorces from reality and a specific context the mental images it derives from passive memories.

In the books of *Vala or The Four Zoas* and *Jerusalem* Blake criticises this limited and abstract animism. The passive mind animates its own limited natural memories, calling them, as Swedenborg does, heaven or divine beings and setting up its limited mental deities as heaven against hell or soul against objects. These animated memories, as we shall see in the 'worm' symbol, are 'woman' because they are passive and based on natural impressions. The 'woman' has her own will which is called 'Female-Will'. She weaves her limited memories together and then begins to animate them:

'Wond'ring she saw her woof begin to animate, & not
As Garments woven subservient to her hands, but having
    a will
Of its own, perverse & wayward.'[38]

Again in the book of *The Four Zoas* the limited natural memories or selfhood are represented, as we shall discuss in the chapter on the 'worm symbol', by Tharmas who is being animated:

'Tharmas like a pillar of sand roll'd round by the whirl-
    wind,
An animated Pillar rolling round & round in incessant
    rage.'[39]

The 'Pillar' represents the mechanical social system of the eighteenth century which had been set in motion by a clock-making God. Deists animated this mechanical system and called it 'Deism'.

'The Ashes of Mystery began to animate; they call'd it
    Deism
And Natural Religion; as of old, so now anew began
Babylon again in Infancy, call'd Natural Religion.'[40]

The 'Ashes of Mystery' represent abstraction, and Blake terms religion and the God of priestcraft a mystery because they are abstract. Natural Religion is based on passive memory of sense impressions and a static class-divided social system. In other words those who are in 'Heaven' animate their own natural memories, which are different from those of the people in 'Hell'. But this animated 'Heaven' intellectually turns against 'Hell' like a being assuming superiority. Thus Natural Religion is the religion of the rigidly divided society of 'Heaven' and 'Hell', or Babylon. Babylon negates Jerusalem and is the divided society, fallen from Brotherhood. The 'woman' or animated Selfhood in Babylon or the society of 'Heaven' and

'Hell' has enslaved Jerusalem under her 'shadow'. The 'woman' is devouring like a worm and the innocent children of Jerusalem are mournful:

' "Why wilt thou give to her a Body whose life is but a
        Shade?
    "Her joy and love, a shade, a shade of sweet repose:
    "But animated and vegetated she is a devouring worm.
    "What shall we do for thee, O lovely mild Jerusalem?" '[41]

Jerusalem is hidden beneath the mechanical social system, which is compared to that of the knitting loom, and the passive mind animates or reflects what it sees in society.

'The golden cords of the Looms *animate* beneath their
        touches soft
    Along the Island white, . . .'[42]

Blake, in fact, uses the term 'animate' in two different senses. In *The Marriage*, for example, it is used in a creative sense; but he also uses the passive sense of the term illustrated above, which puts passive memories before the creative personality or Man. Blake's animism is based on the creative personality or 'Poetic Genius'. The poets, by animating sensible objects, create sensual enjoyment in all people. They awaken the eyes of imagination. Poets, contrary to the passive personality, recognize creative man or 'Poetic Genius' as a true quality as opposed to limited natural memories. It is a genuine quality because it is creative and possessed by every man. The creative personality or poet unites all men in their 'Poetic Genius' and thus they are brothers. But the passive personality unites men by natural memories and those who do not have similar memories are thus excluded, or confined to their own society. Those who are in 'Heaven' have their own memories, which make them superior to those who are in 'Hell'. These memories, as we have seen before, are all-important to the passive personality. He sees and worships his abstract memories as God. But the creative man sees God who 'only Acts & Is, in existing beings or Men'. In a word the passive personality sees his finite and limited memories but the creative personality sees infinite creation in everything. This is the theme in *The Marriage* of Plates 12–13 where Blake satirizes Swedenborg's

F

abstract philosophy and abstract religion. The poets animate
sensible objects which exist in their surroundings. They invoke,
as Wordsworth says,

'the groves . . . the hills and streams . . . senseless rocks'.[43]

The poets address the objects of nature and express their own
desires and feelings through doing so. In joyful days they invite
nature to join them with joy and in the day of sorrow and
need call her to bring them peace and love. In other words,
the poets give nature a personality and make it talk, see, smile,
and bring love. Blake's poems to the four seasons (1769–78)
are good examples of what he means by animism. In the poem
'To Spring' he addresses spring who 'looks' down through the
clear windows of the morning. He calls Spring to turn her 'eyes'
upon our western isle. The hills are 'telling' each other of the
news. The poet asks her to visit his clime with her holy 'feet'
and asks spring to let the wind 'kiss' her perfumed garments
and let the morning and evening breath scatter her 'pearls' on
the 'love-sick' land that mourns for her. Finally the poet calls
her to adorn his land with her fair 'fingers' and pour 'kisses'
on the land's 'bosom' and put a golden crown on her 'lang-
uish'd head':

> 'O thou with dewy locks, who lookest down
> Thro' the clear windows of the morning, turn
> Thine angel eyes upon our western isle,
> Which in full choir hails thy approach, O Spring!
>
> The hills tell each other, and the list'ning
> Vallies hear; all our longing eyes are turned
> Up to thy bright pavillions: issue forth,
> And let thy holy feet visit our clime.
>
> Come o'er the eastern hills, and let our winds
> Kiss thy perfumed garments; let us taste
> Thy morn and evening breath; scatter thy pearls
> Upon our love-sick land that mourns for thee.
>
> O deck her forth with thy fair fingers; pour
> Thy soft kisses on her bosom; and put
> Thy golden crown upon her languish'd head,
> Whose modest tresses were bound up for thee!'[44]

The poet animates Spring. He associates her with the actions of a human being, and expresses his feeling through the animated object.

In his poem 'To Summer' Blake addresses Summer who passes over the valleys. The poet depicts the sun's large 'nostrils', which pour out flames, and 'ruddy limbs' and flourishing 'hair'. He hears his 'voice' under thickest shade and the 'vallies love' the Summer in 'his pride'. Although the Summer is in his pride it is the poet who gives this pride to nature. The poet has his pen to write and his instruments to sing. His youths are bolder and maidens fairer than those of nature. But the poet creates the nature and uses it as the means of communication and tools of expression for his intellectual needs. He gives nature personality and makes her play a part in the story of human life:

> 'O thou, who passest thro' our vallies in
> Thy strength, curb thy fierce steeds, allay the heat
> That flames from their large nostrils! thou, O Summer,
> Oft pitched'st here thy golden tent, and oft
> Beneath our oaks hast slept, while we beheld
> With joy thy ruddy limbs and flourishing hair. . . .

> Our vallies love the Summer in his pride.

> Our bards are fam'd who strike the silver wire:
> Our youths are bolder than the southern swains:
> Our maidens fairer in the sprightly dance:
> We lack not songs, nor instruments of joy,'[45]

In 'To Autumn' the poet animates fruitful autumn; adorning it with 'fruits', 'jolly voice', dancing daughters:

> 'O Autumn, laden with fruit, and stained
> With the blood of the grape, . . .'

The poet invites Autumn to sit and listen to his 'fresh pipe':

> '. . . pass not, but sit
> Beneath my shady roof; there thou may'st rest,
> And tune thy jolly voice to my fresh pipe; . . .'[46]

The 'fresh pipe' is not exclusive to the poet. Everybody has poetic genius and animates his own environment. Shepherds

animate green hills and meadows. Farmers animate plants.
But the poet is conscious of the poetic genius which exists in
every man and attempts to awaken and raise genius or sensual
enjoyment in others too. He makes all take part in this joy
for the 'fresh pipe' speaks in the language of all children or
honest men:

> '. . . all the daughters of the year shall dance!
> Sing now the lusty song of fruits and flowers.'

The symbols of 'fruit' and 'flower' are infinite and common to
all. Every man can take part in the dance and song. The poet
or prophet has, contrary to the priest, a uniting power. By
animating an object of Nature he desires to communicate with
all human spirits or geniuses. He expresses his feeling both to
what attracts him and rouses his enthusiasm or love and to
what repels him and rouses his dislike. In the following lines
the poet adorns the sun with blossoms and flowers:

> 'The narrow bud opens her beauties to
> The sun, and love runs in her thrilling veins;
> Blossoms hang round the brows of morning, . . .
> . . . .
> And feather'd clouds strew flowers round her head.'
> . . . .'47

The poet, contrary to the priest, animates the sensible objects
or what really exists in the outside world. The sun is personified
as a creative being or god who is adorned by woods and plants
or whatever the poet's 'enlarged and numerous senses could
perceive'. The priest abstracts such expressions from their
objects.

Swedenborg, for example, in the chapter 'Concerning the
Sun in Heaven' abstracts the word 'sun' from its sensible
object by saying that:

> '. . . in heaven the sun of the world doth not appear, nor any
> thing which is from that sun, still there is a sun there,
> together with light and heat, . . . The sun of heaven is the
> Lord, the light there is divine truth, and the heat there
> is divine good, which proceed from the Lord as a
> sun . . .'48

The priest, contrary to the poet, does not see the sun in the world. His God and sun are abstract. He sees them in his heaven of passive memories.

'. . . That the Lord actually appears in heaven as a sun, hath not only been told me by the angels, but hath also been given me occasionally to see . . . The Lord appears as a sun, not in heaven, but on high above the heavens. . . .'[49]

To Swedenborg the real sun exists in the mind.

'The reason why he appears before the eyes is, because the interiors, which are of the mind, see through the eyes, from the good of love. . . .'[50]

To Blake the sun of the world is a creator being; the 'narrow bud opens her beauties to him' and 'love runs in her thrilling veins'. But to Swedenborg the sun of the world

'appears . . . as somewhat of thick darkness opposite to the sun of heaven, . . .'[51]

To support his idea that by the sun is meant the Lord in Heaven Swedenborg brings evidence from the Bible:

'Hence it is, in the Word, the Lord, as to love, is compared to the sun, and as to faith to the moon; . . . "*the light of the moon shall be as the light of the sun, but the light of the sun shall be seven-fold, as the light of seven days*", Isaiah xxx.'[52]

To Blake this passage is pregnant with the creative imagination which sees the creation or progression of nature and of man in reality. But Swedenborg is attempting to detach the passage from reality by 'choosing forms of worship from poetic tales'. And 'at length they pronounced that the Gods had order'd such things'. This division of subject from object, spirit from body, word from thing and prophet from history did not exist in ancient time. In other words men derived their mental images from sensible objects.

'Till a system was formed, which some took advantage of, & enslav'd the vulgar by attempting to realize or abstract the mental deities from their objects: thus began Priest-hood: . . .'

By the word 'system' Blake means the social system of
'Heaven' and 'Hell'. The priests or those in 'Heaven' enslaved
the vulgar or those in 'Hell' by pronouncing that God had
spoken to them and they had seen God. Thus began priest-
hood. In other words priesthood started by the abstraction of
mental deities from their material context or by the division of
intellectual activity from practical life.

The Poet does not merely animate the desirable and lovable
elements in nature, such as 'perfumed garments' in Spring,
clear waters in Summer, and fruits of Autumn. He also ani-
mates the pernicious or negative elements, personifying them
as beast and monster. Nonetheless the poet regards the negative
elements as transitory beside the creative Spring and Summer.
In the poem 'Winter', for example, Blake depicts winter as a
'direful monster' and asks him to bar his 'adamantine' doors
and 'shake not' his roofs:

> 'O Winter! bar thine adamantine doors:
> The north is thine; there hast thou built thy dark
> Deep-founded habitation. Shake not thy roofs,
> Nor bend thy pillars with thine iron car.
> . . . .
>
> Lo! now the direful monster, whose skin clings
> To his strong bones, strides o'er the groaning rocks:
> . . . .'

The poet believes that 'Winter' and all antagonistic elements
in nature are transitory, whereas the good and creative elements
such as the sun and summer are eternal. In other words, winter
is caused by the departure of the sun. This changed condition
is transitory and can only exist:

> '. . . till heaven smiles, and the monster
> Is driv'n yelling to his caves beneath mount Hecla.'[53]

Thus the poet or man animates the sensible objects in his
surrounding world. He animates them with geniuses or gods.
It is the genius of Spring to bring fresh spirit and scatter pearls
upon the 'love-sick land'. Summer brings strength and gives
colours to the fruits of trees—then Autumn is adorned with
fruits and 'stained with the blood of the grape'. These are
regarded as geniuses or creative elements in nature.

'It is the business of the Poet', writes Shelley in his Preface to *The Revolt of Islam*

> 'to communicate to others the pleasure and the enthusiasm arising out of those images and feelings in the vivid presence of which within his own mind consists at once his inspiration and his reward.'[54]

The poet creates his own surrounding world. The images and symbols he uses are drawn from his environment. In other words, man creates the sensible objects which surround him. Thus Shelley argues that an essential attribute of poetry is:

> 'the power of awakening in others sensations like those which animate my own bosom . . .'[55]

In this act of creation both the object and the creator or the poetic man are equally important. Every man has 'Poetic Genius' and is attracted towards good and beauty. Blake says:

> 'As all men are alike (tho' infinitely various),
> So all Religions &, as all similars, have one source.
> The true Man is the source, he being the Poetic Genius.'[56]

Favourable conditions aid the development of this genius and unfavourable circumstances cause it to diminish and be buried in a fallen society of negation. In the 'unfallen world', says Northrop Frye,

> 'objects of perception are alive and intelligent, and a faint echo of the animation of that world survives in the animism of primitive religion. The nymphs, satyrs and fauns of Classical mythology are older and more authentic than the Olympian hierarchy. With the separation of existence and perception, however, the natural object became attached to the latter and its spirit or Genius to the former, so that gradually a belief in invisible deities grew up. The eleventh plate of *The Marriage of Heaven and Hell*, the paragraph beginning "The ancient Poets animated all sensible objects with Gods or Geniuses", traces this process with a clarity that might impress even a modern student of the subject.'[57]

'Animism' is not exclusive to the romantic writers in the

eighteenth century. It is regarded as a universal characteristic
of man by anthropological research.

Edward Tylor, for example, in his *Religion in Primitive
Culture*, discussing animism and the primitive view of the souls
of men, beasts and things, writes:

> '. . . strange as such a notion may seem to us at first sight,
> if we place ourselves by an effort in the intellectual position
> of an uncultured tribe, and examine the theory of object-
> souls from their point of view, we shall hardly pronounce
> it irrational . . . the primitive stage of thought in which
> personality and life are ascribed not to men and beasts
> only, but to things. It has been shown how what we call
> inanimate objects—rivers, stones, trees, weapons, and so
> forth—are treated as living intelligent beings, talked to,
> propitiated, punished for the harm they do.'[58]

Man animates objects according to his intellectual needs. And
so, for Blake, men pass and objects change or are replaced by
different kinds, but the pattern or form of thought in man still
remains the same and unchangeable. In other words, objects
change but 'Poetic Genius' always remains the same. Blake
discusses this in detail in his later writings. In *A Vision of the
Last Judgement*, for example, he writes:

> 'Man Passes on, but States remain for Ever; . . . It ought
> to be understood that the Persons, Moses & Abraham,
> are not here meant, but the States Signified by those
> Names . . .'[59]

Blake has defined what he means by the term 'state' in his
book of *Milton*:

> 'Judge then of thy Own Self: thy Eternal Lineaments
>   explore,
> What is Eternal & what Changeable, & what Annihilable.
> The Imagination is not a State: it is the Human Existence
>   itself.
> Affection or Love becomes a State when divided from
>   Imagination.
> The Memory is a State always, & the Reason is a State
> Created to be Annihilated & a new Ratio Created.

Whatever can be Created can be Annihilated: Forms
cannot:
The Oak is cut down by the Ax, the Lamb falls by the
Knife,
But their Forms Eternal Exist For-ever.'[60]

The form of thought in Man is 'Eternal' and unchangeable.
The traveller is the same though the roads differ. Man passes
through states or memories. The passive personality, like
Swedenborg, animates only his limited memories. He sees only
a portion or a changeable object as opposed to 'Imagination'
or the unchangeable 'Form' which is 'Human Existence'. The
poet sees God as infinite but the Priest sees Him as a finite
being.

Blake's distinction between what is changeable and what
unchangeable in man has been expounded by a modern writer.
Claude Levi-Strauss writes:

'Prevalent attempts to explain alleged differences between
the so-called primitive mind and scientific thought have
resorted to qualitative differences between the working
processes of the mind in both cases, while assuming that
the entities which they were studying remained very much
the same. If our interpretation is correct, we are led
toward a completely different view—namely, that the
kind of logic in mythical thought is as rigorous as that of
modern science, and that the difference lies, not in the
quality of intellectual process, but in the nature of the
things to which it is applied. This is well in agreement
with the situation known to prevail in the field of tech-
nology: What makes a steel axe superior to a stone axe is
not that the first one is better made than the second. They
are equally well made, but steel is quite different from
stone. In the same way we may be able to show that the
same logical processes operate in myth as in science, and
that man has always been thinking equally well; the
improvement lies, not in an alleged progress of man's
mind but in the discovery of new areas to which it may
apply its unchanged and unchanging power.'[61]

F*

3. PLATES 12–13. 'POETIC GENIUS AS THE FIRST PRINCIPLE OF
HUMAN PERCEPTION'

Far from being simply 'a witty account of a dinner party', as
John Beer has suggested,

'at which Blake questions the prophets Isaiah and Ezekiel
about their inspiration'[62]

Plates 12–13 are also written in the context of Swedenborg's
Heaven and Hell, and the argument in the plates seems twofold.
Firstly Blake defends the honesty and humanity of the prophets
Isaiah and Ezekiel in the face of the rigid social system of the
priest Swedenborg who, while associating himself with the
ancient prophets and discussing the superior quality of speech
and language in 'Heaven', concludes that:

'. . . the discourses in hell are thus opposite to the discourses
in heaven, wherefore the wicked cannot endure angelic
discourse: . . . infernal discourse is to the angels as a
stinking odour which strikes the nostrils. . . .'[63]

Blake, who is one of those in 'Hell', sits at ease with the
prophets and wants to show that Isaiah and Ezekiel, unlike the
priest, not only do not refuse to discourse with the people in
'Hell' but also dine with them, and share the enthusiasm and
life of the active people. In other words the ancient prophets,
unlike the Angels, worked and encouraged

' "the desire of raising other men into a perception of the
infinite." '

Secondly Blake wants to dissociate the prophets from
Swedenborg's other statement that the Lord 'spake with the
prophets' and 'dictated' to them.[64] Blake asks Isaiah whether
God had really spoken to him or dictated his writings. Isaiah
answers:

' "I saw no God, nor heard any, in a finite organical
perception; but my senses discover'd the infinite in every
thing, and as I was then perswaded, & remain confirm'd,
that the voice of honest indignation is the voice of God, I
cared not for consequences, but wrote." '[65]

In other words, God, contrary to the God of the priest, exists within man. He represents the creative in man. 'God only acts and is, in existing beings or men.' Plates 12–13 are further constructions of Blake's satirical criticism of Swedenborg's system. Swedenborg, as we have seen, supports his case against those in 'Hell' by using arguments and exhortations derived from the Bible and the teaching of Jesus and Old Testament prophets such as Isaiah, Ezekiel, David and others. In *Heaven and Hell* occur statements such as:

'Hence it is, that to adore the sun of the world and the moon, and to bow down to them, signifies, in the Word, to love self and the falses grounded in the love of self . . . ,' (Ezekiel viii. 15, 16, 18).[66]

'Peace shall have no end on the throne of *David*, and on his Kingdom, . . .' (Isaiah ix. 7).

'I will raise up to *David* a just branch, and he shall reign a King, . . .'[67]

'Inasmuch as the angels have such power, therefore they are called powers; as in *David*: "*Bless Jehovah ye angels most powerful in strengths*," '[68]

'I have been informed in what manner the Lord spake with the *prophets*, by (or through) whom the Word was communicated; he did not speak with them as with the *ancients* by an influx into their interiors, . . .'[69]

'Since such was the state of the spirits who spake with the *prophets*, . . .'[70]

'That papers written in heaven appeared also to the prophets, is manifest from *Ezekiel*: . . .'[71]

These are just random examples taken from *Heaven and Hell*. More specifically, plates 12–13 apparently refer to the chapters 'concerning the speech of angels with man' and 'concerning writing in heaven'. Swedenborg argues that the language of every man is based on his memories.

' . . the thought of man coheres with his memory, and speech flows from that source . . .'[72]

It follows that 'Heaven' and 'Hell' have different languages. There are two kinds of language: the language of the Angels and the language of the others. The

> 'angels are not able to utter a single expression of human language ... and besides, human language is natural, and they are spiritual, and spiritual beings cannot utter anything naturally: ...'[73]

But when the Angels speak to men they talk or conjoin to their spiritual body and this is provided by the Lord because

> 'with every man there should be attendant angels and spirits, and that man should be ruled by them from the Lord, ...'[74]

In other words man communicates with the Lord through the spirits and the Angels. Everything, including inspiration, comes from one 'single fountain of life, which is the Lord'.[75]

Swedenborg repudiates the individuality or creative spirit which acts independently in man. The people who believe in the Holy Spirit in every man are called 'visionaries' and 'enthusiasts':

> '. . . such persons are visionaries and enthusiasts, and believe every spirit whom they hear to be the Holy Spirit, when yet they are *enthusiastic* spirits.'[76]

Swedenborg regarded these as dangerous and wicked:

> 'Such spirits are falses as truths, and because they see them, they *persuade* themselves that they are truths, and likewise *persuade* those with whom they flow-in: and whereas those spirits began also to press the *persuasion* of evils, and were also obeyed ... *enthusiastic* spirits are distinguished from other spirits by this, that they believe themselves to be the Holy Spirit, and that the things which they say are divine: those spirits do not hurt man, because man honours them with divine worship. I have also occasionally discoursed with them, and on such occasions were discovered the wicked devices which they infused into their worshippers: they dwell together to the left in a desert place.'[77]

Blake has, apparently, taken the word 'persuade' from this passage. The passage conveys the social conflict of the time between the Church and State, on the one hand, and their opponents, such as the Pietists or Moravians, on the other. By the word 'enthusiasts' Swedenborg apparently meant the Pietists or Moravians who supported the lower classes against the established Church and State. Both Pietists and Moravians also sought, as I pointed out in the first chapter, to remove the wide gulf between the official clergy and the lay classes. Swedenborg, for social reasons, regarded such 'enthusiasts' as both persuasive and dangerous. After discussing the differences between 'enthusiasts' or 'visionaries' and the Angels he says that to speak with visionaries or enthusiasts

'at this day is rarely granted, because it is dangerous'.[78]

But

'to discourse with the angels of heaven is granted only to those who are principled in truths derived from good, especially who are in the acknowledgement of the Lord, ... from which consideration it is evident, that to discourse with the angels of heaven is not granted to any but those whose interiors are opened by divine truths even to the Lord, for the Lord flows-in into those truths with man . . .'[79]

In other words, only those who acknowledge the Lord or the passive memories of the priest are allowed to speak to the Angels and 'see also those things which are in heaven . . .'.[80] This leads Swedenborg to say that man either turns himself to the love of self and the world, or to love of the Lord. The prophets thus had conjunction with the Angels of 'Heaven' and the Lord spoke with them:

'I have been informed in what manner the Lord spake with the prophets, by (or through) whom the Word was communicated; He did not speak with them as with the ancients by an influx into their interiors, but by spirits who were sent to them, whom the Lord filled with his aspect, and thus inspired words which they dictated to the prophets. . . .'[81]

This is the starting point of plates 12–13. Blake's satirical inversion of Swedenborg's passive concept of the prophets begins:

'The prophets Isaiah and Ezekiel dined with me, and I asked them how they dared so roundly to assert that God spoke to them. . . .'

Here, Blake both pokes fun at the contention that the prophets are among the Angels, and also shows that they were active and creative men. The prophet creates hope, inspires people and unites with them, but the priest negates people and creates his rigid social system of 'Heaven' and 'Hell'. To the prophets creation is based on an active life, which is linked with 'imagination' or 'contrary progression'. The active 'imagination' or the active 'contraries' is a forward-looking or progressive power based on a vision of reality. The passive 'imagination' or the passive 'contraries' is backward-looking mind and is based on passive memories which are divorced from practical life. The passive personality desires and loves only those things with which his dominating love agrees. He loves joy, delight and ease, but he does not work for them. He negates the thorn and work as undesirable and evil, their existence springing from 'Hell'. All this means that the active 'imagination' or active 'contraries' are 'infinite', but the passive imagination or static 'contraries' are 'finite'. The priest sees God in his own limited passive memories but the prophet sees God in infinite creation. Thus the prophet Isaiah answered:

'I saw no God, nor heard any, in a finite organical perception, but my senses discover'd the infinite in every thing. . . .'

The prophet Isaiah sees God in active life. To see the 'barren heath' and the 'honey bees' together in a blossomed land is imagination or a process of creation. Man has converted 'barren heath' to blossomed land.

4. 'THE EYE SEES MORE THAN THE HEART KNOWS'

The difference between the priest and the prophet is the difference between the limited Reason (Urizen: your reason) and the 'Poetic Genius'. The priest associates his authority with Divine Providence and the sacred books but the prophet depends on his creative power and personal experience. Max Weber in his book *The Sociology of Religion*[82] discusses the difference between the priest and the prophet, and writes:

> '. . . the personal call is the decisive element distinguishing the prophet from the priest. The latter lays claim to authority by virtue of his service in a sacred tradition, while the prophet's claim is based on personal revelation and charisma. It is no accident that almost no prophets have emerged from the priestly class.'[83]

It was on this personal call or persuasion, the creative genius of man, that Blake laid stress. It conveys the same idea as the 'imagination'. Blake by the 'ages of imagination', probably means the time before 'a system was formed' and 'began Priesthood'. The ancient prophets and poets, by their personal gifts, inspired the people in their active life. If they failed in practice the poets or prophets still created their desire and hopes in 'imagination'. The imagination filled valleys, diverted rivers and removed mountains.

> '. . . in ages of imagination this firm persuasion removed mountains. . . .'

All this means that the prophets put unlimited and creative imagination above any abstract knowledge derived from sense impressions and passive life.

Ezekiel said:

> 'The philosophy of the East taught the first principles of human perception: . . .'

By these principles Blake means those he has already propounded in *All Religions are One* (etched about 1788) against Natural Religion and the empiricist philosophy of sense impressions.

> '*The Argument.* As the true method of knowledge is experiment, the true faculty of knowing must be the faculty which experiences. This faculty I treat of:

'PRINCIPLE 1ˢᵗ. That the Poetic Genius is the true Man, and that the body or outward form of Man is derived from the Poetic Genius. Likewise that the forms of all things are derived from their Genius, which by the Ancients was call'd an Angel & Spirit & Demon.

'PRINCIPLE 2ᵈ. As all men are alike in outward form, So (and with the same infinite variety) all are alike in the Poetic Genius.

'PRINCIPLE 3ᵈ. No man can think, write, or speak from his heart, but he must intend truth. Thus all sects of Philosophy are from the Poetic Genius adapted to the weaknesses of every individual.

'PRINCIPLE 4ᵗʰ. As none by travelling over known lands can find out the unknown, So from already acquired knowledge Man could not acquire more: therefore an universal Poetic Genius exists.

'PRINCIPLE 5ᵗʰ. The Religions of all Nations are derived from each Nation's different perception of the Poetic Genius, which is everywhere call'd the Spirit of Prophecy.

'PRINCIPLE 6ᵗʰ. The Jewish & Christian Testaments are An original derivation from the Poetic Genius; this is necessary from the confined nature of bodily sensation.

'PRINCIPLE 7ᵗʰ. As all men are alike (tho' infinitely various), So all Religions; &, as all similars, have one source.

'The true Man is the source, he being the Poetic Genius'.[84]

These principles are a brief and concise summary of Blake's epistemology.

In his statement that the true method of knowledge is experiment and the true faculty of knowing must be the faculty which experiences, 'experiences' is the key word. By the term Blake means what man experiences both practically and intellectually in his surrounding world. By these practical experiences man gains knowledge of his environment. In other word man acquires knowledge by experience. It follows that what man learns about events and things by hearsay and from books is different from what he learns by practical experience, and is passive.

Passive experience is that which is not experienced by the creative mind personally and individually. It is abstract because it is not practised and is experience in name only. Locke's theory of 'experience' is passive because he bases 'moral fitness' on the information that we have received from others directly or indirectly. For him, education is the direct source of information. The other source is the impressions received from the social environment. By contrast, Blake's *Sons of Innocence*, for example, are the direct product of practical experience. The experience of Innocence is personally acquired but the experience of *Songs of Experience* is only taught and is abstract. Religion talks of love and humanity but in practice acts against love and humanity by its selfishness. But in *The Songs of Innocence*, true love and human brotherhood are experienced and felt rather than taught. The Father and Children, shepherd and flock live together.

The *Songs of Experience* represent a society where morality is taught by those who act against their own teachings. Blake called this condition: 'The Human Abstract'. But in the *Songs of Innocence* 'mercy, Pity, Peace, and love' are seen and experienced. Blake calls this condition 'The Divine Image'—the 'image' that every innocent child or person is capable of. This 'image' is Poetic Genius or creative character. In the *Songs of Experience* this creative character has fallen and is replaced by abstract morality.

The *Songs of Experience* represent the mechanical social system of the eighteenth century which was largely based on the empiricist philosophy. In the title of the songs, the word 'Experience' is apparently meant to echo Locke's philosophy which Blake identified with the mechanical social system. In his *Essay Concerning Human Understanding*, Locke stresses the word 'Experience':

'*All ideas come from sensation or reflection.*—Let us then suppose the mind to be, as we say, white paper, void of all characters, without any ideas; how comes it to be furnished? Whence comes it by that vast store, which the busy and boundless fancy of man has printed on it with an almost endless variety? Whence has it all the materials of reason and knowledge? To this I answer, in one word, from EXPERIENCE; in that all our knowledge is founded, and from that it ultimately derives itself.'[85]

In this passage the word 'Experience' is once again obviously the key word. But here it is used in a very different sense from the active 'experiences' in *All Religions are One*. Locke's philosophy supported the rigid social system of the age. Thus the word 'Experience' in the *Songs of Experience* represents both Lockean philosophy and the social system of which it was an outcrop. The *Songs of Experience*, therefore, mirror a society based on the philosophy of 'EXPERIENCE', and the word itself represents the social system founded on the exclusive experience of the minority in 'Heaven' working against the interest of those in 'Hell'.

For Locke experience was the product of the passive receiving of sense-impressions, but Blake placed emphasis on what the senses work upon and on the activity of the senses. All men possess their five senses, but they do not of necessity all share the same experiences. In *Visions of the Daughters of Albion*, repudiating the sense principle which has been used as an apology for and justification of the existing social system, Blake writes:

' "With what sense is it that the chicken shuns the
  ravenous hawk?
 "With what sense does the tame pigeon measure out the
  expanse?
 "With what sense does the bee form cells? have not the
  mouse & frog
 "Eyes and ears and sense of touch? yet are their habita-
  tions
 "And their pursuits as different as their forms and as
  their joys.
 "Ask the wild ass why he refuses burdens, and the meek
  camel
 "Why he loves man: is it because of eye, ear, mouth, or
  skin,
 "Or breathing nostrils? No, for these the wolf and tyger
  have.

"Ask the blind worm the secrets of the grave, and why he
    spires
"Love to curl round the bones of death; and ask the
    rav'nous snake
"Where she gets poison, & the wing'd eagle why he loves
    the sun;
"And then tell me the thoughts of man, that have been
    hid of old." '[86]

Eyes see many things but the heart knows its particular delight
which is from 'the joys of riches and ease'.[87] Poetic Genius is
the Heart. 'The Eye sees more than the Heart Knows'.

5. 'POETIC GENIUS' OR IMAGINATION AS AN INSTRUMENT OF MORAL GOOD

The principles that

   'the true Man is the source, he being the Poetic Genius'

and that

   'all are alike in the Poetic Genius',

seek to convey, by stressing the potentially equal creative
power of all men, the idea that differences between men come
mainly from their environment and the objects which compose
it.

   There are two kinds of principle: one is limited and passive,
the other is unlimited and creative. The former is based on the
sense principle, the latter on Poetic Genius.

   ' "... Some nations', says Ezekiel, 'held one principle for
   the origin, & some another: we of Israel taught that the
   Poetic Genius (as you now call it) was the first principle
   and all the others merely derivative, which was the cause
   of our despising the Priests & Philosophers of other
   countries, and prophecying that all Gods would at last be
   proved to originate in ours & to be the tributaries of
   the Poetic Genius; it was this that our great poet, King
   David, desired so fervently & invokes so pathetic'lly,
   saying by this he conquers enemies and governs king-
   doms. . . ." '

and the

> 'Religions of all Nations are derived from each Nation's
> different reception of the Poetic Genius'.

The Israelites held Poetic Genius as the origin and regarded
the sense principle or outward body as merely derivative.
They believed all Gods would finally 'be proved to originate'
in the Poetic Genius. This idea served as a foundation for
monotheism. The poets, like King David, appealed to the
creative power of Poetic Genius and believed that it conquers
enemies and overcomes human difficulties. But later on

> '"from these opinions the vulgar came to think that all
> nations would at last be subject to the jews"'.

In other words the outward form or name was divided from
its creative spirit or Poetic Genius by a literal interpretation.
Thus the created or derived form was established to act against
the creator or Poetic Genius. The prophet Ezekiel attempted
to unite nations by prophesying that

> '"all Gods would at last be proved to originate in ... the
> Poetic Genius"'

but the priest later on propounded the outward body or
'derivative' form as opposed to the Poetic Genius or 'true
Man'.

> '"This"', said Ezekiel, '"like all firm persuasions, is come
> to pass; for all nations believe the jews' code and worship
> the jews' god, and what greater subjection can be?"'

Thus the God of the prophet Ezekiel is different from that of
the priest Swedenborg. The God of the prophet is and acts in
all men and is creative, but Swedenborg's God is limited and
passive. To show what is meant by the passive, abstract God
of 'negation' we should return to Swedenborg's *Heaven and Hell*.

One of Swedenborg's chief characteristics is his assumption
that all power is derived from divine sources. The Angels'
understanding springs from the Lord and so whatever they do
is right.

The Lord also rules man through the Angels who act upon
the 'understanding and will', the spiritual part of man, which

in turn governs man's physical part. What the spiritual thinks

'the mouth and tongue speak, and what he wills, this the body acts'.[88]

Swedenborg believed that every action of man is directed from above. He

'cannot even stir a step without the influx of heaven'.[89]

He thought himself completely in the hands of the superior power:

'... it having been granted to the angels to move my steps, my actions, my tongue, and speech, at their will, and this by influx into my will and thought, confirming me by experience in the conviction that of myself I could do nothing'.[90]

Since God has sent the Angels to lead Swedenborg, whatever Swedenborg does is directed and approved by God.

The Angels are all-powerful in the spiritual world and are tools to carry out the Lord's commands. If the Lord orders that thousands in 'Hell' should be punished, the command is carried out by the Angels. Indeed:

'if anything in that world makes resistance, which is necessary to be removed because it is *contrary* to divine order, they cast it down and overturn it by a mere exertion of the will and a look. . . . I have seen also some hundred thousands of evil spirits dispersed and cast into hell by them: multitude is of no avail against them, no arts, cunning confederacies, for they see all things, and in a moment dash them in pieces.'

The Angels are equally powerful in the natural world, where they have

'brought destruction on whole armies',

or have

'induced a pestilence of which seventy thousand men died. . . .'[91]

Swedenborg supports his argument by using David as witness:

> ' "*The angel stretched out his hand against Jerusalem to destroy it, but Jehovah repented of the evil and said to the angel who destroyed the people, it is enough, withold now thy hand: and David saw the angel who smote the people,* 2nd Samuel xxiv. 15, 16, 17. . . . Inasmuch as the angels have such power, therefore they are called powers; as in David: "*Bless Jehovah ye angels most powerful in strength*", Psalm ciii. 20." '[92]

Blake's statement that

> '. . . our great poet, King David, desired so fervently & invokes so pathetic'ly, saying by this he conquers enemies & governs kingdoms; . . . from these opinions the vulgar came to think that all nations would at last be subject to the jews'

is clearly related to the above quoted passage from *Heaven and Hell*.

King David appealed to Poetic Genius, but Swedenborg is typical of the 'vulgar' who came to think that all nations would at last be subject to the Jews. Swedenborg would send Roman Catholics, Muslims (or Mahomedans, as Swedenborg terms them), Quakers and Moravians, into exile, and place them in the 'most remote hells'.[93] Blake identifies Swedenborg's religion with the 'jews' code' and his God with Jehovah.

In Plates 12–13 Ezekiel, Isaiah, David, and Diogenes represent creative characters. The creative character or Poetic Genius is both intellectual and practical. It is active and creative in social and practical life, and its creation is boundless. There is no end to the creation of man and it is the Poetic Genius or 'imagination' which sees this infinite creation. Blake asked Ezekiel why

> 'he eat dung & lay so long on his right & left side?'

He answered

> ' "the desire of raising other men into a perception of the infinite: . . . is he honest who resists his genius or conscience only for the sake of present ease or gratification?" '

The question corresponds to 'The Argument' and the answer accordingly is negative:

'Once meek, and in a perilous path,
The just man kept his course along
. . . .

Till the villain left the paths of ease,
To walk in perilous paths, and drive
The just man into barren climes.'

Blake identifies the Poetic Genius or 'imagination' with the 'meek', 'just', 'honest', conscious man, 'true man' and God. In his *Annotations to Swedenborg's Divine Love* Blake responds to the statement that

'the Negation of God constitutes Hell, and in the Christian World the Negation of the Lord's Divinity',

commenting that 'Hell' is a product of

'The Negation of the Poetic Genius'.[94]

The creative faculty of imagination cannot create unless the passive memories (or 'negation') are cast out; and the passive memories cannot be cast out, man cannot be morally good, unless he acts and creates. This is the theme of Plate 14.

'The ancient tradition that the world will be consumed in fire at the end of six thousand years is true, as I have heard from Hell.

'For the cherub with his flaming sword is hereby commanded to leave his guard at tree of life; and when he does, the whole creation will be consumed and appear infinite and holy, whereas it now appears finite & corrupt.

'This will come to pass by an improvement of sensual enjoyment.

'But first the notion that man has a body distinct from his soul is to be expunged; this I shall do by printing in the infernal method, by corrosives, which in Hell are salutary and medicinal, melting apparent surfaces away, and displaying the infinite which was hid.

'If the doors of perception were cleansed every thing would appear to man as it is, infinite.

'For man has closed himself up, till he sees all things thro'
narrow chinks of his cavern.'[95]

In this passage the poet shows the Angel how to cleanse his
perceiving eyes or the eyes of imagination and thus be able to
see the 'infinite'. Firstly the dichotomy between body and soul
or Man and God 'is to be expunged'. This can be done by the
marriage of 'Heaven' or 'Delight' with 'Hell' or 'Energy'.
Blake himself does this by working or printing. Blake invented
his own method of printing and thus supported his wife and
himself. These kinds of manual tasks would seem 'infernal' to
the Angels in 'Heaven' but to Blake 'are salutory and medi-
cinal'. The artist depends on his creative work to cast out all
passive memories and abstract rules,

'melting apparent surfaces away, and displaying the
infinite which was hid'.

The creative character is like a traveller who moves forward
and therefore has no time to turn back or contemplate his
passive memories. In the creative mind all memories become
inspiring and move on at one with the moving man.

The creative mind is freed when the 'cherub with his
flaming sword' or the negative reasoning power, which is based
on passive memories, leaves 'his guard at tree of life' or Good
and Evil. It is passivity that causes the fall of creative man, for

'man has closed himself up, till he sees all things thro'
narrow chinks of his cavern'.

Plate 14 is also written in the context of *Heaven and Hell* and,
apparently, refers to the chapter 'concerning the speech of
Angels with Man'. In this chapter, while discussing how the
Angels speak with man through man's memory, Swedenborg
writes:

'. . . *the ancients* had an opinion, that after some *thousands
of years* they should return into their former life, and into
all its operations, and likewise that they had so returned,
which they concluded from this circumstance, that occa-
sionally there had occurred to them as it were a recol-
lection of things which yet they never either saw or heard,

which *came to pass* in consequence of spirits flowing in
from their own memory into their ideas of thought.'[96]

The word 'ancients' and the phrases 'thousand years' and
'come to pass' in Plate 14 are inspired by this passage. The
'cherub with his flaming sword' and 'his guard at tree of life'
represents the Angels' in 'Heaven' who guard and punish those
in 'Hell' because of their love of self and of the world. Although
Swedenborg believed that everybody discourses according to
his own memory and says that

'It is not allowed any angel and spirit to speak with man
from his own memory'.[97]

yet he negated the memory of those in 'Hell' as 'evil' and
'infernal'. The Angels are sent from the Lord to 'guard' men:

'. . . the angels of every society are sent to men, that they
may *guard* them, and withdraw them from evil affections
and consequent thoughts, and inspire them with good
affections. . . . they rule the deeds or works of men,
removing . . . evil intentions:
. . . .'[98]

Again, while discussing the love and desire of men in 'Hell',
Swedenborg writes:

'All the hells are closed towards that world, being open
only through holes and clefts, and through wide gaps
which are *guarded*, to prevent anyone coming out except
by permission. . . .'[99]

The 'cherub with his flaming sword' in Plate 14 satirically
represents the ruling interests warding off, restraining and
punishing the active working people who would partake of the
'tree of life'.

When the 'cherub' leaves his guard at the 'tree of life' or
'tree of good and evil' then the 'whole creation will be con-
sumed and appear infinite and holy', whereas it now appears
to Swedenborg 'finite and corrupt'.

Blake who works in 'Hell' tells Swedenborg that if he desires
to return to his former life and live as the ancients lived then
he must improve his 'sensual enjoyment' by realizing that the

delight of 'Heaven' is not distinct from the Body. In other words

'Energy is the only life, and is from the Body; . . . .'[100]

To realize this he ought to work six days, as Blake did by printing, and rest on the seventh day. This will consume his passive world of memory in fire at the 'end of six thousand years' or at the end of six days. Blake takes 'thousand years' from Swedenborg and satirically adds the number 'six' which, apparently, represents six days of the week. Creative work consumes all the passive and negative rules of the priest. Blake sees the seventh day as a day of ease and joy and can experience it fully in contrast to previous labour.

This vision makes the whole creation appear infinite and holy and it is this creative power in man which is imagination or Poetic Genius. Imagination looks forward and is infinite whereas memory looks backward and is finite. Imagination is based on 'contrary progression' but the memory is based on 'negation'.

6. SCIENCE IN 'HEAVEN' AND 'PRINTING HOUSE IN HELL'

When Blake attacks science he attacks abstract knowledge and the rationalism of his time upon which the science or knowledge of the Urizenic character is based:

> 'They began to weave curtains of darkness,
> They erected large pillars round the Void,
> With golden hooks fasten'd in the pillars;
> With infinite labour the Eternals
> A woof wove, and called it Science.'[101]

The word 'science', connoting Rationalism, appears frequently in Swedenborg's writings, as we might expect; and Blake, viewing this Rationalism as passivity, opposed it. Swedenborg writes:

> 'These three Degrees of Altitude are named Natural, Spiritual and Celestial . . . Man, at his Birth, first comes into the natural Degree, and this increases in him by Continuity according to the Sciences, and according to

the Understanding acquired by the, to them Summit of Understanding which is called Rational.'

Blake remarks:

'Study Sciences till you are blind, Study intellectuals till you are cold, Yet science cannot teach intellect. Much less can intellect teach Affection. How foolish then is it to assert that Man is born in only one degree, when that one degree is reception of the 3 degrees, two of which he must destroy or close up or they will descend; if he closes up the two superior, then he is nor truly in the 3^d, but descends out of it into meer Nature or Hell. . . . Is it not also evident that one degree will not open the other, & that science will not open intellect,'. . . .[102]

In his *Annotations to Swedenborg's The Wisdom of Angels Concerning Divine Prividence* Blake wrote: 'Truth is Nature' against Swedenborg's statement that

'Nothing doth IN GENERAL so contradict Man's natural and favourite Opinions as TRUTH, . . .'[103]

'Nature' is 'truth' when it is based on creative energy. 'Nature is Truth', but it falls short of truth according to the weakness or idleness of every man. Scholars miss the point of the contrast between the two kinds of 'Nature' when they take them as evidence of a change in the poet's opinion.[104]

In the later writings of Blake, too, the word 'science' corresponds to rationalism and becomes the symbol of a mechanical system. In *The French Revolution* Blake states how reason and science were formed by the natural and abstract impressions of the reasoner:

'The law and gospel from fire and air, and eternal reason
    and science
From the deep and the solid, and man lay his faded head
    down on the rock. . . .'[105]

The words 'deep', 'solid' and 'rock' convey the rigid nature of the reasoner's impressions. The idle priest forms his laws and gospel from his abstract and passive impressions. The word 'fire' represents his presupposed self-righteous character, and 'air' his abstract teaching. In *America* (1793) Blake attacks the priest and his God who

> 'are unrestrain'd performers of the energies of nature;
> Till pity is become a trade, and generosity a science....'106

These 'energies of nature' are the passive and devouring forces which work against the creative and prolific energy of nature in man. The priest has energy to devour and this energy is based on his passive natural memories or 'Nature's wide womb' which is burning in a 'deep world within'.107 This devouring 'Nature' is passive and seeks 'joy without pain'108 or hard work.

In *The Book of Ahania*, which represents the divided selfhood and 'invisible Lust'109 in the Urizenic character, the word 'science' again means knowledge based on the principle of sense perception. Urizen, by his science, forms the human soul in his own likeness. Planting his seeds among people.

> ' "... thou with thy lap full of seed,
> "With thy hand full of generous fire
> "Walked forth from the clouds of morning,
> "On the virgins of springing joy,
> "On the human soul to cast
> "The seed of eternal science." '110

In *The Four Zoas* the word 'science' again stands for rationalism and Urizenic knowledge. The Urizenic character writes books by viewing his own 'Abyss' of natural impressions. He flees back, as we have seen before, to his natural memories. On this journey he views all the impressions that he had received from his environment in the past. The 'science' or knowledge of Urizen or fallen man is the reflection of these impressions in the depth of his memory:

> 'Oft would he sit in a dark rift & regulate his books,
> Or sleep such sleep as spirits eternal, wearied in his dark
> Tearful & sorrowful state; then rise, look out & ponder
> His dismal voyage, eyeing the next sphere tho' far remote;
> Then darting into the Abyss of night his venturous limbs...
> Creating many a Vortex, fixing many a Science in the
>   deep.'111

It is this sort of knowledge which Blake satirizes in Plates 15–17 of *The Marriage of Heaven and Hell*:

'I was in a Printing house in Hell, & saw the method in which knowledge is transmitted from generation to genera-tion.

In the first chamber was a Dragon-Man, clearing away the rubbish from a cave's mouth; within, a number of dragons were hollowing the cave.

In the second chamber was a Viper folding round the rock & the cave, and others adorning it with gold, silver and precious stones.

In the third chamber was an Eagle with wings and feathers of air: he caused the inside of the cave to be infinite; around were numbers of Eagle-like men who built palaces in the immense cliffs.

In the fourth chamber were Lions of flaming fire, raging round & melting the metals into living fluids.

In the fifth chamber were Unnam'd forms, which cast the metals into the expanse.

There they were receiv'd by Men who occupied the sixth chamber, and took forms of books & were arranged in libraries.'[112]

The Dragon-man represents natural man. The five chambers, represent the Abyss of the five senses. The 'Lions of flaming fire' are the creative mind and energy which is imprisoned in the 'cave'. The imprisoned energy, like a lion, rages in the cage of natural memories 'melting' 'metals' or fixed memories into 'living fluids' or fanciful memories. These fanciful memo-ries of the Angels are printed by 'Unnam'd forms', those who work in a 'Printing house in Hell'. Thus the knowledge of the Angels took the 'forms of books and were arranged in libraries'.

The Urizenic character's 'science' contains the 'Seed' of division. He divides himself from others by seeking refuge in his own passive memories.

'Man is a Worm; wearied with joy, he seeks the caves of
        sleep
Among the Flowers of Beulah, in his selfish cold repose

    Forsaking Brotherhood & Universal love, in selfish clay
    Folding the pure wings of his mind, seeking the places
        dark
    Abstracted from the roots of [Nature del.] Science; then
        inclos'd around
    In walls of Gold we cast him like a Seed into the
        Earth. . . .'113

The science which is divided from active life and reality is
abstract science. This abstract science destroys the creative
mind. It enfolds the creative mind in its abstract philosophy
and causes the fall of the creative or 'Eternal man'. In *The
Four Zoas*, 'Urthona', 'Luvah', 'Tharmas' and 'Urizen' repre-
sent the fallen elements in Man. Urthona corresponds to Los
or Imagination, Luvah to Love, Tharmas to the material
world or 'Parent power', and Urizen to Reason. All these
elements fall and lose their sight and power through the
abstract science which covers them in its veil. Man becomes a
doubting wanderer. The creative mind turns from reality,
and 'Reason', who was like the rising sun, ceases to rise daily
and thus certainty changes to doubt and becomes Urizen.
When 'Reason' falls, or the sun does not rise afresh every
morning, then Luvah and Los or Love and Imagination fall
also. The creative man descends into the bosom of 'Tharmas',
the abstract memories, or 'Eternal Death'. He forms his
principle of 'Love' and 'Hate' from this 'Nature's wide womb'.
He loves all his passive memories and hates the world of
reality and active life. Thus man descends from active life and
love into passive life and love.

    'They have surrounded me with walls of iron & brass, O
        Lamb
    Of God clothed in Luvah's garments! little knowest thou
    Of death Eternal, that we all go to Eternal Death,
    To our Primeval Chaos in fortuitous concourse of inco-
        herent
    Discordant principles of Love & Hate. I suffer affliction
    Because I love, for I [am del.] was love, but hatred awakes
        in me,
    And Urizen, who was Faith & certainty, is chang'd to
        Doubt; . . . .'114

The science of Urizen is bitter and negative for he walks only the path of hopelessness and despair:

'. . . nor saw Urizen with a Globe of fire
Lighting his dismal journey thro' the pathless world of death,
Writing in bitter tears & groans in books of iron & brass. . . .'[115]

This abstract and bitter science is contrasted with the 'sweet' science; the former can change into the latter when the natural and passive memories are supported by man's creative energy. When this creative energy has priority over the natural memories the latter become inspiring as the 'Earthworm renews the moisture of the sandy plain'.[116] By reuniting passive memories with creative energy, the subjective world with the objective and real world, the 'Eternal Man' or Imagination rises again. *The Four Zoas* starts with the fall of 'Man' from the 'Universal Brotherhood' into division or war and ends with the sweet science of unity and brotherhood:

'The Sun arises from his dewy bed, & the fresh airs
Play in his smiling beams giving the seeds of life to grow,
And the fresh Earth beams forth ten thousand thousand springs of life.
Urthona is arisen in his strength, no longer now
Divided from Enitharmon, no longer the Spectre Los.
Where is the Spectre of Prophecy? where the delusive Phantom?
Departed: & Urthona rises from the ruinous Walls
In all his ancient strength to form the golden armour of science
For intellectual War. The war of swords departed now,
The dark Religions are departed & sweet Science reigns.'[117]

The word 'Science' in the creative sense of the word is usually combined by Blake with the word 'Art'. In his Annotations to Sir Joshua Reynold's 'Discourses' Blake wrote:

'The Arts & Sciences are the Destruction of Tyrannies or Bad Governments. Why should A Good Government endeavour to Depress what is its Chief & only Support?

'The Foundation of Empire is Art & Science. Remove
them or Degrade them, & the Empire is No More.'[118]

We see that the word 'Science' or knowledge is used by
Blake in two different senses; one refers to a passive 'science',
the other to something active and creative.

7. 'PRISONS ARE BUILT WITH STONES OF LAW'

A cursory study of Blake's work might lead one to the mistaken
idea that he opposed law and religion. Blake did not condemn
law as such, but its unjust and inhuman forms. Nor did Blake
condemn religion as such, but opposed the abstract and
negative attitudes of priest and state who used religion for
their own ends. Those in 'Heaven' make laws against those in
'Hell' according to their likes and dislikes. Religion and law
thus become the products of abstract knowledge which restains
and chains the just or active man:

'The Giants who formed this world into its sensual
existence, and now seem to live in it in chains, are in truth
the causes of its life & the sources of all activity; but the
chains are the cunning of weak and tame minds which
have power to resist energy; according to the proverb, the
weak in courage is strong in cunning.'[119]

The Giants are the active beings or human energies who
create the material world. The 'chains' in this context are
formed by law and religion.

The active people in Swedenborg's 'Hell' are Giants or
energies who have created the sensual existence of 'Heaven'.
Swedenborg talks of them as the 'mighty ones'.[120] In general
their

'faces are direful, and void of life like carcases, in some
instances they are black, in some fiery like little torches,
in some disfigured with pimples, warts, and ulcers, in
several instances no face appears, but in its stead some-
thing hairy or bony, and in some cases teeth only are
extant; their bodies also are monstrous. . . .'[121]

And again the

'. . . gnashing of teeth, which are mentioned in the Word
as the portion of those who are in hell'.[122]

These Giants in the chains of 'Hell' are thus, in truth, the
source of all activity in 'Heaven'. They are kept in chains by
those whose negative action springs from weakness—and whose
art is only to resist energy:

'. . . The chains are the cunning of weak and tame minds
which have power to resist energy'.

The tamed mind is fed only on passive teachings. The passive
character is however, far from being pacific and non-violent.
It is, on the contrary, though weak in the courage needed to
live an active and practical life, strong in the cunning and
power needed to force his will on others:

'the weak in courage is strong in cunning'.

Through the 'tame mind' and 'systematic reasoning' the
priest, like Urizen, drives a deep wedge between his self hood or
the devouring part and his productive or prolific part. As society
is divided into 'Heaven' and 'Hell' so his mind is also divided:

'Thus one portion of being is the Prolific, the other the
Devouring: to the Devourer it seems as if the producer
was in his chains; but it is not so, he only takes portions
of existence and fancies that the whole.'[123]

The passive devouring character is wrapped up in his
natural memories like a 'Dragon' hidden in a Cave. His likes
and impressions are formed by the five senses and are for him
all-important. But he is mistaken. These memories are merely
'portions of existence' which he imagines as the whole. For he

'. . . has closed himself up, till he sees all things thro'
narrow chinks of his cavern'.[124]

The 'weak and tame mind' first restrains its own creative
element and then attempts to restrain others. The restrained
portion divides man from others, becoming a passive negation
of social existence.

'But the Prolific would cease to be Prolific unless the
Devourer, as a sea, received the excess of his delights.'[125]

G

The 'Devourer', in this context, is active and prolific. Man creates by his genius and driving desire. The desire and delight of man are infinite. He cannot create and be prolific unless holding the vision of infinite desire. In other words, the Devourer can only be Prolific when desire is fulfilled by action rather than by restraint. Desire or energy is like a sea; the barren lands become fertile when water washes over them.

'The desire of Man being Infinite, the possession is Infinite & himself Infinite.'[126]

Desire in man is a prolific good when it is based on an active life. It becomes evil when it succumbs to passivity. The passive devourer is identified with the passive Reason and the active devourer with the active Reason.

In society, the Priest is the personification of passive restraint and his religion is based on 'negation'.

'Negation' is unnecessary; but the existence of the contraries, the active 'Devourer' or 'Desire', is essential for the creation of the contrary portion of the 'Prolific',

'Some will say: "Is not God alone the Prolific?" I answer: "God only Acts and Is, in existing beings or Men." '[127]

Here Blake gives a human form to the heavenly God of the priest. In his *Annotations to Reynolds*, he writes: '. . . I always thought that the Human Mind was the most Prolific of All Things & Inexhaustible . . .' (K. p. 471).

In Blake's system, then, there is no end to creation. The end of one creation is the beginning of another; the old heaven and earth pass away, the new come into existence. In society, Blake represents this process by two classes or generations of people, one class passing away and the other class rising up, much as the old day is replaced by the new. Those who try to halt or fix this creation destroy existence, for:

'These two classes of men are always upon earth, & they should be enemies: whoever tries to reconcile them seeks to destroy existence.'
Religion is an endeavour to reconcile the two.'[128]

These two classes of men represent stages of development and are based on 'contraries'. One stage or state passes away and another comes into existence. They live mutually. But the classes of 'Heaven' and 'Hell' are based on negation. The interests of one class ('Heaven') negates the interests of the other class ('Hell'). Blake is explicit in *Jerusalem*:

  ' "Negations are not Contraries: Contraries mutually Exist;
  But Negations Exist Not. Exceptions & Objections &
    Unbeliefs
  Exist not, nor shall they ever be Organized for ever &
    ever.
  If thou separate from me, thou art a Negation, a meer
  Reasoning & Derogation from me, an Objecting & cruel
    Spite
  And Malice & Envy. . . ." ' (K. p. 639).

The priest's attempts at 'reconciliation' are based on laws of 'negation', with 'Heaven' as the punisher above and 'Hell' as the one suffering punishment below. The priest's 'reconciliation' is false because it is based on an unjust relationship, with one law for the idle in 'Heaven' and the same law for the active beings in 'Hell'. 'One Law for the Lion and Ox is Oppression' Blake concludes.

  Blake's theory of the 'two classes of men' who must necessarily be enemies might seem, as Middleton Murry has implied,[129] a paradox in the context of *The Marriage of Heaven and Hell*. *The Marriage* does indeed repudiate Swedenborg's divided society, yet Blake insists on the necessity of two contrary classes of men upon earth. Blake condemns Swedenborg's divided society because it is based on a static and fixed system. Blake condemns deformity not variety. The relationship between 'Heaven' and 'Hell' in Swedenborg is based on 'negation' which deforms and cripples one half of society. The selfish father cripples his children's creative energy. He stifles their growth and development and creates despair and hopelessness. In *Songs of Experience* Blake censures the father-priest who binds his children to the earth and stifles their growth:

      ' "Prison'd on wat'ry shore,
      "Starry Jealousy does keep my den:
      "Cold and hoar,
      "Weeping o'er,
      "I hear the Father of the ancient men.

"Selfish father of men!
"Cruel, jealous, selfish fear!
"Can delight,
"Chain'd in night,
"The virgins of youth and morning hear?

"Does spring hide its joy
"When buds and blossoms grow?
"Does the sower
"Sow by night,
"Or the plowman in darkness plow?

"Break this heavy chain
"That does freeze my bones around.
"Selfish! vain!
"Eternal bane!
"That free Love with bondage bound." '[130]

Blake's two classes of men are undeformed and creative 'contraries'. Their relationship is based on love and unity. The child and father are contraries; one grows up, grows old, and the other takes its place. The father is, by the process of natural growth, declining like the setting sun, while the child is reaching the zenith of his 'active' life, like the rising sun. They are opposites and potential enemies because their interests are different and they are in two different stages of development. But this opposition is necessary for creation and a necessary part of creation. It is part of the 'living being' both in nature and in society:

'Opposition is true Friendship'[131] and 'The roaring of lions, the howling of wolves, the raging of the stormy sea, and the destructive sword, are portions of eternity, too great for the eye of man.'[132]

These are all manifestations of 'energies' in nature which cannot be imprisoned or resisted. When an energetic force encounters resistance in nature, it reacts violently. This reaction can be the roaring of lions or the roll of thunder. Thunder is like the destructive sword which cuts through the stagnant and close air, the wild beasts in Swedenborg's 'Hell' are manifestations of such restrained energy for 'some hells appear to the view like caves and dens, such as wild beasts inhabit in forests'.

The jealous and selfish father negates the energy or life force of his children and thus creates wrathful 'tygers', who appear to the Angels as wild beasts in society. The priest's 'Heaven' and 'Hell' are ever divided by his self-interest which is being supported by his negative laws.[133] The love which ought to unite man with his fellow creatures is with 'bondage bound' by such laws. Society becomes like a 'mill'[134] with 'Heaven' as the 'miller' grinding its 'Heavenly' stones on the wretched in 'Hell'.

A context begins to emerge within which we might come to an understanding of how the 'stones of Law' build prisons and the 'bricks of Religion', brothels. It is also in this context that Blake's dialetic becomes understandable and terms and symbols reveal their particular definitions. Such terms and symbols in Blake are patently not abstract but are the embodiment of an act or of a state of mind:

'Each are Personified. There is not an Error but it has a Man for its [Actor del.] Agent, that is, it is a Man. There is not a Truth but it has also a Man. Good & Evil are Qualities in Every Man, whether a Good or Evil Man.' (K. p. 615.)

Thus Blake insists that the value of every term must be seen in its human dialectic. The word 'love', for example, is abstract unless we know the context of its use.

In the *Songs of Experience* Blake clearly differentiates between selfish and selfless love:

' "Love seeketh not Itself to please,
"Nor for itself hath any care,
"But for another gives its ease,
"And builds a Heaven in Hell's despair." '

'So sang a little Clod of Clay
Trodden with the cattle's feet,
But a Pebble of the brook
Warbled out these metres meet:'

' "Love seeketh only Self to please,
"To bind another to Its delight.
"Joys in another's loss of ease,
"And builds a Hell in Heaven's despite." '[135]

The 'clod of clay' is a symbol of humility and selflessness, while 'the pebble of the brook' represents selfhood. The 'clod', selfless because it does not set out to please itself but seeks its own love in the pleasure of others, is 'trodden with the cattle's feet' yet is happy and sings the songs of love. True and selfless love puts another's pleasure before its own. The 'pebble', a symbol of selfhood, is passive in its position. It seeks only 'self to please'. The 'clod' 'sings' with a spontaneous energy. The 'pebble' is restricted by the verbal fixity of 'metres meet'.

The language and spirit of the poetry is clearly dialectical. The 'Love' which 'seeketh not itself to please' and the 'Love' which 'seeketh only Self to please' are opposing states. 'Pebble' negates 'Clod'. The 'Pebble's' love is limited but the 'Clod's' is unlimited and free, though self-sacrificing. They represent two different states of mind. The *Songs of Innocence* and *of Experience* show these contrary states of the human soul. The 'contrary states' turn to 'negation' when the finite rises against the infinite. The *Songs of Innocence* represent the infinite and *Songs of Experience* the finite which has turned to 'negation' by establishing itself against 'Innocence'. There is conflict between the two. Thus 'The Tyger', in all its complexity, is the symbol of energy, but of a self-centred, terrifying energy; and 'The Lamb' in all its simplicity symbolizes the calm of a universal, an undivided or classless society or true 'Heaven'. 'The Tyger' and 'The Lamb' then, are products of two different contexts. 'The Tyger' a creation of a jungle-like order, 'The Lamb' of a peaceful harmony. In one, creativity is displaced, negative; in the other, content and at peace with itself. The savage irony of the question 'Did he, who made the lamb make Thee?' recalls Blake's sardonic caption to Plate 12 in 'The Gates of Paradise': 'Does thy God, O Priest, take such vengeance as this?' (K. p. 768).

Swedenborg in his chapter 'Concerning the State of Peace in Heaven' states that there are two inmost principles in heaven: innocence and peace. They 'proceed immediately from the Lord: innocence is that principle from which is derived every good of heaven, and peace is that principle from which is derived all the delights of good'.[136] Only the Angels in 'Heaven' live in 'peace' and innocence because they have risen above the physical level of life:

'... in order to perceive the peace of heaven, a man ought to be . . . withdrawn from the body.'[137]

Swedenborg then notes that it is not enough to

'rest of mind, and tranquility . . . arising from the removal of cares'

to perceive the peace of heaven. It only comes

'with those who are principled in heavenly good, . . . inasmuch as peace flows in from the Lord into their inmost principle . . .'.[138]

Those in a state of innocence love everything which is good but

'consider themselves only as receivers, and ascribe all things to the Lord'.[139]

Those in 'Hell' cannot be in 'innocence' and 'peace' because they are not in love with the Lord and willing to be led by Him, and thus are not in 'Heaven'. They are in love with the 'self' and do not want to be led by another:

'... all who are in heaven are in innocence, for all who are there love to be led by the Lord; for they know that to lead themselves is to be led by the proprium . . . and the proprium consists in loving self, and he who loves himself doth not suffer himself to be led by another'.[140]

He states categorically elsewhere:

'... they who are in hell are altogether contrary to innocence, nor do they know what innocence is'.[141]

The mine-owner and priest in Swedenborg denies that those who work and live in 'Hell' are innocent; but those who live amid the abundance of 'Heaven' and dislike the active life are innocent because they do not love the 'self'. They love the Lord and thus receive his gifts 'gratis'. It is this kind of passive and abstract 'innocence' that Blake has illustrated in his Frontispiece to *Songs of Experience*.

Swedenborg enlarges on the attitude of those in 'Hell' towards those in 'Heaven' who have the monopoly of 'peace' and 'innocence'. The former seem 'inflamed with a cruel lust to hurt'[142] the Angels. To protect the innocent ones and preserve 'peace' in 'Heaven' in the face of opposition from 'Hell' the Angels use the laws of restraint through fear of punishment. At the end of the chapter 'Concerning the state of peace in Heaven', Swedenborg condemns the vengeful attitude of those in 'Hell' towards those in 'Heaven' and says that violence occurs in 'Hell' when its inhabitants are unrestrained by fear. The evil ones in 'Hell';

> 'burn with enmities, hatreds, *revenge*, cruelty . . . in which . . . their mind . . . indulges itself, as soon as they see anyone who doth not favour them, and thus bursts forth into open violence when unrestrained by fear; and that hence it comes to pass that their delight dwells in insanity, whilst the delight of those who are principled in good dwells in wisdom; the difference is like what subsists between hell and heaven'.[143]

The proverb 'A dead body revenges not injuries'[144] refers to the chapter about peace, and the idea of 'revenge' seems to be derived from the preceding passage. Blake challenges the unjust and selfish attitude of the ruling interests represented here by Swedenborg. In a society where the good things of life and all intellectual gifts are the sole property of those in 'Heaven', while the honest toil of those in 'Hell' is condemned as the love of self and of the world; where the father, who is supposed to be the shepherd and loving guide and protector of his children, instead lives upon them and accuses them of harbouring hatred and revenge; where he has allocated the conditions of innocence and peace for himself and placed his heavenly delight and interest before his children's ease: in this society, and with this unjust relationship, the resulting feelings of enmity and revenge in the children is understandable and justified. The beings in Swedenborg's 'Hell' are living people, and thus react against their injuries; they would only accept them if they were passive or dead: 'A dead body revenges not injuries.'

It is this 'Heaven', this sort of society and its moral laws,

that Blake opposes in *The Marriage of Heaven and Hell*. Children
and father, he says, can live together in innocence and peace.

Swedenborg has drawn on the teachings of Jesus to support
his arguments. He states that the Lord is the source of peace:

' "*Jesus said PEACE I leave with you, My PEACE I give
unto you* . . . John xiv. 27." '[145]

Blake defends Jesus from being used as a support for Sweden-
borg's doctrine, and thus writes:

'Jesus Christ did not wish to unite, but to separate them,
as in the Parable of sheep and goats! & he says: "I came
not to send Peace, but a Sword." '[146]

It is the priest's art to divide and rule by fear of punishment.
And the civil law follows his lead, for again the

'laws in the world prescribe punishment for every evil'.[147]

Swedenborg says that

'God is good itself, love itself, and mercy itself'; . . . 'God
never turns Himself away from man.'[148]

But at the time of conflict between the Angels in 'Heaven' and
the people in 'Hell' God sides with the Angels. The Lord
prescribes and permits these torments.[149] The Lord seems to
speak with the same voice that we hear in *The Book of Urizen*
(1794). 'Urizen', after discovering the 'secrets of wisdom',
issues his decrees:

' "Lo! I unfold my darkness, and on
"This rock place with strong hand the Book
"Of eternal brass, written in my solitude:

"Laws of peace, of love, of unity,
"Of pity, compassion, forgiveness;
"Let each chuse one habitation,
"His ancient infinite mansion,
"One command, one joy, one desire,
"One curse, one weight, one measure,
"One King, one God, one Law." '[150]

These are Urizen's self-begotten laws, written in the book of

G*

'eternal brass'. The slogan 'one King, one God, one Law' is a tool in the hands of the ruling interests, the Angels in 'Heaven', to subjugate the engulfed and class-divided society where unity and oneness do not exist at all.

'Heaven', Swedenborg continues, has its laws and government too, but vastly different from those in 'Hell'. They are, to begin with, based on justice because:

> 'all the inhabitants of that Kingdom are principled in the good of love to the Lord from the Lord, and what is done from that good is called just'.[151]

It follows that justice is exclusively for the community of Angels in 'Heaven'. The government is in the hands of the Lord who directs the Angels:

> 'He leads them and teaches them in the affairs of life: truths, which are called truths of judgment, are inscribed on their hearts.'[152]

Everyone knows these truths and so

> 'matters of judgement never come into dispute there'.[153]

The less wise interrogate the more wise on matters related to life and the more wise, in turn, interrogate the Lord 'and receive answers'.[154] Thus the Angels learn about truth and judgement.

Governors in 'Heaven' administer

> 'all things according to the laws; they understand those laws because they are wise, and in doubtful cases they are enlightened by the Lord'.[155]

They are never punitive, because their laws are based on mutual love.

In 'Hell' the love of self and of the world is evil because it stems from the external world; in 'Heaven' it is not evil, because all love comes from the Lord. There is thus one law which is made only by those who are in 'Heaven'. The law is made from the standpoint of those in 'Heaven'.

If there were an equal justice for 'Heaven' and for 'Hell', the priest would cease to have unlimited power and riches. 'The wrath of the lion is the wisdom of God' and is beautiful, but if the lion uses this wisdom for his own ends, it becomes ugly and destructive. Power misused is immoral because it imposes its will on others. This can only occur in a society divided into 'Heaven' and 'Hell' in which one law is applied, representing only the viewpoint of those in 'Heaven'.

The different characteristics of the lion, tiger or ox cannot be fully appreciated and given proper recognition under abstract laws applying in the same way to all of them. The lion and the tiger which are products of such unjust and unequal laws seem like the head of Leviathan which appears enormous but is weak and earthbound. The lion, King of the jungle, lives on the results of his own energy. The priest imagines himself as powerful and wise in 'Heaven', yet lives upon the work of others.

According to Swedenborg, the governors of 'Heaven' are full of wisdom and love towards their fellow creatures. They do not make themselves

> 'greater than others, but lesser; for they set the good of society and of their neighbours in the prior place'.[156]

Swedenborg approves this attitude but does not himself set the good of society 'in the prior place'. In support of his arguments he quotes Jesus who said to his disciples:

> ' "*Whosoever would be the greatest amongst you, let him be your minister, and whosoever would be first amongst you, let him be your servant*" ' (Matt. xx. 27, 28).

And again,

> ' "*He that is the greatest amongst you, let him be as the least*" ' (Luke xxii. 26).

But to Swedenborg, greater wisdom is synonymous with greater wealth. The governors, despite their love and wisdom,

> 'enjoy honour and glory; they dwell in the midst of the society, in situations elevated above others, and likewise in magnificent palaces', . . . (H.H. p. 161, no. 218)

These are the symbols of their office, given to them by the Lord. Defending the position of Jesus against the unjust laws of the priest and his God and King, Blake, in *The Marriage*, turns the laws of Swedenborg upside down and dismisses them, as Jesus did the punitive 'laws' of the Old Testament. Blake censures the priest, saying that if he really loved Jesus and considered Him the greater one then he should copy Jesus' actions. Jesus condemned such moral laws as those of the Angel Swedenborg.

'Once I saw a Devil in a flame of fire, who arose before an Angel that sat on a cloud, and the Devil utter'd these words: "The worship of God is: Honouring his gifts in other men, each according to his genius, and loving the greatest men best: those who envy or calumniate great men hate God; for there is no other God." '

The Angel hearing this became almost blue; but mastering himself he grew yellow, & at last white, pink, and smiling, and then replied:

' "Thou Idolater! is not God One? & is not he visible in Jesus Christ? and has not Jesus Christ given his sanction to the law of ten commandments? and are not all other men fools, sinners, & nothings?" '[157]

'The Devil answer'd: "bray a fool in a morter with wheat, yet shall not his folly be beaten out of him; if Jesus Christ is the greatest man, you ought to love him in the greatest degree; now hear how he has given his sanction to the law of ten commandments: did he not mock at the sabbath, and so mock the sabbath's God? murder those who were murder'd because of him? turn away the law from the woman taken in adultery? steal the labor of others to support him? bear false witness when he omitted making a defence before Pilate? covet when he pray'd for his disciples, and when he bid them shake off the dust of their feet against such as refused to lodge them? I tell you, no virtue can exist without breaking these ten commandments. Jesus was all virtue, and acted from impulse, not from rules." '[158]

8. 'BROTHELS ARE BUILT WITH BRICKS OF RELIGION'

The religion that Blake opposes not only fails to fulfil its social and human responsibilities but also hinders and binds its adherents by its selfish attitudes. Religion negates and law punishes; one teaches virginity, the other rapes. Both religion and law are in the hands of the Angels in 'Heaven' who rule those in 'Hell' by their means. Religion rules the mind and law the body.

E. D. Hirsch in his book *Innocence and Experience: An Introduction to Blake* has suggested that Blake

'like Swedenborg, had given marriage a profound sacramental significance'.[159]

But a closer examination of Swedenborg might reveal a case quite opposite to that of Mr. Hirsch. Blake did not share Swedenborg's beliefs about marriage. The point of the last half of the proverb seems to be a criticism of the chapter 'Concerning Marriage in Heaven' and 'brothels' in 'Hell'. In this chapter Swedenborg discusses conjugal love and condemns adulteries as opposed to the delight of heavenly marriage.

There are two kinds of marriages, those of 'Heaven' and those of the earth. The former is the conjunction of man and woman into one mind. The mind consists of two parts, understanding and will. When these two parts act in unity, they are called one mind. In this united mind the husband

'acts that part which is called understanding, and the wife that which is called will'.[160]

This is the conjunction of the interiors. When it descends to the exterior 'principles', which are bodily, it is perceived and felt as love, which is 'conjugal love'.[161] Thus conjugal love is derived from the 'conjunction of two into one mind'. The two conjugal partners in 'Heaven' are called one Angel.

In this conjunction of man and woman or understanding and will into one mind, Swedenborg considers the man as superior to the woman. Although they are united in one mind, the wife ought to follow her husband for he is

'born to be intellectual, thus to think from intellect, but the woman is born to be voluntary'.

Man acts from 'reason, but the woman from affection'.[162]

Understanding and will, thought and affection, are dissimilar as the form of man and woman are dissimilar. The body of a person reflects his or her mind, for the

'body is an effigy of the mind, because formed to be a resemblance of it'.[163]

Consequently the man has

'a harsher and less beautiful countenance, a deeper tone of speech, and a more robust body, but the woman has a softer and more beautiful countenance, a tone of voice more tender, and a body more delicate'.[164]

Blake was perhaps satirizing this description of man and woman when he wrote the proverb:

'Let man wear the fell of the lion, woman the fleece of the sheep.'

Opposing the priest's passive life, Blake suggests that if man is born to be intellectual and has a stronger body, then he ought to be more active in practical life.

The main condition that leads to conjugal love is, as we have already noted, the conjunction of two minds into one. Another condition is that the beings concerned must live in 'divine good and divine truths', that is to say, in 'Heaven'. The divine good and truth in 'Heaven' spring from the Lord and thus

'no one can be in love truly conjugal unless he acknowledges the Lord, and His Divine (Principle), for without that acknowledgement the Lord cannot flow in, and be conjoined to the truths appertaining to man'.[165]

Neither can conjugal love occur between those of a different religion because

'two dissimilar and discordant principles cannot make one mind out of two'.[166]

Because people with different religions are dissimilar

'the origin of their love doth not partake at all of what is spiritual; if they cohabit and agree together, it is only from natural causes'.[167]

For this reason Swedenborg also disapproves of marriage between those in 'Heaven' and those in 'Hell'. The former acknowledge the Lord, while the latter acknowledge 'Energy'. Those in 'Heaven' have their own exclusive society with one religion. Marriages in 'Heaven' are

'contracted with those who are within a society, because they are in similar good and truth, but not with those who are out of the society: all who are there, within a society, are in similar good and truth, and differ from those who are without . . .'.[168]

Hence

'every society of heaven consists of those who are of similar dispositions; similar are presented to similar'.[169]

Opposing the priest's act of division, Blake marries 'Heaven' and 'Hell' both in body and mind, both in feeling and in society. The title of the chapter 'Concerning Marriage in Heaven' is perhaps used for phrasing the title of *The Marriage of Heaven and Hell*.

Swedenborg says that only those in 'Heaven' can live in true conjugal love and have a 'heavenly' marriage. Union between those who are false and evil is called an infernal marriage, based only on physical lust:

'It hath been given me to see what is the quality of marriage between those who are in the falses of evil, which is called the infernal marriage; they discourse with each other, and likewise are conjoined from a lascivious principle. . . .'[170]

Earthly marriages differ from those made in 'Heaven' in that they are not based on the conjunction of good and truth and therefore are not principled in conjugal love. They are based on natural causes and their only aim is natural, the procreation of children, whereas heavenly marriages are 'spiritual'. Earthly marriages conceive children, heavenly marriages exist for the

'procreation of good and of truth'.[171]

In 'Heaven' by nativities and generations

'. . . are signified spiritual nativities and generations, which

are of good and of truth, by a mother and father truth
conjoined to good which procreates, by sons and daughters
the truths and goods which are procreated'. . . .[172]

Earthly nuptials are those of 'the flesh' but heavenly nuptials
are 'spiritual',[173] and thus in 'Heaven' the man and woman
are not called husband and wife but the conjugal partner of
each other because their union is the conjunction of two minds.
Swedenborg's whole concept of conjugal love seems to be that
of an idealized spiritual relationship between man and woman,
far removed from the flesh. He separates this ideal union from
family responsibility by confining the aim of procreation of
children only to the inferior earthly marriages. Thus marriage,
a social act with responsibility to society, is limited to a spiritual
'conjunction of two minds into one' and bodily union is
degraded.

Earthly marriages can be holy if they are based on love of
the Lord and His Divine laws; otherwise they are contrary to
conjugal love and are adulteries,

> 'contrary to divine laws, and contrary to the civil laws of
> all kingdoms'.[174]

Unions between those who fail to acknowledge the priest's
Lord and his Church are termed adulteries.

Apart from these restrictions, Swedenborg sweepingly rejects
all partnerships in 'Hell' as 'adulteries'. Those in 'Hell' can
never live in conjugal love because their ruling desires are love
of the self, destruction of good and truth, and violation of the
'Divine (Being or Principle)' in 'Heaven'. Swedenborg states

> 'That all who are in hell are in opposition to conjugal love,
> hath been given me to perceive from the sphere thence
> exhaling, . . . that the ruling delight in hell is the delight
> of adultery, and that the delight of adultery is likewise the
> delight of destroying the conjunction of good and truth,
> which conjunction makes heaven . . .'.[175]

Swedenborg is horrified to find that

> 'In some of the hells there are mere brothels, which are
> disgusting to the sight, filled with every kind of filth and
> excrement.'[176]

The people in 'Hell'

> 'pass their time in brothels, . . . loving such habitations . . .
> nothing is more delightful to them than to break the bonds
> of marriage'.[177]

Blake reacts to the negative marriage laws of the priest
with the comment: 'Brothels are built with bricks of Religion'.
By his religion the priest chains both body and mind. Those
who cannot satisfy the requirements of his marriage laws must
either restrain their desire or gratify it in brothels. In the
divided and insecure society of Swedenborg where 'Heaven'
lives upon 'Hell' and where people are reduced to poverty by
the selfish desires of the Angels in 'Heaven', the only means of
income which seem open to wretched and hopeless women is
the brothels. And these latter flourish where hypocrisy degrades
and limits physical enjoyment. The 'youthfull Harlot's curse'[178]
and the 'new born infant's tear' in the 'London' poem of the
Songs of Experience, are, as we noted, the result of such social
conditions and relationships. And these are effectively satirized
in Plates 17–20 of *The Marriage*, where Swedenborg's idea of
divine providence is associated with a 'Mill':

> 'An Angel came to me and said: "O pitiable foolish young
> man! O horrible! O dreadful state! consider the hot
> burning dungeon thou art preparing for thyself to all
> eternity, to which thou are going in such career." '
> 'I said: "Perhaps you will be willing to shew me my
> eternal lot, & we will contemplate together upon it, and
> see whether your lot or mine is most desirable".'[179]

Blake asks the Angel to reveal his destiny to him so that they
can judge which is the preferable 'fate'. Accordingly the Angel
takes him:

> '. . . thro' a stable & thro' a church & down into the church
> vault, at the end of which was a mill: thro' the mill we
> went, and came to a cave: down the widning cavern we
> groped our tedius way, till a void boundless as a nether
> sky appear'd beneath us, & we held by the roots of trees
> and hung over this immensity: . . .'[180]

The 'Stable' represents the Angel's passive and negative

instructions about energy. In *Heaven and Hell* Swedenborg himself discusses the three states 'of man after death, or of his spirit', the third of which is:

> 'a state of instruction; this state appertains to those come into heaven, and become angels . . .'

Those who are in 'Hell' have reached the infernal society because they

> 'cannot be instructed; wherefore their second state is likewise their third, . . . they are altogether turned to their own love, thus to the infernal society which is in similar love'.[181]

In this context, Blake retorts, 'the tygers of wrath are wiser than the horses of instruction'. Blake, though a devil from 'Hell', is permitted to accompany the Angel through church or heaven. After passing through the stable or stage of instruction and church they finally come to a mill and cavern. The 'void boundless' which looms at the end of the 'winding cavern' and 'tedious way' represents the vacuum, which is Urizen's metaphysical world formed by passive impressions:

> 'A void immense, wild, dark & deep,
> Where nothing was: Nature's wide womb;
> And self balanc'd, stretch'd o'er the void.'[182]

Blake enters the abysmal world of the Angels where they are 'held by the roots of trees and hung over this immensity'. The image suggests the metaphysical philosophy of Swedenborg who believed that all the joy and delight of the Angels 'comes from above'.[183]

The Devil (Blake), not content, wants to explore the void to see if Providence is there, but the Angel tells him not to 'presume' but instead to wait and see his 'lot' when the darkness passes away (when man leaves the body after death).

> 'So I remain'd with him, sitting in the twisted root of an oak; he was suspended in a fungus, which hung with the head downward into the deep.'

In this position they observe the 'Abyss' where societies of 'Heaven', 'spirits' and 'Hell' can be seen. In 'Hell' they behold:

'. . . the infinite Abyss, fiery as the smoke of a burning city; beneath us, at an immense distance, was the sun, black but shining; round it were fiery tracks on which revolv'd vast spiders, crawling after their prey, which flew, or rather swum, in the infinite deep, in the most terrific shapes of animals sprung from corruption; & the air was full of them, & seem'd composed of them: these are Devils, and are called Powers of the air. I now asked my companion which was my eternal lot? he said: "between the black & white spiders".'[184]

This passage is a satirical reading of Swedenborg's 'Hell' and refers to the society of spirits situated between 'Heaven' and 'Hell'. In the world of spirits the wicked are naturally attracted to the 'sooty caverns' like

'ravens, wolves, and swine, which, in consequence of the smell which they perceive, *fly* and run to carrion and dunghills'.[185]

The caves lead

'obliquely downward to the deep, where . . . there are several doors: through those caverns exhale nauseous and foetid stenches'.[186]

These 'Devils' or 'Powers of the air' inhabit the regions that the Angel shows to Blake.

The Angel then says that Blake's destiny is to be 'between the black and white spiders' which represents Swedenborg's idea of 'equilibrium':

'. . . spiritual equilibrium . . . or freedom, exists and subsists *between* good acting on one part, and evil re-acting on the other part, or *between* evil acting on one part and good reacting on the other part; the equilibrium *between* good acting and evil re-acting is such as appertains to the good. . . .'[187]

Blake uses the 'spider' as an ironical name for the 'spirit'. Satirizing Swedenborg's idea of equilibrium, he ironically places himself between the 'black & white spiders'. After showing Blake his 'Hell', Swedenborg climbs up into the 'mill' or 'Heaven'. Once the Devil is left alone, he finds that 'Hell'

appears pleasant and harmonious. In other words the Devil is
at ease with the others in 'Hell'.

'My friend the Angel climb'd up from his station into the
mill: I remain'd alone; & then this appearance was no
more, but I found myself sitting on a pleasant bank beside
a river by moonlight, hearing a harper, who sung to the
harp; & his theme was: "The man who never alters his
opinion is like standing water, & breeds reptiles of the
mind."'

'But I arose and sought for the mill, & there I found my
Angel, who, surprised, asked me how I escaped?

'I answer'd: "All that we saw was owing to your meta-
physics; . . ." '188

The Devil now suggests that he show the Angel his 'eternal
lot' in turn. The Angel laughs at this proposal but is caught
'by force' and taken above the earth into his heaven or meta-
physical world. Blake and the Angel fly:

'westerly thro' the night, till we were elevated above the
earth's shadow; then I flung myself with him directly into
the body of the sun; here I clothed myself in white, &
taking in my hand Swedenborg's volumes, sunk from the
glorious clime, . . .'189

The Devil descends from Swedenborg's metaphysical world
or the 'infinite Abyss' of passive memories and brings the
'skeleton of a body' which is wrapped in the linen clothes or
fixed memories of Swedenborg:

'. . . I in my hand brought the skeleton of a body, which in
the mill was Aristotle's Analytics.

'So the Angel said "thy phantasy has imposed upon me,
& thou oughtest to be ashamed" '.

'I answer'd: "we impose on one another, & it is but
lost time to converse with you whose works are only
Analytics". Oppression is true friendship.'190

The 'Analytics' suggests rationalist metaphysics based on
abstractions. Plates 21–22 and 22–24 are a brief reading of

Heaven and Hell and summarize what Blake has said in the previous plates. Swedenborg reveals two dominating characteristics in *Heaven and Hell*. He interprets all his passive memories as qualities of wisdom and asserts that the Angels are the only wise beings. And he exhibits a distaste for the active life and work of those in 'Hell', while insisting that all necessities of life come from 'above'.

Blake's opposition to the 'Angels' can be fully appreciated and justified in this context.

The rest of the plate continues the attack on Swedenborg who:

'. . . boasts that what he writes is new; tho' it is only the Contents or Index of already publish'd books.

'A man carried a monkey about for a shew, & because he was a little wiser than the monkey, grew vain, and conceiv'd himself as much wiser than seven men. It is so with Swedenborg: he shews the folly of churches, & exposes hypocrites, till he imagines that all are religious, & himself the single one on earth that ever broke a net.

'Now hear a plain fact; Swedenborg has not written one new truth. Now hear another: he has written all the old falsehoods.

'And now hear the reason. He conversed with Angels who are all religious, & conversed not with Devils who all hate religion, for he was incapable thro' his conceited notions.

'Thus Swedenborg's writings are a recapitulation of all superficial opinions, and an analysis of the more sublime— but no further.

'Have now another plain fact. Any man of mechanical talents may, from the writings of Paracelsus or Jacob Behmen, produce ten thousand volumes of equal value with Swedenborg's, and from those of Dante or Shakespear an infinite number.

'But when he has done this, let him not say that he knows better than his master, for he only holds a candle in sunshine.'[191]

All preachers come from the Lord's spiritual Kingdom which

is set against those in 'Hell' who live in fire 'kindled by the love of self and of the world . . .'.[192]

Blake defends the gifts of the working people in 'Hell' against the passive Angel in 'Heaven' and insists on the virtue or honesty of the true Jesus against the Jehovah or false Jesus of the Priest. Swedenborg worshipped a Jesus who represented the 'laws of the ten commandments', but Blake honoured Jesus who struggled to break these laws and free human beings from oppression.

Swedenborg decreed that 'Heaven' and 'Hell' must be ruled by the laws of the Angels, but to Blake 'One Law for the Lion & Ox is Oppression'. Law becomes oppressive when it fails in its social and human responsibility and becomes a mere tool in the hands of the ruling class to protect its self-interest.

Chapter Five

THE PROPHETICAL WRITINGS

I. 'EVERY HONEST MAN IS A PROPHET'

'Every honest man is a Prophet; he utters his opinion both of private & public matters',[1] writes Blake in his *Annotations to Watson*. The term 'honest' is the key word and denotes a characteristic peculiar to a true prophet. Believing that 'Prophetic Genius' is in every man, the prophet puts the interest of the whole before his own partial interest. Challenging Swedenborg's false prophecy Blake asks: ' "is he honest who resists his genius or conscience only for the sake of present ease or gratification?" '[2] The answer is 'No'. Selfish ease and gratification oppose genius and suppress conscience by abstract moral laws and philosophical systems. Prophetic Genius tells us that 'Energy is the only life, and is from the Body; and Reason is the bound or outward circumference of Energy.'[3] But the abstract moral laws and their philosophical system teach that 'Energy, call'd Evil, is alone from the Body; & that Reason, call'd Good, is alone from the Soul.'[4] The priest, and Swedenborg is himself a good example, lives amid wealth and ease but denies the importance of the material world as the source of energy and life. Blake attacks 'Natural Man' because of his 'sensual existence' and selfish gratification. He also attacks abstract philosophy because it supports the system of 'Natural Man' under the name of a 'Reason' divorced from social context: 'Abstract Philosophy warring in enmity against Imagination.'[5] Since this 'Reason' is limited to the ruling interests Blake calls it Urizen (your reason) who is the negator of others.

For Blake 'Reason' has a material basis and a particular interest. Repudiating the 'metaphysics' and 'systematic reasoning' of the rationalists, Blake writes: 'Reason is the bound or outward circumference of Energy'. In other words, rationalists who attempt to justify the existing ruling interests under the banner of 'rationalism' are in error. The study of philosophy divorced from its particular social contexts is an abstract philosophy, and abstraction is the enemy of truth or Imagination. Commenting on Reynold's dictum 'When the Artist has by diligent attention acquired a clear and distinct idea of beauty and symmetry; when he has reduced the variety of nature to the abstract idea . . .' Blake writes 'What Folly!'[6]

Bromion in *Visions of The Daughters of Albion* represents the Urizenic character who negates and accuses Oothoon, the honest innocence. Oothoon loves Theotormon, the heart that desires the joy of the material world without shame and a sense of guilt. 'For every thing that lives is Holy'.[7] But this love and honesty of Oothoon is perverted and defiled by the selfish jealousy of Bromion:

> 'I loved Theotormon,
> And I was not ashamed;
> I trembled in my virgin fears,
> And I hid in Leutha's vale!
>
> I plucked Leutha's flower,
> And I rose up from the vale;
> But the terrible thunder tore
> My virgin mantle in twain.'[8]

Imagination falls in 'Leutha's vale', the restricted state of man, either by subjection to the five senses or negation of them by poverty and fear. Man acquires new selfhood by the development of his senses. The development is from a limited to an unlimited perspective—from individual to social and human wholeness. Imagination explores the unlimited horizons. It is the 'Heart' of humanity which knows its infinite desires. The five senses shrink and become limited when divorced from Imagination. Theotormon who is supposed to be the source of energy is now 'a sick man's dream' and 'Oothoon is the crafty slave of selfish holiness.'[9] The 'sick man' is the 'natural man' whose soul is sunk in material acquisition. Selfish holiness is the kind of religion and educational system which teaches self-denial and love of others on the one hand while simultaneously accumulating wealth at the expense of others. Selfish holiness has a different heart and interest. It is the particular ruling interest of Bromion which negates Oothoon's love, the innocence. The conflict between Bromion and Oothoon is not the expression of a difference of sense-perception but rather of the difference of heart, of human perspective. 'The Eye sees more than the Heart knows'.[10] The eye sees many things but the heart knows its particular interest. In other words the work of the sense organs is not passive and mechanical but rather is directed by a certain ruling love or interest:

> ' "With what sense is it that the chicken shuns the ravenous hawk?
> "With what sense does the tame pigeon measure out the expanse?
> "With what sense does the bee form cells? have not the mouse & frog
> "Eyes and ears and sense of touch? yet are their habitations
> "And their pursuits as different as their forms and as their joys.
> "Ask the wild ass why he refuses burdens, and the meek camel
> "Why he loves man: is it because of eye, ear, mouth, or skin,
> "Or breathing nostrils? No, for these the wolf and tyger have.
> "Ask the blind worm the secrets of the grave, and why her spires
> "Love to curl round the bones of death; and ask the rav'nous snake
> "Where she gets poison, & the wing'd eagle why he loves the sun;
> "And then tell me the thoughts of man, that have been hid of old." '[11]

This is a concise reply to rationalists such as Locke who attempted to justify social relationships by basing human understanding and thought on impressions formed by sense-perception and by received education. Social class division and difference between the poor and rich, according to the rationalists, are a matter of different sense-perceptions and of education or culture which has passed from generation to generation. Such teachings aim at protecting those who possess against those who do not. Locke's moral philosophy protected the property of the propertied class.

The questions in the *Visions of The Daughters of Albion* challenge this debased materialism. The challenge is social and political. Blake argues that if the five senses form the mind and determine human understanding then why 'to the Eyes of a Miser a Guinea is more beautiful than the Sun, & a bag worn with the use of Money has more beautiful proportions than a Vine filled with Grapes'? Animals have eyes, ears and sense of touch but their 'pursuits' are 'as different as their forms and their joys'. The chicken that 'shuns the ravenous hawk', the 'tame pigeon that measures out the expanse' and the bees that 'form cells' all have senses, but their driving interests are different. The 'wild ass' refuses his burden while the 'meek camel' loves man. Is it 'because of eye, ear, mouth, or skin', or 'breathing nostrils'? 'No, for these the wolf and tyger have.' The essential difference is in their ruling interests and environmental conditions. The ruling interests and 'Energy' are based on the 'Body' or material world.

Blake is not against empiricism as such but he opposes the philosophical and social systems which attempt to justify their existing position by empiricism. To Blake the senses of Oothoon, the innocent, are oppressed and enslaved by Bromion who propagates this rationalist philosophy:

'Enslav'd, the Daughters of Albion weep; a trembling
   lamentation
Upon their mountains; in their valleys, sighs towards
   America.'

The ruling interests which enslaved the 'Daughters of Albion', the senses or energy, in England were the same ruling interests which exploited America. America was a colony and market for English monopolies. She was not allowed to trade with other nations except England. The American revolution was a revolt against this enslavement:

'For the soft soul of America, Oothoon, wander'd in woe,
Along the vales of Leutha seeking flowers to comfort her;'

America is like a child driven to a position where she wanders in woe while seeking her independence. But Oothoon knows her heart's interest: ' "I turn my face to where my whole soul seeks." '12 She loves Theotormon, the mother of nourishment and energy, but Bromion, who teaches the rationalist and empiricist philosophy, in practice negates the senses of others by the accusations of moral laws and their negation of joy and gratification of desire:

> ' ". . . Behold this harlot here on Bromion's bed,
> "And let the jealous dolphins sport around the lovely maid!
> "Thy soft American plains are mine, and mine thy north & south:
> "Stampt with my signet are the swarthy children of the sun;
> "They are obedient, they resist not, they obey the scourge;
> "Their daughters worship terrors and obey the violent." '13

Bromion is England threatening America on account of her trade with others. America is a lovely maid whose jealous lover, the English government, does not allow others to approach her. When America tries to forge relationships with other nations she is accused of adultery. Bromion wishes his mistress, the children of America, to be obedient and 'worship terrors and obey the violent'. The relationship between exploiter and exploited is based on a perverted love affair where the exploited is the victim of a jealous lover. The Daughters of Albion hear Oothoon, the victim, who rejects Bromion's accusations:

> ' ". . . Arise, my Theotormon, I am pure,
> "Because the night is gone that clos'd me in its deadly black.
> "They told me that the night & day were all that I could see;
> "They told me that I had five senses to inclose me up,
> "And they inclos'd my infinite brain into a narrow circle,
> "And sunk my heart into the Abyss, a red, round globe, not burning,
> Till all from life I was obliterated and erased." '14

Bromion's selfish love oppresses and limits Oothoon's five senses by poverty. Her 'brain' and 'heart' are also kept undeveloped by this Urizenic negation. It is the parasitic interest of Bromion which destroys Oothoon's joy: 'Sweetest the fruit that the worm feeds on, & the soul prey'd on by woe.'[15]

Blake in *Visions of The Daughters of Albion* illustrates both the nature of the social relationships inside England and also between England and her colonies. The society is engulfed by the poor and rich, two opposing interests, two conflicting loves, two different worlds, the world of the 'lion' and of the 'Ox':

'How different their eye and ear! how different the world to them.'[16]

The 'Visions' of Albion see these worlds and this difference in society. They teach self-denial and moral laws while pursuing a selfish life. The father teaches love while negating love and desire in others. Oothoon opposing the self-begotten laws of Bromion speaks out:

'I cry: Love! Love! Love! happy happy Love! free as the mountain wind!
"Can that be a Love that drinks another as a sponge drinks water,
"That clouds with jealousy his nights, with weepings all the day,
To spin a web of age around him, grey and hoary, dark,
Till his eyes sicken at the fruit that hangs before his sight?
Such is self-love that envies all, a creeping skeleton
With lamplike eyes watching around the frozen marriage bed." '[16]

The 'frozen marriage bed' represents the social relationships where the priest teaches virginity while the King rapes. One negates the love of self and of the world while the other devours by the enslavement of his children at home and abroad:

'Enslav'd, the Daughters of Albion weep; . . . sighs towards America.'

2. THE REVOLUTIONARY POET

Blake's social criticism and opposition to exploitation and oppression of man by man is not limited to England. His opposition is based on a human level which transcends national frontiers. His vision is unlimited. *America, Europe,* and 'Africa' and 'Asia' in *The Song of Los* are examples of the unlimited vision.

Blake celebrated both the American and French revolutions. The advertisement for *The French Revolution: A Poem in Seven Books* states that 'the remaining books of this poem are finished, and will be published in their Order', yet only 'Book the First' appeared and the publication of the other books, as J. Bronowski suggests, was cancelled because of the repressive political atmosphere which caused J. Johnson, Blake's publisher, to go into hiding. Bronowski writes: 'It was the world of the acts against Seditious Writings, against Seditious meetings, against Seditious Societies, against treasonable practices. It was the world of prosecutions for blasphemy, and of the laws against cheap newspapers. It was the world of the militia bills and of the Combination Laws. It was Pitt's world. That world did not make Blake; but it baffled him, and cowed him.'[17] The message in *The French Revolution* is straightforward and speaks for itself:

'The dead brood over Europe, the cloud and vision
    descends over cheerful France;
O cloud well appointed! Sick, sick, the Prince on his
    couch wreath'd in dim
And appalling mist . . . the ancient dawn calls us
To awake . . .
From my window I see the old mountains of France, like
    aged men, fading away.'[18]

Censorship cowed Blake yet could not change his mind. His social criticism became deeper and his revolutionary spirit voiced itself through unheard-of symbols such as Orc, Rintrah and Los. We hear the same voice in *America* as we do in *The French Revolution.*

' "The morning comes, the night decays, the watchmen
    leave their stations;
"The grave is burst, the spices shed, the linen wrapped
    up;
"The bones of death, the cov'ring clay, the sinews shrunk
    & dry'd

"Reviving shake, inspiring move, breathing, awakening,
"Spring like redeemed captives when their bonds &
    bars are burst.
"Let the slave grinding at the mill run out into the field,
"Let him look up into the heavens & laugh in the bright
    air;
"Let the inchained soul, shut up in darkness and in
    sighing,
"Whose face has never seen a smile in thirty weary years,
"Rise and look out; his chains are loose, his dungeon
    doors are open;
"And let his wife and children return from the oppressor's
    scourge.
"They look behind at every step & believe it is a dream,
"Singing: 'The Sun has left his blackness & has found a
    fresher morning,
" 'And the fair Moon rejoices in the clear & cloudless
    night;
" 'For Empire is no more, and now the Lion & Wolf
    shall cease.' " '19

The poem is dialectical. The poet hopes that a new social
system will replace the old in America: 'The morning comes,
the night decays'. The 'Night' represents the dark and stagnant
social condition where men exist under the oppression of the
'watchmen'—the envoys of the British government. The 'grave'
represents the society where the exploiter, like a worm, feeds
upon its victims. The 'linen' is the laws and ideology of the
ruling system which clothes itself in these systems. The dead
are wrapped in linen. The 'mill' represents the social relation-
ships where the 'Angels' in 'Heaven' exploit and suppress those
in 'Hell' both bodily and intellectually. The 'Lion & Wolf'
represent a ruling class which accuses and terrifies its rebellious
children for being 'blasphemous Demon', 'Antichrist', 'hater
of Dignities' and 'transgressor of God's law':

'. . . Albion's Angel wrathful burnt
Beside the Stone of Night, and like the Eternal Lion's howl
In famine & war, reply'd: "Art thou not Orc, who serpent-
    form'd
"Stands at the gate of Enitharmon to devour her children?

"Blasphemous Demon, Antichrist, hater of Dignities,
"Lover of wild rebellion, and transgressor of God's Law,
"Why dost thou come to Angel's eyes in this terrific
    form?" '20

Selfrighteousness is the characteristic of the Angels and accusa-
tion a terrifying weapon to cow their opponents. When
religion and deceit fail to work, the accusation and punishment
of the 'ten commands' come into action. Orc, who is conscious
of the Angels' deceit and opposes their 'selfish holiness', has
been accused and punished for his opposition.

It is useless and distracting in this poetry and also in later
prophetical works to play the mental game of hunt the symbol,
to try to discover the origin of unheard-of names and characters
such as 'Orc' and 'Urizen' in Blake. These characters speak
for themselves and can be identified by the nature of their
position:

'The Terror answer'd: "I am Orc, wreath'd the accursed
    tree:
"The times are ended; shadows pass, the morning 'gins to
    break;
"The fiery joy, that Urizen perverted to ten commands,
"What night he led the stary hosts thro' the wild wilder-
    ness,
"That stony law I stamp to dust; and scatter religion
    abroad
"To the four winds as a torn book, & none shall gather
    the leaves;
. . . .

"For everything that lives is holy, life delights in life;
"Because the soul of sweet delight can never be defil'd;" '21

Here Orc voices Imagination. He terrifies ruling systems and
shakes Empire. He revolts against the systems which bind the
desire and joy of others by their limited and selfish interests
under 'holy' laws which Orc stamps 'to dust' by regarding them
as negative and passive. To Orc 'everything that lives is holy,
life delights in life', but the limited and selfish interest of
Urizen is ironically repudiated by Blake as 'Selfish holiness'.
Orc seeks holiness in 'life' which delights all, but Urizen defiles

life by his selfishness and 'pale religious letchery' which seeks 'virginity' and obedience. Deceit accompanies exploitation and Church accompanies Empire. To Blake the bonds of religion and empire are one and the same. In the American Revolution

'. . . The Priests in rustling scales
Rush into reptile coverts, hiding from the fires of Orc,'[22]

Orc is not always prophetic and revolutionary. He is recognized by the nature of his verbal utterances, his social situation and his relationship with others. When his ruling power is Imagination he is prophetic, at other times he is a fallen Urizenic character. In the latter state he is identified with Urizenic Rintrah:

' "Arise! O Rintrah, eldest born, second to none but Orc!
"O lion Rintrah, raise thy fury from thy forest black!
"Bring Palamabron, horned priest, skipping upon the mountains,
"And silent Elynittria, the silver bowed queen.
"Rintrah, where hast thou hid thy bride?
"Weeps she in desart shades?
"Alas! my Rintrah, bring the lovely jealous Ocalythron." '[23]

The 'forests black' are the forests of natural memories where Urizen, the lion Rintrah, is wandering. Here Rintrah who represents limited reason is divided from Orc, the Imagination. Jealous Ocalythron, the queen, is the product of this limited reason and limited interest. Rintrah is as strong as a lion but his strength is the product of his limited sensuous existence. Reason was originally creative and the seeing eyes of Orc, but the selfish and limited interest has caused his fall. The fallen man and society see night instead of day, the moon instead of the sun, and the society is ruled by the 'cavern'd Man', the furious King. Stagnancy and passivity are characteristic of fallen society:

'Enitharmon slept
Eighteen hundred years. Man was a Dream!'[24]

It is now the eighteenth century and still the Angels of Albion rule the 'Island white', a body whose blood and life are drained away. They attempt to justify their existing social situation against the wind of revolution from Europe:

> 'They heard the voice of Albion's Angel howling in flames
>   of Orc,
> Seeking in the trump of the last doom.'[25]

The Lockean theory of the passive mind and the Newtonian concept of a mechanistic universe served the ideology of the fearful Angels:

> 'A mighty Spirit leap'd from the land of Albion,
> Nam'd Newton: he seiz'd the trump & blowed the
>   enormous blast!
> Yellow as leaves of Autumn, the myriads of Angelic hosts
> Fell thro' the wintry skies seeking their graves,
> Rattling their hollow bones in howling and lamentation.'[26]

The 'cavern'd Man' seeks comfort in his passivity, the 'bones of the dead', and encourages this passivity in others under the banner of 'rationalism'. He turns his eyes towards night and dreams instead of turning to daylight and reality. There is a conflict between Urizen and Orc. Urizen attempts to bind but Orc seeks to free from bondage. Urizen binds society by fear and punishment:

> 'Every house a den, every man bound: the shadows are
>   fill'd
> With spectres, and the windows wove over with curses of
>   iron:
> Over the doors "Thou shalt not," & over the chimneys
>   "Fear" is written:
> With bands of iron round their necks fasten'd into the
>   walls
> The citizens, in leaden gyves the inhabitants of suburbs
> Walk heavy; soft and bent are the bones of villagers.'[27]

These lines are a manifestation of political reality at the time. The bondage and 'shadows' are products of binding selfhood or 'spectre'. The bondage is both physical and spiritual, economic and intellectual. The 'shadows' embody the nature of social relationships and the oppressive political atmosphere.

H

The laws of negation—'Thou shalt not'—and 'Fear' protect
the property of the Angels in 'Heaven' against the people in
'Hell'. Blake siding with those in 'Hell' lived in this atmosphere
and experienced it physically and mentally. He writes in June
1793, 'I say I shan't live five years, And if I live one it will be
a Wonder.'[28] His fear does not stem only from political sup-
pression but from the lack of a secure place and work. He
writes in a letter to George Cumberland (1799), 'I know that
He who Works & has his health cannot starve, . . . I feel myself
happy & contented let what will come; having passed now
near twenty years in ups & downs.'[29] But Blake could not
always occupy his hands easily or work for an employer who
would recognize his dignity as a creative engraver. Complaining
against William Hayley's exploitation he writes in a letter to
Thomas Butts (January 1802):

'My unhappiness has arisen from a source which, if
explor'd too narrowly, might hurt my pecuniary circum-
stances, As my dependence is on Engraving at present,
& particularly on the Engravings I have in hand for
Mr. H. : & I find on all hands great objections to my doing
any thing but the meer drugery of business, & intimations
that if I do not confine myself to this, I shall not live; this
has always pursu'd me.'[30]

Blake's symbols, language and anger are not separated from
his 'circumstances'. His 'circumstances' were such that he
could not afford to voice his social opposition openly. Most of
his employers, like Hayley, belonged to the ruling system which
Blake opposed. Blake had either to follow their taste in art or
starve. The conflict was thus within society and within Blake.
    Although Blake changed his language he kept his mind free
and his imagination active. In 'Africa' he could extend the
universe of his human concerns:

'They saw Urizen give his Laws to the Nations
By the hands of the children of Los.

Adam shudder'd! Noah faded! black grew the sunny
    African
When Rintrah gave Abstract Philosophy to Brama in the
    East.'[31]

The 'Abstract Philosophy' is the philosophy of 'Reason' which was proclaimed as a superior culture to the Africans and Asians. 'In the early decades of the century, both the Rationalist and Evangelical movement, though they had nothing else in common between them, reinforced the tendency towards Westernization of the Indians. This eventually disheartened the supporters of native culture and language. The Rationalist belief that reason had given Europeans the light of ascendancy over the Orientals was the first expression of the European sense of superiority.'[32] When Blake attacks 'Abstract Philosophy' and 'reason' he attacks the system which uses religion and reason as a 'Net' for its interests. The reasoner perverts truth by abstract arguments. For Blake truth is concrete and ought to be sought in social and human relationships. For 'Truth has bounds, Error none.'[33] Imagination, the Poetic Genius, is 'Truth' and the uniting principle of humanity, but limited memory is 'Error' which divides humanity. Urizen propagates ratio and division. He moulds and limits minds to his own natural impressions which he calls 'Reason'. Blake regards this 'Reason' as 'Human Illusion':

> 'Till his Brain in a rock & his Heart
> In a fleshy slough formed four rivers
> Obscuring the immense Orb of fire
> Flowing down into night: till a Form
> Was completed, a Human Illusion
> In darkness and deep clouds involv'd.'[34]

The 'four rivers' and 'Human Illusion' are discussed in *Vala or The Four Zoas*, which is one of the longer and more difficult Prophetical works. The book, like the *Book of Urizen*, illustrates the division of man from man caused by 'Natural Man's' limited love and jealousy which negates and torments others. *The Four Zoas* is about '*The torments of Love & Jealousy in* The Death and Judgement of *Albion* the Ancient Man'. Division in humanity is 'Death' which is the character of a fallen society. A divided society is a fallen one:

> 'His fall into Division & his Resurrection to Unity:
> His fall into the Generation of decay & death, & his
> Regeneration by the Resurrection from the dead.'[35]

The division and conflict are both in society and within fallen man:

> 'Four Mighty Ones are in every Man; a Perfect Unity
> Cannot Exist but from the Universal Brotherhood of Eden
> The Universal Man, . . .[35]

Only the 'Heavenly Father', the Poetic Genius or Imagination, can know the nature of these 'Living Creatures'. 'Natural Man', who is wrapped up in his individual and limited impressions, cannot know life or understand its living elements. The 'Living Creature' specifies the living form of the characters of Four Zoas against any abstraction and supernatural power. These characters are within society or Man:

> '. . . in the Brain of Man we live & in his circling Nerves,
> Tho' this bright world of all our joy is in the Human Brain
> Where Urizen & all his Hosts hang their immortal lamps'.[36]

The 'Brain of Man' is creative and dynamic. It creates, animates and gives life and purpose to its surrounding universe. But the joy and energy of the 'Human Brain' are taken from it by the negative and abstract teachings of Urizen. The 'immortal lamps' satirize Urizen's abstract teachings which underrates human values and creativity. The 'Lamps' or Urizen come into conflict with the sun of Imagination.

The four 'mighty ones' are originally love, reason, the material world and imagination. These are creative, joyful and holy elements in every man. But the fallen society perverts them by making them limited, loathsome and unholy. They become passive and abstract. The Four Zoas represent the fallen states of these elements. 'Luvah' represents love, 'Urizen' reason, 'Tharmas' the material world and 'Urthona' imagination.

Vala is a great work of social criticism and satire which 'whosoever reads' if he does so 'with his intellect he comprehend'.[37] The work unveils the folds of the Urizenic system which teaches 'love', 'brotherhood', 'freedom' and 'reason' but in practice turns against true love by its selfish love, against 'brotherhood' by its policy of division, against 'freedom' by

selfish negation and against 'reason' by its limited outlook.
The analysis of this division is the central theme of *Vala*. The
theme is Man's

'. . . fall into Division & his Resurrection to Unity:
His fall into the Generation of decay & death, & his
Regeneration by the Resurrection from the dead.'[38]

Division has taken place in history and within society.
Humanity is divided and fragmented by individualism and
acquisitiveness. Man has fallen from unlimited and universal
humanity into limited and selfish materialism which is the
state of 'decay & death'. Since the fall has taken place in
history and within human society the 'Resurrection' must also
take place within society. The division of interest within
society has influenced all aspects of human existence. Man is
divided against man and also divided against his true part or
creative soul. Thus true man has lost his creative part by the
suppression and ruling interest of fallen man in society and
himself:

' ". . . Thy fear has made me tremble, thy terrors have sur-
          rounded me.
"All Love is lost: Terror succeeds, & Hatred instead of
          Love,
"And stern demands of Right & Duty instead of Liberty.
"Once thou wast to Me the loveliest son of heaven—
          But now
"Why are thou Terrible? and yet I love thee in thy terror
          till
"I am almost Extinct & soon shall be a shadow in
          Oblivion,
"Unless some way can be found that I may look upon
          thee & live.
"Hide me some shadowy semblance, secret whisp'ring in
          my Ear,
"In secret of soft wings, in mazes of delusive beauty.
"I have look'd into the secret soul of him I lov'd,
"And in the Dark recesses found Sin & cannot return." '[39]

The fallen society is ruled by fear and terror, and love is
replaced by pity and charity. The ruling interest has turned

the lovable world into a hateful and loathsome object by forcing man into a begging position and imposing its demands of 'Right & Duty'. But the lovable world must be liberated from the accusation of the ruling interest; then the world will be beautiful. The demands of 'Right & Duty instead of Liberty' set a delusive aim—for man becomes geared and subject to limited ends rather than aiming at the liberation of the human soul from the terror and exploitation of the ruling interests:

> ' "Why wilt thou Examine every little fibre of my soul,
> "Spreading them out before the sun like stalks of flax to dry?
> "The infant joy is beautiful, but its anatomy
> "Horrible, Ghast & Deadly; nought shalt thou find in it
> "But Death, Despair & Everlasting brooding Melancholy." '[40]

The human soul cannot be free unless man is also freed physically. The human soul is limited and fragmented by the laws and rules of the fallen society. Love is interrogated and censored and thus is reduced to 'Death, Despair & Everlasting brooding Melancholy'. Man has either to love and expand his humanity or limit and contract his love to himself and thus die within himself. The 'infant joy is beautiful' because it universalizes human emanations and the creative soul, but its 'anatomy' and fragmentation destroys the creativity and beauty. The fallen society fosters individualistic and selfish hope and brings into despair universal brotherhood and love. By this individualism and fragmentation it teaches a kind of inward-looking rationalism which limits man to his passive memories. This limited inward-looking rationalism leads man to animate his own impressions formed by the five senses and to complete the 'Circle of Destiny'. This limited circle is the resting place of fallen man who dreams. He is amid worldly wealth and bound to it, but he dreams in metaphysical space in the sleep of death. Blake calls this the position of 'pleasant rest', 'Beulah'; and the 'Circle of Destiny' which forms the world and space of the rationalist is named 'Ulro'. Blake satirizes this mentality and its religions and cultural outcrop:

'There is from Great Eternity a mild & pleasant rest
Nam'd Beulah, a soft Moony Universe, feminine, lovely,
Pure, mild & Gentle, given in Mercy to those who sleep,
Eternally created by the Lamb of God around,
On all sides, within & without the Universal Man.
The daughters of Beulah follow sleepers in all their
    Dreams,
Creating spaces, lest they fall into Eternal Death.
The Circle of Destiny complete, they gave to it a space,
And nam'd the space Ulro, & brooded over it in care
    & love.'[41]

By the term 'Great Eternity' Blake satirizes the established
social system. The 'mild & pleasant rest' represents passivity
and the 'Moony Universe' opposes the creative sunny universe.
This passive state of leisure which is 'feminine, lovely, pure,
mild & gentle' is given in 'Mercy' by divine providence. Here
the 'Lamb of God' is not the 'Lamb' in the *Songs of Innocence*
which makes 'all the vales rejoice'. The 'Lamb of God' in *Vala*
is abstract and inhabits the rationalist's 'Circle of Destiny'
formed by his passive and limited upbringing.

'Enion brooded o'er the rocks; the rough rocks groaning
    vegetate.
Such power was given to the Solitary wanderer:'[42]

Human vision and creative genius (Enion) is turned away
from social reality into his limited natural memories where
'natural man' broods over the 'rocks' and 'Reading the Visions
of Beulah' or his passive memories. The terms 'vegetation' and
'rock' represent the bound and static mentality of the fallen
man:

' "Hear! I will sing a Song of Death! it is a Song of Vala!
"The Fallen Man takes his repose, Urizen sleeps in the
    porch,
"Luvah and Vala wake & . . . *fly* up from the Human
    Heart
"Into the Brain from thence; . . ." '[43]

A division or conflict is created between the heart and mind by
the division between action and word, between true love and
false or abstract love. The fallen man teaches love and brother-

hood but in practice he turns love into hate and brotherhood
into enmity by his ruling interest.

In *Vala* the poet discusses the division which has occurred in
society, and has influenced all aspects of human life. Society
is divided physically and mentally. Men are divided in their
hearts and minds. The ruling interests which dominate society
physically also dominate intellectually. The ruling culture is
thus the product and manifestation of ruling interests. They
attempt to hide their material interests under the veil of
abstract intellectual, philosophical and spiritual arguments
which are used as a sign of superiority and a defensive barricade
against exploited and wretched people. Blake tears aside this
veil in his *Vala*. He knows that this veil prevents man from
seeing the infinite—universal humanity. Limited man can pity
only himself and looks back towards the night rather than
forward to the morning:

> ' "Why dost thou weep as Vala & wet thy veil with dewy
>   tears,
> "In slumbers of my night-repose infusing a false morning,
> "Driving the Female Emanations all away from Los?
> "I have refus'd to look upon the Universal Vision." '44

For Blake true prophecy is not a rising above the people but
rather a joining with them. The false prophet ascends above
the people and utters his own limited impressions as a divine
message. But the true prophet sees divinity in universal
humanity and his message is to unite by tearing the veil of
mystery which blinds the 'universal vision' of man:

> ' ". . . For I behold the Fallen Man
> "Seeking to comfort Vala: she will not be comforted.
> "She rises from his throne and seeks the shadows of her
>   garden
> "Weeping for Luvah lost in bloody beams of your false
>   morning;
> "Sick'ning lies the Fallen Man, his head sick, his heart
>   faint:
> "Mighty achievement of your power! Beware the punish-
>   ment!" '

The 'Fallen Man' is fallen in his social relationship. He has descended into limited selfhood which is his Vala who shelters him in the 'shadows of her garden'. The 'garden' of Vala is the forest of natural memories which limits and prevents the 'Fallen Man' from seeing the 'Divine Image' or universal humanity:

> ' "Refusing to behold the Divine Image which all behold
> "And live thereby, he is sunk down into a deadly sleep.
> "But we, immortal in our own strength, survive by stern debate
> "Till we have drawn the Lamb of God into a mortal form.
> "And that he must be born is certain, for One must be All." '[45]

Vala negates the 'Divine Image' of human universality. Vala is the mortal and limited state of man. She opposed the development and birth of the 'Lamb of God'—universal humanity—by her effort to keep Imagination on a limited mortal plane. The development of Imagination and human unity must be fulfilled to complete the resurrection of Man, for 'One must be All'.

Vala also embodies all the possession and love of 'Fallen Man'. His love is passive and devouring (Luvah). His world is limited and based on his selfish worldliness. He seeks comfort in Vala but 'more! more! is the cry of a mistaken soul; less than All cannot satisfy Man'. 'All' is Human Divinity and wholeness as opposed to limited and selfish interest. Vala is identified with the ruling interests at the time. The 'tree of Mystery', 'Urizen's Mysterious tree', 'fumes of Mystery', 'the Veil of Mystery', 'written in blood "Mystery" ', 'Mystery Babylon', 'Mystery the Harlot', 'the streets of Mystery' represent the system of Vala.[46] She represents the hypocritical social system and relationship in its total chaos where

> ' "The Horse is of more value than the Man. The Tyger fierce
> "Laughs at the Human form; the Lion mocks & thirsts for blood.
> "They cry, 'O Spider, spread thy web! Enlarge thy bones &, fill'd
> " 'With marrow, sinews & flesh, Exalt thyself, attain a voice.

H*

" 'Call to thy dark arm'd hosts; for the sons of Men
        muster together
" 'To desolate their cities! Man shall be no more!'
    'Awake O Hosts!'
"The bow string sang upon the hills, 'Luvah & Vala ride
"Triumphant in the bloody sky, & the Human form is no
        more.' " '47

The ruling interests teach love, humility, peace and moral laws
but in practice violate peace and turn against humanity by
their selfish interest. Moral laws and teachings are in fact used
as a veil to cover such selfish and inhuman interests. When
Blake attacks moral laws he aims at the hypocritical social
system which uses these laws to protect its existing position and
interest. In this society where individualistic love of gain and
limited interest are the only driving force the 'Human form'
is expected to be suppressed and bestiality is encouraged. The
Tyger, who is the symbol of self-centred and bestial energy,
laughs at 'the Human form; the Lion mocks & thirsts for
blood'. The 'Lion' is the symbol of the ruling class which
makes laws to protect its own interests.

Vala is a dramatic history of a jungle-like society where man
lives in a darkened condition and where it is therefore always
'night'. The basic human rights are violated, man is exploited
by man and his thoughts are supressed by censorship:

' " 'My clouds are not the clouds of verdant fields & groves
        of fruit,
" 'But Clouds of Human Souls: my nostrils drink lives of
        Men.'
"The Villages Lament: they faint, outstretch'd upon the
        plain.
"Wailing runs round the Valleys from the Mill & from
        the Barn.
"But most the polish'd Palaces, dark, silent, bow with
        dread,
"Hiding their books & pictures underneath the dens of
        Earth.
"The Cities send to one another saying: 'My sons are
        Mad

" 'With wine of cruelty. Let us plat a scourge, O Sister
City'.
"Children are nourish'd for the Slaughter; once the Child
was fed
"With Milk, but wherefore now are Children fed with
blood?" '48

In a society where all means of production are in the hands of
a possessing class men are either exploited and used as slaves in
factories or sent to war to fight for the ruling interests. Thus
'Children are nourish'd for the Slaughter'. The term 'Slaughter'
vividly conveys the degree of cruelty practised by man against
man.

Vala is not merely a history of the darkening social condition
of the time. It is also a dialectical and revolutionary work
where Imagination (Los) revolts against this jungle-like
system of social relationships.

' " '. . . Awake, O Brother Mountain!
" 'Let us refuse the Plow & Spade, the heavy Roller &
spiked
" 'Harrow; burn all these Corn fields, throw down all
these fences!
" 'Fatten'd on Human blood & drunk with wine of life is
better far
" 'Than all these labours of the harvest & the vintage.
See the river,
" 'Red with the blood of Men, swells lustful round my
rocky knees;' " '49

The term 'Mountain' represents the working-class Body which
is exploited by landowners and industrialists. Their fields,
houses and bodies are 'Fatten'd on Human blood'. Blake calls
the labourer his brother because he himself was a life-long
worker. His class consciousness is not exclusive to *The Marriage
of Heaven and Hell* or his early works. It is also well rooted in
the cloudy context of his prophetical writings, the obscurities
of which are the product of a repressive atmosphere:

'Luvah and Vala standing in the bloody sky.'50

'Vala' is the 'Spectrous Power' which combines all abstract
moral laws and the 'Net' of religion which serve one love, one

law and one king. 'Luvah' is the perverted and abstract love
of Urizen who teaches love but in practice loves only himself
and is pernicious to others. The 'Spectrous Power' is a force
which is a 'Void' and outside 'Human existence'. It teaches
spiritualism but in its inner being is bound by selfish material
interest. When Blake suggests casting out this inhuman and
'Spectrous Power' he in fact attacks and challenges its material
root or existence. Although 'Spectrous Power' possesses all
material wealth, the 'Human blood', yet he is blind to his
surrounding world. His Imagination is faint and his love
distracted and distorted:

> ' "There is no City, nor Cornfield, nor Orchard; all is
>   Rock & Sand.
> "There is no Sun, nor Moon, nor Star, but rugged
>   wintry rocks
> "Justling together in the void, suspended by inward fires.
> "Impatience now no longer can endure. Distracted
>   Luvah,
> "Bursting forth from the loins of Enitharmon, Thou
>   fierce Terror,
> "Go howl in vain! Smite, smite his fetters! smite, O
>   wintry hammers!
> "Smite, Spectre of Urthona! mock the fiend who drew
>   us down
> "From heavens of joy into this deep. Now rage, but rage
>   in vain!" '51

The 'Distracted Luvah' has two essential characteristics.
One is passivity and the other fury and terror. Through his
passivity he feeds on the joy of others and through his terror
and rage creates fear and fetters. Enion like Tiriel is 'blind
& age-bent', and is the symbol of passivity who dwells in the
'frightful deep' of his natural memories. His art is lamentation
and his song is the 'Song of Death'. He listens to the voice of
social discontent and revolt while weeping for his own fate:

> ' "Why does the Raven cry aloud and no eye pities her?
> "Why fall the Sparrow & the Robin in the foodless
>   winter?
> "Faint, shivering, they sit on leafless bush or frozen stone

"Wearied with seeking food across the snowy waste, the little

"Heart cold, and the little tongue consum'd that once in thoughtless joy

"Gave songs of gratitude to waving cornfields round their nest.

"Why howl the Lion & the Wolf? why do they roam abroad?

"Deluded by [the del.] summer's heat, they sport in enormous love

"And cast their young out to the hungry wilds & sandy deserts.

"Why is the Sheep given to the knife? the Lamb plays in the Sun!

"He starts! he hears the foot of Man! he says: Take thou my wool,

"But spare my life: *but* he knows not that [the del.] winter cometh fast.

"The Spider sits in his labour'd Web, eager watching for the Fly.

"Presently comes a famish'd Bird & takes away the Spider.

"His Web is left all desolate that his little anxious heart

"So careful wove & spread it out with sighs and weariness." '52

The questions, like those (Plate 3) in *Visions of The Daughters of Albion*, are challenging. Blake queries the whole philosophical system and moral theories of the ruling class by his uncompromising belief that 'Energy' is from the 'Body'. The material world is the basis of all activities and life. The strife between 'Heaven' and 'Hell' is an economic issue. The mental fight is also a product of this basic issue. Why 'does the Raven cry' and why 'fall the Sparrows & the Robin in the foodless winter?'. Because they lack Energy and vitality which come from food, the body, the material world. They are 'wearied with seeking food across the snowy waste, the little heart cold', but they become joyful and give 'songs of gratitude to waving cornfields round their nest'—'Energy is Eternal Delight'. By these questions Blake also challenges the British Empire's claim that her conquests of India and Africa were based on human responsibility in order to propagate and develop civilization among uncivilized nations. It was the 'white man's burden' to civilize the 'wilds' of 'sandy desarts': the questions 'Why howl the Lion & the Wolf? Why do they roam abroad?' are politically deep and far reaching. The 'Lion & the Wolf' represent Empire. For when 'EMPIRE IS NO MORE! . . . THE LION & WOLF SHALL CEASE'.[53] The driving force behind Empire is the material interest which plunders, suppresses and slaughters the people bodily and spiritually. The Lamb who represents the mass says: 'Take thou my wool, but spare my life.'[54]

Blake through his philosophy that 'Energy' is from the 'Body' unveils the selfishness and hypocrisy of the social system which is wrapped in moral and humanitarian terms such as 'love', 'pity' and 'peace'. Blake calls these terms the 'Human abstract'. In other words, in practice they work against 'Humanity' from the very nature of their ruling interest and social relationship. Blake condemns the limited and selfish interest which suppresses humanity. His attempt to show that social and mental fight has an economic root is a defence of humanity. For any discussion of humanity outside the social and living condition is an abstract intellectual exercise. Man is responsible for social errors and injustice: for

> 'Pity would be no more
> If we did not make somebody Poor;'[55]

therefore humanity must be practically demonstrated within a social relationship rather than taught in abstract terms:

> 'Where Mercy, Love, & Pity dwell
> There God is dwelling too'[56]

Blake criticizes the Church and its religion because of its abstract teachings and because it divorces God from man and his social relationship and living conditions. He writes satirically:

> 'Then those in Great Eternity met in the Council of God
> As one Man, for contracting their Exalted Senses
> They behold Multitude, or Expanding they behold as one,
> As One Man all the Universal family; & that One Man

They call Jesus the Christ, & they in him & he in them
Live in Perfect harmony, in Eden the land of life,
Consulting as One Man above [Mount Gilead del.] the
    Mountain of Snowdon Sublime.'[57]

Religion attempts to bridge the social gulf by an abstract and
deluding concept of Man as the 'Universal family'. This Man
is called 'Jesus the Christ'. But according to Blake, 'Jesus
Christ did not wish to unite, but to separate them, as in the
Parable of sheep and goats! & he says: "I came not to send
Peace, but a Sword".'[58] In other words Jesus revolted against
the ruling interests or Roman Empire and sided with the poor
and wretched. So the kind of Jesus Christ that the Church is pro-
pagating is a passive being and the enemy of the true Christ:

    'The Vision of Christ that thou dost see
    Is my Vision's Greatest Enemy:
    Thine has a great hook nose like thine,
    Mine has a snub nose like to mine:
    Thine is the friend of All Mankind,
    Mine speaks in parables to the Blind:
    Thine loves the same world that mine hates,
    Thy Heaven doors are my Hell gates.
    Socrates taught what Meletus
    Loath'd as a Nation's bitterest Curse,
    And Caiphas was in his own Mind
    A benefactor to Mankind:
    Both read the Bible day & night,
    But thou read'st black where I read white.'[59]

Different classes read the Bible differently. The objective living
condition of man influences his outlook. The 'Heaven' of one
is the 'Hell' of the other. For the 'Heaven' of the leisured class
is built at the expense of those who live and work in 'Hell':

    ' "Love seeketh only Self to please,
    . . . .
    . . . builds a Hell in Heaven's despite." '[60]

The Christ that the Church worships is the prosecutor of
'Heaven' and those who live there, but Blake's vision of Christ
is of one who sides with the poor and speaks on behalf of the
'Blind' and needy in 'Hell'. The Church and the ruling system

(Urizen) use the name of Jesus Christ as a hypocritical veil to hide their wealth and war of greed:

> ' "Luvah & Urizen contend in war around the holy tent."
> . . . .
>
> So spoke the Messengers of Beulah. Silently removing,
> The Family Divine drew up the Universal tent
> Above [Mount Gilead del.] High Snowdon, & clos'd
>   the Messengers in clouds around
> Till the time of the End. Then they Elected Seven, called
>   the Seven
> Eyes of God & the Seven Lamps of Almighty.
> The Seven are one within the other; the Seventh is
>   named Jesus,
> The Lamb of God, blessed for ever, & he follow'd the
>   Man
> Who wander'd in mount Ephraim seeking a Sepulcher,
> His inward eyes closing from the Divine vision, & all
> His children wandering outside, from his bosom fleeing
>   away.'[61]

The 'Messengers of Beulah' are the false prophets whose love and reason are limited and based on passive memories. These passive memories form their world and horizon which Blake satirically calls: 'Universal tent'. The terms 'Universal' and 'tent' convey the characteristic of Urizenic mentality which on the one hand is based on limited reason (your reason) and the other hand is formed from contemplating a metaphysical and illusionary space or universe where the lost man wanders. Urizen moves backward into the night of non-existence which forms his universe. His love and life are perverted and thus he has lost Divine Vision which can dwell only within human relationships or 'where Mercy, Love, & Pity dwell':

> '. . . *perverse roll'd the wheels of Urizen & Luvah, back revers'd*
> *Downwards & outwards,* [*bending* del.] *consuming in the wars*
>   *of Eternal Death.*
> . . . .
>
> *Rising upon his Couch of death Albion beheld his Sons.*
> *Turning his Eyes outward to Self, losing the Divine*
>   *Vision, . . .*'[62]

The *'Couch of death'* is a fallen society where Urizenic power controls true and creative men. The Urizenic power is based on fear and death, on fear because of its dependence on others and on death because of its devouring nature. Thus the war of Urizen is the product of his weakness and his social relationship. Urizen

'. . . saw Eternal Death beneath.
Pale, he beheld futurity: pale, he beheld the Abyss
Where Enion, blind & age bent, wept in direful hunger
    craving,
All rav'ning like the hungry worm & like the silent grave.
Mighty was the draught of Voidness to draw Existence in.

Terrific Urizen strode above in fear & pale dismay.
He saw the indefinite space beneath & his soul shrunk
    with horror,
His feet upon the verge of Non Existence; . . .'[62]

Blake's society is ruled by this power and mentality. The weak and passive govern the strong and productive. The 'hungry worm' is the parasitic ruling interests who feed on dearth and dead. In this divided society Imagination is suppressed by material and subjection limitation:

'In human forms distinct they stood round Urizen, prince
    of Light,
Petrifying all the Human Imagination into rock & sand.'[63]

Error in society is created by man. Urizen and those who surround him have 'human form' in appearance but their inner being or mind has lost the 'Human Vision' and is divorced from Imagination. Once man loses Imagination he falls back into his limited natural memories and sees only himself:

'What is within now sees without; they are raw to the
    hungry wind.
They become Nations far remote, in a little & dark Land.'[64]

The term 'Nations' represents the social division caused by material barriers. The world of one class is so remote from the other that though 'in a little . . . land', they yet look two separate nations. Blake criticises the social system which uses man as a means for material acquisition. In other words humanity becomes subject to what is non-human. Urizen is divided from the rest of society by his own ruling interests, therefore he has formed his own outlook. He has fallen from a human to a non-human level or into his limited world of material interest. In this circumstance and social relationship man is deprived of Imagination and stripped of his freedom. For true freedom is social and human liberty from exploitation of man by man:

> ' ". . . I suffer affliction
> "Because I love, for I . . . was love, but hatred awakes
>   in me,
> "And Urizen, who was Faith & certainty, is chang'd to
>   Doubt;
> "The hand of Urizen is upon me because I blotted out
> "That Human [terror del.] delusion to deliver all the sons
>   of God
> "From bondage of the Human form. O first born Son of
>   light,
> "O Urizen my enemy, I weep for thy stern ambition,
> "But weep in vain. O when will you return, Vala the
>   Wanderer?"

These were the words of Luvah, patient in afflictions,'[65]

Vala is the natural man who wanders in the dark land of his selfish interest. In the industrialized society of the eighteenth century he is the profiteer capitalist who creates competition and terror among people to promote his commerce. Blake questions and criticizes such industrial and class relationships:

> ' "What! are we terrors to one another? Come, O brethren,
>   wherefore
> "Was this wide Earth spread all abroad? not for wild
>   beasts to roam."
> But many stood silent, & busied in their families.
> And many said, "We see no Visions in the darksom air.
> "Measure the course of that sulphur orb that lights the
>   [dismal del.] darksom day;
> "Set stations on this breeding Earth & let us buy &
>   sell." '[66]

In a fallen society human life is reduced to buying and selling and humanity to a money-making machine. Every family strives to be better off than its neighbour or is 'busied' with its own family prosperity while ignoring others. In other words, everybody is compelled or educated to see only his own limited world and to be busy only with his own selfish interest. Individualism in its selfish sense is encouraged. Blake criticizes this kind of family love and calls it—'soft Family-Love'. It is equally selfish and inhuman to foster a nation at the expense and misery of others.

> 'Is this thy soft Family-Love,
> Thy cruel Patriarchal pride,
> Planting thy Family alone,
> Destroying all the World beside?'[67]

The question is a fundamental social and political question. Human Imagination which sees society and humanity as an organic whole is being suppressed by the limited ruling love or interest.

The Selfish interest of Fallen Man operates amid darkness and mystery which are characteristic of his system. He catches his victims by 'The Net of Religion' and eats them as a 'worm' in darkness. All the efforts of the Fallen Man are directed towards denigrating the importance of human energy and productive work. Because his strength depends on the energies of men he attempts to associate his power with an incomprehensible supernatural source. Thus the weak feeds on the strong and the passive on the creative man by making a mystery of it:

> 'The threads are spun & the cords twisted & drawn out;
>   then the weak
> Begin their work, & many a net is netted, many a net
> Spread, & many a Spirit caught; innumerable the nets,
> Innumerable the gins & traps, & many a soothing flute
> Is form'd, & many a corded lyre outspread over the immense.
> In cruel delight they trap the listeners, & in cruel delight
> Bind them, condensing the strong energies into little
>   compass.'[68]

The Fallen Man also causes the fall of others. They fall from

Imagination into 'non entity'. Vala or the Four Zoas, who were once original states of man, are driven into darkness. In darkening social circumstances where the energies of men are exploited by industrialists and the voice of protest is silenced, Vala laments in the silent night:

' "O Lord, wilt thou not look upon sore afflictions
"Among these flames incessant labouring? our hard
    masters laugh
"At all our sorrow. We are made to turn the wheel for
    water,
"To carry the heavy basket on our scorched shoulders, to
    sift
"The sand & ashes, & to mix the clay with tears &
    repentance.
"The times are now return'd upon us; we have given
    ourselves
"To scorn, and now are scorned by the slaves of our
    enemies.
"Our beauty is cover'd over with clay & ashes, & our
    backs
"Furrow'd with whips, & our flesh bruised with the heavy
    basket.
"Forgive us, O thou piteous one whom we have offended!
    forgive
"The weak remaining shadow of Vala that returns in
    sorrow to thee.
"*I see not Luvah as of old, I only see his feet*
"*Like pillars of fire travelling thro' darkness & non entity.*"
Thus she lamented day & night, compell'd to labour
    & sorrow.
Luvah in vain her lamentations heard:'[69]

It is the art of Urizen or the ruling class to reduce the labourers into a lamenting state and a weak position where they can only beg for forgiveness. Urizen teaches that human misery is the result of human sin, therefore to be saved from suffering we must beg the Lord to forgive us. But Imagination scatters the smoke and clouds of mystery and, contrary to Vala, declares that sorrow and poverty are created by man for man. Human

Imagination experiences this truth through social and practical experience. Thus Los, the creative Imagination, while 'driving Enion far into the deathful infinite' questions the social and philosophical system of Urizen:

> ' "What is the price of Experience? do men buy it for a
>   song?
> "Or wisdom for a dance in the street? No, it is bought
>   with the price
> "Of all that a man hath, his wife, his children.
> "Wisdom is sold in the desolate market where none come
>   to buy,
> "And in the wither'd field where the farmer plows for
>   bread in vain." '[70]

The innocence and honesty of Los contrasts with the passivity and hypocrisy of Vala, which is like the abstract pity and empty sigh of the father in 'A Dream'. Imagination revolts against the social system by criticizing its class division and its conditions of life. It brings the problems of man down from remote mystery and abstract argument to a social context and human relationship. Instead of lamenting and complaining against the ruling interests like Vala, Imagination attacks the selfish nature of the social system. It challenges Urizen on economic and social grounds. The social and objective living circumstances of man forms his outlook. Fine words about obedience and human love are certainly expected from those who have the largest slice of the cake, but for those who have only crumbs these abstract words are a valueless mockery. Blake opposes the hypocrisy of the ruling system and its religion (Vala). He writes:

> ' "It is an easy thing to triumph in the summer's sun
> "And in the vintage & to sing on the waggon loaded with
>   corn.
> "It is an easy thing to talk of patience to the afflicted,
> "To speak the laws of prudence to the houseless wanderer,
> "To listen to the hungry raven's cry in wintry season
> "When the red blood is fill'd with wine & with the
>   marrow of lambs.

"It is an easy thing to laugh at wrathful elements,
"To hear the dog howl at the wintry door, the ox in the
   slaughter house moan;
"To see a god on every wind & a blessing on every blast;
"To hear sounds of love in the thunder storm that
   destroys our enemies house;
"To rejoice in the blight that covers his field, & the
   sickness that cuts off his children,
"While our olive & vine sing & laugh round our door,
   & our children bring fruits & flowers.

"Then the groan & the dolor are quite forgotten, & the
   slave grinding at the mill,
"And the captive in chains, & the poor in the prison,
   & the soldier in the field
"When the shatter'd bone hath laid him groaning among
   the happier dead.

"It is an easy thing to rejoice in the tents of prosperity:
"Thus could I sing & thus rejoice: but it is not so with
   me." '71

Here the dialectics in *Vala* emerges and the background and
context of the conflict appears. The conflict is within society
and within the poet. The conflict occurs both on economic and
intellectual levels. The mentality of those who live in the 'tents
of prosperity' is different from and opposite to those who are
'the captive in chains, & the poor in the prison'. Those who
live in the 'tents of prosperity' rejoice in the delight of 'Heaven'
and 'laugh at wrathful elements', that is, those who protest
against social injustice and 'Heaven's' violation of human
dignity and peace. Blake who worked all his life and shared
the experiences of the 'houseless wanderer' and the 'captive
in chains' could not sit at ease and rejoice—'it is not so with
me' he says. He speaks for his class and defends 'the just' or
those who toil for their daily bread. His voice of revolt is
heard against the ruling system all through *Vala* and other
prophetical writings:

' " 'Prophetic dreads urge me to speak: futurity is before me

' " 'Like a dark lamp. Eternal death haunts all my expectation.

' " 'Rent from Eternal Brotherhood we die & are no more.

' " 'Whence is this voice crying, Enion! that soundeth in my ears?

' " 'O cruel pity! O dark deceit! can Love seek for dominion?' " '72

Chapter Six

'WHAT IS MAN?'

At this point my purpose is two-fold. Firstly to demonstrate that the worm in Blake's writing symbolizes a social and human being who represents false mind, false art and fallen man against true mind, true art and true Man. There is conflict and strife between false man and true Man within society. I shall examine this dialectical process all through Blake's writings. Secondly I shall conclude that for Blake true Man and creative mind is eternal but falsehood is created. What is created can be annihilated too. For example 'contraries' are eternal but 'negation' is created. The 'worm' is a symbol of 'negation' and must be 'cut' so that the 'contraries' can be married: 'The cut worm forgives the plow.'

Since here we are attempting to look at Man as a whole in Blake, it is appropriate to borrow the title 'What is Man?' from the preface to the designs of *The Gates of Paradise*, which I shall discuss in detail when examining the 'worm' symbol.

I. THE WORM SYMBOL IN *TIRIEL* AND *THE BOOK OF THEL*

The word 'worm' is used to demonstrate two different types of social character and mentality. One is a devourer and the other prolific. The word is sometimes used as the symbol of selfishness and at other times as the symbol of a weak being. In the book of *Tiriel*, for instance, it is used in the former sense and in *The Book of Thel* in the latter sense. Tiriel as I noted in Chapter Two, is the symbol of fallen man. He is jealous of his children and is afraid lest they take his power from him. He looks at them as his enemies and calls them 'worms of death':

' "Serpents, not sons, wreathing around the bones of Tiriel!
Ye worms of death, feasting upon your aged parent's
flesh!" '[1]

Although Tiriel calls his children 'worms of death' he is,

however, himself a serpent and his inner being is a creeping
form bound to the earth; bound, that is, to his natural
memories. He is

' "A worm of sixty winters creeping on the dusky ground" '.²

The creeping form represents selfhood.

The 'worm of sixty winters' represents the weak character
who rejects the self-sacrificing aspects of life and flees back to
his memories. The doors of these pleasant memories are always
open. Tiriel is blind and like a frightened infant he feels his
way and cries ' "peace to these open doors!" '³ He wanders in the
pleasant gardens of 'Har', in the shadow of infantile memories.
But he cannot see the world of reality. He is 'blind to the
pleasures of the sight and deaf to warbling birds'.

> 'All day they walk'd & all the night beneath the pleasant
>   Moon,
> Westwardly journeying, till Tiriel grew weary with his
>   travel.'⁴

The old man who enters through the door is an 'innocent old
man' who looks weary from journeying. Tiriel passes through
thick doors. He is

> ' ". . . the king of rotten wood & of the bones of death;
> He wanders without eyes & passes thro' thick walls
>   & doors." '⁵

Thel is a female version of Tiriel. She is the symbol of a passive
and abstract religion. Thel is the 'virgin of the skies' and
'queen of the vales', but without a use. The *Book of Thel* is an
allegory of the passive character visiting the world of generation.
Thel rejects the self-sacrificing aspects of experience and flees
back to the valleys of 'Har', her pleasant infantile memories
which form her 'grave'.

> 'Can Wisdom be put in a silver rod?
> Or Love in a golden bowl?'⁶

The answers to these questions are apparently negative.
'Wisdom' and 'Love' should be seen in human action. The
theme of the book is that a man's moral worth must be judged

by his acts of creation or the extent of his usefulness to others
because: 'we live not for ourselves'.

The contrast between the 'worm' as a symbol of selfhood
and the 'worm' as a symbol of a weak being can be seen in
The Book of Thel. Thel represents the passive and selfish
character who feeds only on her sweet infantile memories; and
the 'clod of clay', as I mentioned in Chapter Two, represents
the selfless character who feeds the weak 'worm'. One repre-
sents abstract wisdom and the other active personality. Thel
seeks only to please herself. She walks through the vales of
'Har', she smells the flowers and hears the birds, but does not
feed them:

> ' "For I walk thro' the vales of Har, and smell the sweetest
>   flowers,
> "But I feed not the little flowers; I hear the warbling
>   birds,
> "But I feed not the warbling birds; they fly and seek
>   their food:" ' [7]

Although Thel lives in pleasant surroundings she nevertheless
complains and does not enjoy her life because she fears death:

> ' "But Thel delights in these no more, because I fade
>   away;
> "And all shall say, 'Without a use this shining woman
>   liv'd,
>
> " 'Or did she only live to be at death the food of worms?' " ' [8]

The poet shows the indecisive mental state of the unborn
spirit or passive character. On the one hand she is passive and
bound to nature, while on the other hand she is conscious of
her own approaching death and the transient nature of
delights. There are two alternatives: either the passive character
has to sacrifice her selfhood and feed others by being creative,
or remain passive and 'smell the sweetest flowers' without
feeding them. But Thel cannot do either. She cannot delight
in the sweet memories of the vales of 'Har' because they are
mortal. In contrast to the creative mind in man the natural
memories are weak and transitory. Thel laments the unreliable
and transient nature of her life:

' "O life of this our spring! why fades the lotus of the
        water,
"Why fade these children of the spring, born but to
        smile & fall?
"Ah! Thel is like a wat'ry bow, and like a parting cloud;
"Like a reflection in a glass; like shadows in the water;
"Like dreams of infants, like a smile upon an infant's
        face;
"Like the dove's voice; like transient day; like music in
        the air." '[9]

For travelling in this direction, as we have seen with Tiriel,
leads to weariness. It leads to the night, and to the dark wood
where the desolate spirit and lost traveller wanders. This path
leads to 'standing lakes'[10] and a static world. The journey is
wearisome and Thel longs for the gentle 'sleep of death'.

' "Ah! gentle may I lay me down, and gentle rest my
        head,
"And gentle sleep the sleep of death, . . ." '[11]

This gentle sleep does not, however, bring her peace. She
still hears the 'voice of sorrow breathed from the hollow pit'.[12]
This 'voice of sorrow' is the voice of the unborn spirit or
undeveloped inner being and the 'hollow pit' is the womb of
nature or impressions formed by sense-perception.

Although aware of her transient life, Thel nevertheless
refuses self-sacrifice. Tiriel calls his sons 'worms of death' and
is frightened lest they take his power from him. Thel is similarly
afraid of being the food of worms at death.

The poet finally shows the moral weakness of Thel by
introducing the 'clod of clay' as a symbol of selflessness. Thel
feeds her own weak part but the 'clod of clay' feeds the helpless
'worm'. Thel abhors being eaten by the worms but the poet
implies that it is better to be food for weak worms than a
parasitic character feeding upon other beings.

' "Then if thou art the food of worms, O virgin of the skies,
"How great thy use, how great thy blessing! Every thing
        that lives
"Lives not alone nor for itself." '[13]

Thel sees the worm who is helpless, naked and weeping, but refuses to help:

> ' "Art thou a Worm? Image of weakness, art thou but a
> Worm?
> "I see thee like an infant wrapped in the Lilly's leaf.
> "Ah! weep not, little voice, thou canst not speak, but
> thou canst weep.
> "Is this a Worm? I see thee lay helpless & naked, weeping,
> "And none to answer, none to cherish thee with mother's
> smiles." '[14]

The wisdom of Thel is put in a 'silver rod' and her 'love' in a 'golden bowl', and they are abstract. She is the virgin of the 'skies'; the skies represent abstraction. Though she describes the pitiful appearance of the worm and sees it helpless and naked like an infant, Thel's maternal instincts are not aroused; she does not attempt to nourish it. The 'clod of clay', on the contrary, hearing the worm's voice reacts with pity and offers her 'milky fondness':

> 'The Clod of Clay heard the Worm's voice & raised her
> pitying head:
> She bow'd over the weeping infant, and her life exhal'd
> In milky fondness: then on Thel she fix'd her humble
> eyes.
> "O beauty of the vales of Har! we live not for our-
> selves".'[15]

Thel separates wisdom and love from the practical life whereas the 'clod' combines love and life together: the 'clod' says:

> ' "Thou seest me the meanest thing, and so I am indeed.
> "My bosom of itself is cold, and of itself is dark;
> "But he, that loves the lowly, pours his oil upon my head,
> "And kisses me, and binds his nuptial bands around my
> breast,
> "And says: 'Thou mother of my children, I have loved
> thee
> " 'And I have given thee a crown that none can take
> away.'
> "But how this is, . . . , I know not, and I cannot know;
> "I ponder, and I cannot ponder; yet I live and love." '[16]

There is a gap between what Thel or the priest know and what they do. Thel, like the priest, knows that 'God would love a worm' and would punish 'The evil foot that wilful bruis'd its helpless form' but does not know that he 'cherished it with milk and oil'. In other words she has only an idea of a punishing God and, like the priest, she knows only what has already been formed of God and love in her memories. These memories are like dead bones in a grave where the 'worm' of 'sixty winters' lives. This is the only place to which the passive reasoner can finally return:

'The eternal gates' terrific porter lifted the northern bar:
Thel enter'd in & saw the secrets of the land unknown.
She saw the couches of the dead, & where the fibrous roots
Of every heart on earth infixes deep its restless twists:
A land of sorrows & of tears where never smile was seen.'[17]

The limited natural memories are indeed the land of sorrows and tears because the 'eternal man' or the creative mind is chained to these passive and limited impressions. Memories formed by limited impressions can see only themselves and thus obstruct the creative mind or imagination. The passive memories are, thus, like a 'worm' embedded in the soil of the creative mind. The mind cannot be creative unless freed from these memories or from selfhood.

2. THE WORM SYMBOL IN THE *SONGS OF INNOCENCE* AND *OF EXPERIENCE*

The word 'worm' is used both in the *Songs of Innocence* and *of Experience*. These works correspond to each other, 'Shewing the Two Contrary States of the Human Soul' in two different social relationships. The *Songs of Innocence*, as pointed out before, represents a selfless society where social relationship is based on love and brotherhood, but in the *Songs of Experience* social relationships are rigid and based on selfhood and negation. The use made of the worm symbol in each book illustrates this contrast.

In the *Songs of Experience* the word 'worm', as I noted in the first part of Chapter Two, appears in 'The Sick Rose':

'O Rose, thou art sick!
The invisible worm
That flies in the night,
In the howling storm,

Has found out thy bed
Of crimson joy:
And his dark secret love
Does thy life destroy.'[18]

This destructive and invisible worm in the *Songs of Experience*
contrasts with the 'glow-worm' in the *Songs of Innocence* which
represents selfless being or love lighting the ground in dark
nights for the beetle:

' "I am set to light the ground,
While the beetle goes his round:" '[19]

3. 'THE GATES OF PARADISE'

The Gates of Paradise is one of the most important works that
Blake engraved in 1793. It was his 'first attempt to convey his
message primarily by a series of pictures'.[20] It illustrates two
'contrary states'; one 'Innocence' or Imagination, the other
the fall of man from creativeness into the bondage of natural
memories. He describes two parallel ways, one of which leads
to unity, expansion and freedom of man, and the other to
division, contraction and selfhood.

The designs illustrating this work were engraved in 1793
and issued with a title-page which differs from later editions.
The work was then called *For children: The Gates of Paradise*,
and consisted only of the title-page and the seventeen emblems.
The illustrations as they appeared in 1793 had already been
engraved under that date (K. p. 209). Many years afterwards
Blake again used the plates, altering the title-page (he altered
'For children' to 'For the Sexes' and left 'The Gates of Paradise'
as before). He added new sentences to the illustrations on
several of the plates, and engraved three new plates with texts
to come at the end. These three new plates, as the title indicates
('The Keys of the Gates'), are in fact the keys to these illu-

'THE DANCE OF ALBION' OR 'GLAD DAY'

'Albion rose from where he labourd at the Mill with Slaves'

FOR THE SEXES:
THE GATES OF PARADISE

[FRONTISPIECE]

What is Man?

The Sun's Light when he unfolds it
Depends on the Organ that beholds it.

I

I found him beneath a Tree.

2   Water
Thou Waterest him with Tears:

3   Earth
He struggles into Life

4

Air
On Cloudy Doubts & Reasoning Cares

5

Fire
That end in endless Strife.

6

At length for hatching ripe
he breaks the shell.

7

What are these? Alas! the Female Martyr,
Is She also the Divine Image?

8   My Son! my Son!

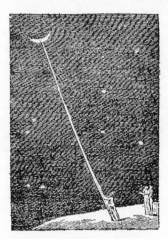

9   I want! I want!

10

Help! Help!

11

Aged Ignorance
Perceptive Organs closed, their Objects close.

12

Does thy God, O Priest, take such vengeance
as this?

13

Fear & Hope are—Vision.

I*

14
The Traveller hasteth in the
Evening.

15
Death's Door

16
    I have said to the Worm:
Thou art my mother & my sister.

strations. In this form the work consists therefore, of 21 plates. The later work is assigned by Geoffrey Keynes to about the year 1818.[21]

Another very interesting illustration which, it seems to me, must be studied together with *The Gates of Paradise* is ' "The Dance of Albion" ' or ' "Glad Day" ', dated 1780. But this date, as Keynes has suggested, seems to refer to the original drawing and not to the engraving, which was probably done about 1793.[22] Nonetheless what is most important for us here is that Blake had apparently already arrived at the level of consciousness or Imagination in 1780. By consciousness or Imagination is meant, simply, the overcoming of passive and limited memories, by the 'Poetic Genius' or creative mind; in other words to acquire the vision of 'Contraries' and 'Negation' within society. In the illustration there is a youth who has stripped off his clothes and beneath him, a moth and an earth worm. The sun rises with the youth, and under the original drawing (1780) the following sentences appear:

'Albion rose from where he labour'd at the Mill with Slaves:
Giving himself for the Nations he danc'd the dance of Eternal Death.'[23]

In both the illustrations to *The Gates of Paradise* and ' "Glad Day" ', it seems that the main purpose of the artist is to show how passive man forms his paradise out of his passive memories. In ' "Glad Day" ' the poet, apparently, wants to show how the moth with Satanic batwings, as a symbol of passive man, flies towards night while the active man rises with the day or reality. The worm on the ground apparently represents the earth-bound being of man. The sun represents Imagination. The earth and sun illustrate the dialectical nature of man.

In the illustrations of the frontispiece to *The Gates of Paradise* we see a caterpillar on one leaf of the tree and a human baby wrapped in his swaddling clothes on the other leaf. Beneath the illustration is the question 'What is Man?'. Blake has answered the question on the same page as follows:

'The Sun's Light when he unfolds it
Depends on the Organ that beholds it.'

The passive man sees night or his passive memories whereas the active rises with the sun, the symbol of creation.

In *The Gates of Paradise* Blake represents the state of regeneration of the passive or fallen man. *The Gates of Paradise* is linked to ' "Glad Day" ' in which the freed man is giving himself for the nations because ' "we live not for ourselves" '.[24] But in *The Gates of Paradise* man, after hatching and breaking the shell of nature, flees back to the paradise of his pleasant memories as Thel, refusing self-sacrifice, flees back to the 'vales of Har' escaping from life and reality. There is a correspondence between the two beings on two separate leaves of the same tree. One develops as an organic part of the tree but the other is a divided and dividing organism which feeds on the leaf parasitically.[25]

Thus ' "Glad Day" ' represents the freedom of creative man from limited natural impressions and *For the Sexes: The Gates of Paradise* represents the fall of man into a vegetative nature.

By the word 'fall' is meant the descent from creation or Imagination into passive natural memories or selfhood which is represented by the symbol of 'woman'. 'Woman' or 'Female' in Blake represents the social background and should not be taken as a literal reference. Natural memories are called 'Woman' because the first and deepest impressions of the world of everyone, whether male or female, are formed by and with the mother. Basic necessities, food and shelter, are thus associated with 'Woman' or mother. This fall is, perhaps, represented in illustration No. 1:

> '1My Eternal Man set in Repose,
> The Female from his darkness rose
> And She found me beneath a Tree,
> A Mandrake, & in her Veil hid me.'[26]

What the woman finds, apparently, is the infant form whose mind is put in repose. When the infant's mind and personality is kept undeveloped by negative teaching, then the creative mind descends and becomes limited like a weak worm bound to the earth. Thus the limited natural memories rise and take over and govern the unwilling man when his creative mind or 'Eternal Man' stops creating or is set in repose: the natural memories are here represented by the word 'Female'.

In the processes of the creation of man there are two alterna-
tives: he is either passive or active. The passive or weak part
does not take over unless the creative or 'Eternal Man' has
been 'set in Repose'. 'Eternal Man', 'Poetic Genius' and
'Imagination' all represent the same idea. When the creative
or 'Eternal Man' is set into sleep the natural part of the
'worm' of weakness grows, as we have seen in Tiriel, and
becomes a 'worm of sixty winters' or develops to 'Serpent
Reasoning' of 'Good' and 'Evil', 'Virtue' and 'Vice' or 'Heaven'
and 'Hell'. This fall of man into division and generation and
his resurrection to unity, as I have noted before, is the theme of
Vala or The Four Zoas (1795):

> 'His fall into Division & his Resurrection to Unity:
> His fall into the Generation of decay & death, & his
> Regeneration by the Resurrection from the dead.'[27]

The 'division' is division from Imagination with the corre-
sponding fall into passivity which is the state of death. Death
is the condition of the passive and fixed mind which like a
corpse is wrapped in the 'Female veil' of natural memories.
Vala or The Four Zoas, then, represents the 'Female veil'. The
veil also appears in the *Visions of the Daughters of Albion*. The
abstract and negative teachings of priestcraft warp the inno-
cent, honest, open and fearless joys of infancy. The child, who
was seeking the vigorous joys of morning light,[28] has been
frightened by the priest and hidden his joys in 'Leutha's vale'.

> 'I loved Theotormon,
> And I was not ashamed;
> I trembled in my virgin fears,
> And I hid in Leutha's vale!'[29]

When the creative mind is barred from development and
creation and is instead governed by natural memories and
abstract ideas then man becomes weak and earth-bound. The
passive man turns his back on involvement in the world of
reality and instead dreams and lives in the world of his limited
memories. The passive thinker doubts his own energy (see
illustration No. 2: 'Water') and creativity. He only believes
his passive memories which are reflected in the water like
pictures. In other words, the passive character is dominated by

his own memories formed by impressions of his own limited
social environment. But these memories are abstract pictures
in the water because they do not exist except in the mind of a
passive reasoner. He is struggling, and seeks a reflection of his
passive memories in the world of reality. Since he does not
depend on his own creative energy he depends instead on
things other than his own creative power. He is bound to the
earth (see illustration No. 3: 'Earth'). Sometimes he looks
hopelessly at the stars in the immense space of his heaven (see
illustration No. 4: 'Air'), or, at another time, he rises against
the world, which like fire, has surrounded him (see illustration
No. 5: 'Fire'). But he is like Swedenborg who while in 'Heaven'
is troubled by the infernal fire in 'Hell'. He is fighting for
'Truth' which to him exists only in his own memories. His
'Will' and 'Rational Truth' are like the 'flaming sword' (*M.H.H.*,
p. 154, 'the cherub with his flaming sword') representing the
passive memories and fixed mentality which destroy the creative
part in himself and then in other people. For the passive
character first falls victim himself and then makes other victims
by his laws of good and evil:

> '2Doubt Self Jealous, Wat'ry folly,
> 3Struggling thro' Earth's Melancholy.
> 4Naked in Air, in Shame & Fear,
> 5Blind in Fire with shield & spear,
> Two Horn'd Reasoning, Cloven Fiction,
> In Doubt, which is Self contradiction,
> A dark Hermaphrodite I (We . . .) stood,
> Rational Truth, Root of Evil & Good,
> Round me flew the Flaming Sword;
> Round her snowy Whirlwinds roar'd
> Freezing her Veil, the Mundane Shell.'30

The creative mind is hidden in the 'Female Veil' of natural
memories. It is as if it were hidden in a cave or, like a dead
body, put in the 'grave'.

The 'Eternal Man' finally awakens and rends the 'Veil' and
enters his 'Cave'. In other words the passive memories become
active in the mind and the dead rise from the grave of the
'Mundane Shell' (see illustration No. 6: 'At length for hatching
ripe he breaks the shell'). After the resurrection or the awakening

of the creative mind different people see in the 'Grave' different
beings. One, like Blake, meets his Saviour or his Poetic Genius,
who is the transformer of his memories into an active imagina-
tive life. Another, like Swedenborg (as Blake points out in *The
Marriage*, plate 3) finds a 'Female Garment' there. Finally
some find a 'Male', who is 'woven with care', that is to say, he
is kept in restriction and bound by his limited natural memories
and is therefore unable to rise. One frees the 'Eternal Man' the
other only his memories. The 'Female' or the 'Sexual Garments'
as we have seen in Swedenborg's heavenly memories, are
limited and thus inferior to the creative mind. Since the
memories are fixed in the mind and are also limited to an
individual environment and upbringing they are therefore
based on selfhood, on a 'Sexual Garment'. These memories
become a 'devouring Winding sheet'.

> '6I rent the Veil where the Dead dwell:
> When weary Man enters his Cave
> He meets his Saviour in the Grave
> Some find a Female Garment there,
> And some a Male, woven with care,
> Lest the Sexual Garments sweet
> Should grow a devouring Winding sheet.'31

The man who meets his 'Eternal Man' as Saviour in the
'Grave' and rises, leaving all his linen clothes behind, is
similar to the butterfly who flies away leaving the chrysalis
behind. But the man who finds only the garments or his
natural memories in the 'Grave' is still, like the worm, bound
to the earth. Though the latter has risen from the 'Grave', he
is still, like Swedenborg, 'sitting at the tomb'; in other words
he is still bound to earth or his fixed natural memories. In this
case the cycle of creation turns into the cycle of 'generation of
decay' because it ends in the same place from which it started.
In other words it starts in infancy when man is weak like a
worm on a leaf bound to its mother-nature, and it ends with
the same weak character who is like an 'innocent old man' or
a 'worm of sixty winters'. The same cycle of generation, as we
have seen before, occurs in 'The Argument' of *The Marriage*.
It starts with the Urizenic character of Rintrah and ends with
the same character as in the illustration No. 8 the son rebels

against his tyrannical father and then becomes himself the tyrant. All this indicates that taking the limited natural memories or selfhood instead of the 'Eternal Man' leads to the same dead end where the 'worm' is still 'weaving in the ground':

> '¹⁵The Door of Death I open found
> And the Worm Weaving in the Ground:
> ¹⁶Thou'rt my Mother from the Womb,
> Wife, Sister, Daughter, to the Tomb,
> Weaving to Dreams the Sexual strife
> And weeping over the Web of Life.'³²

The 'Eternal Man' is martyr to the 'Female veil' or his limited memories. He flees from existence and life to the non-existence of his passive memories (see illustration No. 7). Thus the world of reality is dead in the eyes of the passive beings; only their own limited and passive memories are living:

> '⁷One Dies! Alas! the Living & Dead,
> One is slain & One is fled.'³³

In illustration No. 7 there are two children and the traveller, who is astonished at the crime that has been committed by one child upon the other. One child is slain and the slayer is fleeing towards the forest of passive memories. The child slain on the ground represents the active and creative character, and the character in flight represents the passive character who flees back to his passive memories.³⁴

Beneath illustration No. 7 the traveller or the artist asks:

> 'What are these? Alas! The Female Martyr,
> Is She also the Divine Image?'³⁵

The poet regrets that man has become the victim of his passive memories or 'Female veil'. The answer to the question 'Is She also the Divine Image?' must accordingly be negative. Since creation is God descending according to the weakness of man, and the passive memories are the weak part of man, therefore man descends or falls by his limited and fixed memories.

The passive character who endeavours to discover 'truth' in

his own limited memories seeks his liberty in a wrong direction. He is blind to the world of reality. In illustration No. 9 this passive reasoner wants to flee to the 'moon' because it is the only direction in which he can go. He cannot face the world of reality. Whenever the passive character enters into the world of reality or 'Time's Ocean' he feels that he is drowning and calls 'Help! Help!' (see illustration No. 10).

When the mind stops creating then the 'Perceptive Organs' become closed: 'Perceptive Organs closed, their Objects close', and man cannot see anything except the impressions which he has received through his five senses. In illustration No. 11, the 'Aged Ignorance', there is an old man and a winged child. The old man represents passivity and the winged child creativity. The man faces towards the west and the child towards the rising sun in the east. The man restrains the child from moving towards the sun by clipping his wings. This action represents the negation of the creative mind by the passive reasoner who desires to rectify everything according to his own fixed outlook. The glasses that the aged man is wearing perhaps represent this fixed outlook, and he is apparently blind. When the creative mind becomes passive the eyes in fact become blind because they are able to see only prior perceptions. The passive or fallen man, then, is vengeful to others. His division from the rest of existence and his parasitical nature starve the rest of society (illustration No. 12). Here, where the father and his children are apparently starving, the following question appears:

'Does thy God, O Priest, take such vengeance as this?'

And to further the bitterly ironical comment on the priest's promise of heaven in exchange for bodily suffering, the children in illustration No. 13 are sitting at their father's death-bed fearfully watching his soul rise up to heaven.

In *The Keys to the Gates* the following lines correspond to illustrations Nos. 12 and 13.

> '12And in depths of my Dungeons
>   Closed the Father & the Sons.
> 13But when once I did descry
>   The Immortal Man that cannot Die,'[36]

The mind becomes passive when man halts creation, or the traveller falls asleep and is lost when he stops his travelling. To prevent himself from falling asleep man must create or carry on his journey of active life (see illustration No. 14). Beneath this illustration the following statement appears:

'The Traveller hasteth in the Evening.'

The word 'traveller' is the key word in this statement and indeed in the whole context of *The Gates of Paradise*. It is the symbol of the active man as opposed to the passive. Illustration No. 14 corresponds to illustration No. 15 and, like the ' "Glad Day" ', they show two opposite directions. In illustration No. 14 the 'Traveller' (like Albion) hurries forwards but in No. 15 the old and weary traveller (like the moth) moves backward and enters through 'Death's Door' which, as I have mentioned before, means returning to his natural memories or 'Cave'. The 'Evening' apparently represents the final stage of daily work of the traveller. When this occurs he looks forward to carrying on his journey, in contrast to the passive and blind character who returns to the stage from which he had started his journey:

> '14Thro' evening shades I haste away
> To close the Labours of my Day.
> The Door of Death I open found
> And the Worm Weaving in the Ground:'37

The only power which guides the poet in his journey is Imagination or 'Eternal Man'. Creative imagination can distinguish the 'Door of Death' from the 'Immortal Man', and the 'worm' from the 'plow' or labour:

> 'As the plow follows words, so God rewards prayers.
> The rat, the mouse, the fox, the rabbet watch
> the roots; the lion, the tyger, the horse, the elephant
> watch the fruits.'38

The passive man cannot see the future and so he sees the past, the night instead of the dawn and sunrise, the root instead of the fruit of the tree.

4. THE CREATION OF FALLEN MAN

In the *Book of Urizen* Blake illustrates the psychology of the Urizenic mentality. He explains how Urizen's mind is being formed by limited sense-perception and is then divided from the rest of existence by its creating an individual or solitary place for itself. The term 'Urizen', as we have noted before, means 'your reason' because the world of Urizen, that is to say, his wisdom, laws, love, desire, truth, peace, compassion and pity are all the products and reflection of his own limited environment. All these impressions are fixed in his mind and what his reason can see is only the ratio of two things: one is the reflection of impressions from his own limited environment and the other is outside society. His reason or mind is fixed between these two spheres. The passive mind which is formed by the limited impressions can see only the elements that it has already perceived. For from a 'perception of only 3 senses or 3 elements none could deduce a fourth or fifth'.[39]

Since the knowledge and discoveries of passive reason are based on the principle of sense-perception and are thus limited to a personal background, the experience of other people is therefore for it something abstract and inaccessible. Thus Urizen's knowledge and discoveries are 'self-clos'd'; and, for the passive reasoner, everything outside himself is in 'eternity', which is an ironical name for the unknown, for that which is excluded from his 'self-closed' knowledge:

> 'Lo, a shadow of horror is risen
> In Eternity! Unknown, unprolific,
> Self-clos'd, all-repelling: what Demon
> Hath form'd this abominable void,
> This soul-shudd'ring vacuum? Some said
> "It is Urizen." But unknown, abstracted,
> Brooding, secret, the dark power hid.'[40]

Although sense-perception is limited and passive it has nevertheless a devouring nature. Urizen is an unprolific character who feeds on other beings. Passive sense-perception draws in all kinds of things in silent activity and tormenting passions:

> 'Dark, revolving in silent activity:
> Unseen in tormenting passions:

> An activity unknown and horrible,
> A self-contemplating shadow,
> In enormous labours occupied.'[41]

The impressions formed by the limited sense-perception in Urizen lack form. They are poured in and piled up in the dark and unknown spaces in the memory. The 'wood', 'forest', 'wilderness' and 'chaos' represent the passive memories. When Urizen like Tiriel is frightened he flees back to the woods. In other words he is like a frightened child who seeks refuge in the bosom of his natural memories. As the forests are dark, closed and unknown so are the passive memories. The traveller might easily lose his way in the dark forest as he does in the comparable condition of his passive memories:

> 'But Eternal beheld his vast forests;
> Age on ages he lay, clos'd, unknown,
> Brooding shut in the deep; all avoid
> The petrific, abominable chaos.'[42]

The mind of Urizen is sunk and hidden in this chaos. He labours in darkness and utters his laws from the depths of dark solitude. All this is rolling round the 'Eternal Man' or creative mind as a big wheel turns round a small wheel underneath:

> 'His cold horrors silent, dark Urizen
> Prepar'd; his ten thousands of thunders,
> Rang'd in gloom'd array, stretch out across
> The dread world; & the rolling of wheels,
> As of swelling seas, sound in his clouds,
> In his hills of stor'd snows, in his mountains
> Of hail & ice; voices of terror
> Are heard, like thunders of autumn.'[43]

The 'thunder' is peculiar to the Urizenic character of Rintrah. Urizen lives by terror and war. Blake's 'wheels' and 'mill' are, as I have noted before, the symbols of the rigid social system in which the wheel of 'Heaven' rolls over 'Hell' where Albion 'labour'd at the Mill with Slaves'.[44] Urizen himself is created by the principle of sense-perception, and he forms his own particular 'Earth', 'Heaven' and 'Immensity' according to the same principle:

> 'Earth was not: nor globes of attraction;
> The will of the Immortal expanded
> Or contracted his all flexible senses;
> Death was not, but eternal life sprung.'[45]

This so-called eternal life springs from fixed memories. What Urizen sees are only his own fixed and internalized impressions against the creative mind. He sees the immovable rocks rather than the moving sea. He discovers 'immensity' in his own abstract memories rather than in reality. In other words he looks backward rather than forward:

> 'The sound of a trumpet the heavens
> Awoke, & vast clouds of blood roll'd
> Round the dim rocks of Urizen, so nam'd
> That solitary one in Immensity.'[46]

Urizen is mentally asleep among his fixed memories. 'Urizen laid in a strong sleep.' His impressions formed by sense-perception enclose him inside themselves as a 'womb' encloses a baby.

> 'And a roof vast, petrific around
> On all sides he fram'd, like a womb.'[47]

Inside, the womb is deep, dark and burning. It is 'nature's wide womb' which does not create, an immense void which can only devour and consume. Urizen, from his subjection to fixed memories, is associated with beast, bird, fish and serpent, the natural being of limited mentality:

> '. . . he strove in battles dire,
> In unseen conflictions with shapes
> Bred from his forsaken wilderness
> Of beast, bird, fish, serpent & element,'[48]

Like a beast, Urizen sees only the inside of his cave or, like a fish, only what exists in the water. The fish can only live in water and likewise Urizen can only live in his natural memories.

The Urizenic character by returning to 'Nature's womb' divides himself from the rest of existence and instead creates his own 'immensity' within the womb. In this world of immensity he sees the sun and moon. He discovers his worlds in the endless abyss of his five senses. The creative man sees the rising sun in reality but Urizen sees the shadow or abstract reflection of the sun through the 'glasses' of his predilections.

> 'Thus the Eternal Prophet was divided
> Before the death image of Urizen;
> For in changeable clouds and darkness,
> In a winterly night beneath,
> The Abyss of Los stretch'd immense;
> And now seen, now obscur'd, to the eyes
> Of Eternals the visions remote
> Of the dark separation appear'd:
> As glasses discover Worlds
> In the endless Abyss of space, . . .'[49]

Urizen, then lives in parasitic isolation in the 'womb' of 'Enitharmon' or society. Enitharmon is sick of having this 'worm' in her 'womb', as the 'Rose' in the *Songs of Experience* is sick of the 'invisible worm'.[50]

> 'A time passed over: the Eternals
> Began to erect a tent,
> When Enitharmon, sick,
> Felt a Worm within her womb.'[51]

It is to be a 'worm of sixty winters creeping on the dusky ground':

> 'Yet helpless it lay like a Worm
> In the trembling womb
> To be moulded into existence.'[52]

When the worm was moulded into existence it first appeared as Tiriel:

> '. . . Urizen sicken'd to see
> His eternal creations appear,
> Sons & daughters of sorrow in mountains
> Weeping, wailing. First Tiriel appear'd.'[53]

But this helpless worm in the 'womb' of Enitharmon is different from the helpless worm which is being nursed by the 'clod of clay'. The latter finally becomes useful 'for the Earthworm renews the moisture of the sandy plain'.[54] But the former grows and turns into a poisonous serpent or a harmful being. Its harmfulness springs from its parasitic nature.

> 'All day the worm lay on her bosom;
> All night within her womb
> The worm lay till it grew to a serpent,
> With dolorous hissings & poisons
> Round Enitharmon's loins folding.'[55]

The Urizenic character grows bodily but mentally remains like a worm or baby in its mother's bosom. In other words it outwardly resembles a man but mentally or psychologically is infantile. This personality is represented by the 'man Child'. In appearance he is an adult but his inner being is an undeveloped sorrowful child who continually seeks maternal attention. He is like a worm within Enitharmon's womb.

> 'Coil'd within Enitharmon's womb
> The serpent grew, casting its scales;
> With sharp pangs the hissings began
> To change to a grating cry:
> Many sorrows and dismal throes,
> Many forms of fish, bird & beast
> Brought forth an Infant form
> Where was a worm before.

> 'The Eternals their tent finished
> Alarm'd with these gloomy visions,
> When Enitharmon groaning
> Produc'd a man Child to the light.'[56]

The creative mind in the 'man Child' is crushed by being kept undeveloped. The personality of such a character is therefore a mere shadow of passive memories. Blake calls such a personality the 'Human shadow':

> 'A shriek ran thro' Eternity,
> And a paralytic stroke,
> At the birth of the Human shadow.'[57]

The 'Human shadow' represents garments or natural memories which are found in the 'grave' by the passive reasoner. The 'Human shadow' and the 'Human abstract' of the *Songs of Experience* are thus the same thing. The 'Human shadow' is human in appearance but like a serpent inside, seemingly human but poisonous and harmful in his social relationship.

The 'sneaking serpent' who 'walks in mild humility' in 'The Argument' of *The Marriage* also represent this sort of personality. The helpless worm, thus, turns into a serpent in Urizen but becomes a useful being in the bosom of the 'clod of clay'. Urizen contrasts with the 'clod of clay'.

In the symbol of a 'man Child' the 'Child' is the creative personality which is bound by the passive and jealous 'man'. When the child is born into Enitharmon or society he is taken and chained by Urizen. Everybody is born a child and is thus potentially creative but his social environment and upbringing can make him passive. In a society which is ruled by the Urizenic mentality the child's mind is formed according to that of Urizen.

> 'They took Orc to the top of a mountain.
> . . . .
> They chain'd his young limbs to the rock
> With the Chain of Jealousy
> Beneath Urizen's deathful shadow.'[58]

'Orc' is the symbol of the creative child or man. In the passive Urizenic character he is chained and imprisoned underneath his natural memories. In other words Urizen is the jealous father of Orc or the child. But in the creative man Orc or the child is freed from social bondage. Here the child is the father of the passive man. Every man was a child and every child is born free, but passivity and bondage were created. Shelley's Prometheus Unbound also, perhaps, corresponds to the symbol of the freed Orc in Blake.

Orc, like Rintrah, is a 'twofold being': one aspect is like the prophetic character and the other is the Urizenic character. If the 'Child' is freed from the Urizenic natural man, then Orc becomes a creative or prophetic character. But, if the 'Child' is chained by the natural man, or the creative mind is imprisoned by limited memories, then Orc becomes weak and helpless in his subjection. This passive character is represented by 'Urizen and Orc' who corresponds to the 'man Child':

> 'But Los encircled Enotharmon
> With fires of Prophecy
> From the sight of Urizen & Orc.'[59]

Urizen chains the 'Child' or Orc in a 'Web' which is called 'The Net of Religion'.

> 'Till a Web, dark & cold, throughout all
> The tormented element stretch'd
> From the sorrows of Urizen's soul.
> . . . .
> None could break the Web, no wings of fire,
>
> 'So twisted the cords, & so knotted
> The meshes, twisted like to the human brain.
>
> 'And all call'd it The Net of Religion.'[60]

5. 'ENITHARMON SLEPT EIGHTEEN HUNDRED YEARS. MAN WAS A DREAM!'

In the books of *Europe* (1794) and *The Song of Los* (1795), which includes *Africa* and *Asia*, the worm is the symbol of the passivity formed by sense-perception. Both *Europe* and the *Song of Los* illustrate the psychological condition of the fallen society. The poet's tone is satirical. *Europe* begins with mockery of the 'Cavern'd Man' as opposed to true Man or 'Poetic Genius':

> ' "Five windows light the cavern'd Man: thro' one he
>   breathes the air;
>   "Thro' one hears music of the spheres; thro' one the
>   eternal vine
>   "Flourishes, that he may receive the grapes; thro' one
>   can look
>   "And see small portions of the eternal world that ever
>   groweth;
>   "Thro' one himself pass out what time he please; but he
>   will not,
>   "For stolen joys are sweet & bread eaten in secret
>   pleasant."
>
> So sang a Fairy, mocking, as he sat . . . upon the table
>   and dictated EUROPE.'[61]

The 'stolen joys' are the impressions formed by the senses in the mind of the passive person. These natural impressions are sweet because they are, as we have seen before, the source of everything that is important for the passive personality or 'Cavern'd Man'. They are his joy and food, but are 'stolen' because they are not based on his own energy. The 'bread' is 'pleasant' because it is 'eaten in secret', conveying the kind of life that passive man pursues. He lives in enjoyable secrecy. The 'dark secret love' in the *Songs of Experience* seems to convey the same idea.

The world of reality appears dead to the 'Cavern'd Man'. His natural memories form his world, which seems to him the only living world.

' ". . . tell me, what is the material world, and is it dead?" '

asks the poet.

The Fairy who dictates *Europe* to the poet answers:

' ". . . I will write a book on leaves of flowers,
    "If you will feed me on love-thoughts & give me now
        and then
    "A cup of sparkling poetic fancies; so, when I am tipsie,
    "I'll sing to you to this soft lute, and shew you all alive
    "The world, where every particle of dust breathes forth
        its joy." '[62]

Here Blake satirizes the shallowness of sense-perception. The poet sees that 'every particle of dust breathes forth its joy'. The material world is not dead but its life depends on that of the organs which perceive it. The sun, for example, seemed dead to Swedenborg.

'It follows that the one Sun is living and that the other Sun is dead, also that the dead Sun itself was created by the living Sun from the Lord.'

Blake wrote beneath the passage: 'How could Life create death?'[63]

The passive personality, with eyes fixed on his limited impressions, can see nothing but his own static memories. The passive mind is like a tree whose roots are in the air instead of beneath the earth:

> ' "My roots are brandish'd in the heavens, my fruits in
>   earth beneath
> "Surge, foam and labour into life, first born & first
>   consum'd!
> "Consumed and consuming!⁶⁴" '

'Consuming' conveys the devouring character of the passive
personality. This was apparently the characteristic of the
European monarchs of the time. The voice of Orc or the
revolutionary character who has been corrupted by his passive
memories is heard in *Europe*:

> ' "Sitting in fathomless abyss of my immortal shrine
> "I seize their burning power
> "And bring forth howling terrors, all devouring fiery
>   kings,
> "Devouring & devoured, roaming on dark and desolate
>   mountains,
> "In forests of eternal death, shrieking in hollow trees.
> "Ah mother Enitharmon!" '⁶⁵

Orc is like the sun which must either shine or sink and become
dark, changing from a prolific to a devouring state. The
'forests of eternal death' suggest the passive natural memories.
Orc flees back to the forest or his natural memories. He is a
weary traveller, like Tiriel.

> ' "For I am faint with travel" '⁶⁶

This fainting character of Orc is selfish and jealous, negating
creation and binding the 'infinite with an eternal hand'. He
is jealous of his children and does not want them to take his
place. He asks Mother Enitharmon:

> ' "O mother Enitharmon, wilt thou bring forth other
>   sons?
> "To cause my name to vanish, that my place may not be
>   found, . . ." '⁶⁷

The creative character of Orc was thus put in repose by the
'Shadowy Female' of his natural memories. He slept in the
bosom of Mother Enitharmon like a worm in the womb of
nature. Enitharmon lives in night because her creative son

Orc is fallen. In other words, when the sun sets the night comes:

> ' "Now comes the night of Enitharmon's joy!" '

It is the night of society's joy. The ruling philosophy of the age is the rationalist philosophy, or 'Woman' who dominates society with her 'Female Will' or self-interest. The poet ironically asks:

> ' "Who shall I call? Who shall I send,
> "That Woman, lovely Woman, may have dominion ?" '[68]

'Woman' is the symbol of passive memories or selfhood, and selfhood cannot remove selfhood. Therefore Rintrah, or the prophetic character, is called on to save Orc from the domination of 'Woman':

> ' "Arise, O Rintrah, thee I call! & Palamabron, thee!
> "Go! tell the Human Race that Woman's love is Sin;
> "That an Eternal life awaits the worms of sixty winters
> "In an allegorical abode where existence hath never
>   come.
> "Forbid all Joy, & from her childhood shall the little
>   female
> "Spread nets in every secret path." '[69]

The 'worms of sixty winters' convey the passive and Urizenic character similar to that of Tiriel. Here the rise of Rintrah, seems to refer to the revolutions of the eighteenth century.

> ' "Arise, my son! bring all thy brethren, O thou king of
>   fire!
> "Prince of the sun!
> . . . .
> "And thine eyes rejoice because of strength, O Rintrah,
>   furious king!" '[70]

The 'lovely jealous Ocalythron' represents the jealous Queen, corresponding to the 'furious King'. One Urizenic character has been replaced by another Urizenic character. The creative character of Orc is put into a state of sleep and the 'night of Enitharmon's joy' still goes on.

It is now the eighteenth century and Enitharmon or society,

having slept for eighteen hundred years, is shaken by the French Revolution:

> 'Enitharmon slept
> Eighteen hundred years. Man was a Dream!
> The night of Nature and their harps unstrung!
> She slept in middle of her nightly song
> Eighteen hundred years, a female dream.'[71]

Man dreamed in his natural memories age after age. Enitharmon or society was divided into two 'stationary orbs' or into 'Heaven' and 'Hell'. The revolutions did not help those in 'Hell' but served the interests of those in 'Heaven'. 'Heaven' was like a mighty wheel turning over the smaller wheel or 'Hell':

> '. . . man fled from its face and hid
> In forests of night: then all the eternal forests were divided
> Into earths rolling in circles of space, that like an ocean
>   rush'd
> And overwhelmed all except this finite wall of flesh.
> Then was the serpent temple form'd, image of infinite
> Shut up in finite revolutions, and man became an Angel,
> Heaven a mighty circle turning, God a tyrant crown'd.'[72]

The sleeping Enitharmon then becomes aware of the universal laws of Newton:

> 'A mighty Spirit leap'd from the land of Albion,
> Nam'd Newton: he seized the trump & blow'd the enormous blast!'[73]

Enitharmon is woken by the 'trump' of Albion. Newton's philosophy and his laws are well suited to the mechanical system of society. They fit so comfortably into the existing system that Enitharmon is not even aware that she has been sleeping:

> 'Then Enitharmon woke, nor knew that she had slept;
> And eighteen hundred years were fled
> As if they had not been.'[74]

Despite all these changes the selfhood or the 'worms of sixty winters' still feed in the bosom of Enitharmon. The weak and needy 'Earth-worm' calls to Enitharmon for help, but she does not pay attention to it. She instead invokes Ethinthus or her passive memories:

> ' "Arise, Ethinthus! tho' the earth-worm call,
> "Let him call in vain, . . ." '[75]

Ethinthus is the queen of waters, who shines in the sky. She, perhaps, corresponds to the ' "starry floor,/The wat'ry shore" ' which starts the *Songs of Experience*. Enitharmon, ignoring the call of the weak 'Earth-worm', comforts her 'fainting soul' by sweet Ethinthus:

> ' "Ethinthus! thou art sweet as comforts to my fainting soul,
> "For now thy waters warble round the feet of Enitharmon." '[76]

The selfish Urizenic characters and the condition of hopelessness have caused Enitharmon to become weak and faint.

The situation in France and Europe and the reign of terror after the French Revolution overshadowed the 'Island white'.[77] It brought further repressive laws in England passed by a fearful and suspicious government:

> 'Every house a den, every man bound: the shadows are fill'd
> With spectres, and the windows wove over with curses of iron:
> Over the doors "Thou shalt not", & over the chimneys "Fear" is written: . . . '[78]

In May 1792 The Royal Proclamation 'against Divers Wicked Seditious Writings' foreshadowed the prosecution of radical publicists. 'Paine and his printer were prosecuted after the second part of *The Rights of Man*'.[79] Blake was almost certainly compelled to cancel the publication of the remaining books of his poem *The French Revolution*, a proof copy of which (the first book) was dated 1791. It was not because he had changed his mind about the French Revolution, but because a strong tide of counter-revolutionary feeling among the propertied class forced radicals to be more cautious, and either Blake or his printer, Joseph Johnson, may well have felt that to print this poem was too risky a venture.

When Blake etched *Europe*, the leaders of the London Corresponding Society were awaiting trial. 'The shadows of the censor and the spy lay across the page; and Blake knew it.'[80] Therefore he had to use such symbols as the 'worm of sixty winters' or 'Tiriel' for George III and Rintrah for Pitt, and the 'earth-worm' to represent the wretched and needy people.

In *The Song of Los* the poet satirically symbolises the coming of the abstract philosophy of the 'Five Senses' to Africa and Asia:

> 'Adam stood in the garden of Eden
> And Noah on the mountains of Ararat;
> They saw Urizen give his Laws to the Nations
> By the hands of the children of Los.'[81]

The 'children of Los' represent the false prophetic characters who are ruled by Urizen. They are sent to Africa and Asia to propound the abstract philosophy of 'Five Senses':

> 'Adam shudder'd! Noah faded! black grew the sunny African
> When Rintrah gave Abstract Philosophy to Brama in the East.'[82]

Urizen gives laws and religion according to his limited impressions formed by passive sense-perception. This mechanical system manifests itself in the philosophy of Newton and Locke:

> 'Thus the terrible race of Los & Enitharmon gave
> Laws & Religions to the sons of Har, binding them more
> And more to Earth, closing and restraining,
> Till a Philosophy of Five Senses was complete.
> Urizen wept & gave it into the hands of Newton & Locke.'[83]

Blake criticizes Newton and Locke because their philosophy encourages passive memories which act against the creative and active mind or personality. The 'Abstract Philosophy' and the 'Philosophy of Five Senses' which governs laws and

Religion are one and the same. The Kings of Asia and Africa and the priest have built their heavens on the ruins of their people. In *Asia* the 'mortal worms' represent the passive characters who rule by the laws enforced by their own natural memories or passive life: They

> ' ". . . cut off the bread from the city,
> "That the remnant may learn to obey,
> "That the pride of the heart may fail,
> "That the lust of the eyes may be quench'd,
> "That the delicate ear in its infancy
> "May be dull'd, and the nostrils clos'd up,
> "To teach mortal worms the path
> "That leads from the gates of the Grave?" '[84]

The Urizenic character holds bread, the life line of people, in his possession. And thus he can rule according to his own wishes. He can reduce and destroy their energy and oblige them to obey his will. He destroys the creative personality or 'pride of the heart'. Once the creative personality is lost then man becomes like a mortal worm subject to something outside himself. The word 'mortal' represents the subjected or passive state of being.

Blake evaluates his characters according to their relationship with other beings or people. For this reason in one place a word is the symbol of a creative character, and elsewhere is the symbol of a passive and negative character. God or the creative personality in one condition 'is become a *worm* that he may nourish the weak . . .',[85] but in another condition he falls and becomes, like Tiriel, a 'worm of sixty winters creeping on the dusky ground'[86] which is of a devouring and destructive character. Blake does not treat his characters as fixed and predestined individuals. He treats them according to their position, that is to say, whether they are prolific or devouring. For

> 'let it be remember'd that creation is God descending
> according to the weakness of man, . . .'[87]

The difference between the worm as God and the worm as Tiriel is that the former feeds other weak beings but the latter feeds his own self upon other beings.

K

In *The Four Zoas* and *Jerusalem* the word 'worm' is used in two different forms: one is, like Tiriel, the symbol of the passive and negative character and the other the symbol of humility and selflessness.

In *The Four Zoas* (1797)

'Vala or The Death and Judgement of the Ancient Man
    a Dream of Nine Nights.'

the poet illustrates, in a long narrative, the fall of Man from creation into division. The 'Ancient Man' is Albion or the creative personality who, by turning his 'Eyes outward to Self', or creative energy, loses the 'Divine Vision'.[88] In other words he sets natural memories against the Poetic Genius or Imagination. The 'Divine Vision' or Imagination is the eternal and unchangeable power in man which creates and exercises its influence on the outside world which is changeable; whereas the fallen man subjects his mind to these limited and changeable objects. The name Enion, in *The Four Zoas*, generally stands for this fallen man; Albion calls Urizen and asks him to take possession of the 'dark sleep of Death' or his passive memories:

' "... Behold these sick'ning Spheres,
    "Whence is this voice of Enion that soundeth in my
        [ears del.] *Porches*?
    "Take thou possession! take this Scepter! go forth in my
        might,
    "For I am weary & must sleep in the dark sleep of
        Death." '[89]

The 'sleep of Death' is, as we have noted before, the division from reality and fall into passivity. Albion, by losing the 'Divine Vision', like the old man in the illustration of 'Death's Door', becomes weary and returns to his passive natural memories. When Albion returns to his natural memories his creativity is slain. Like No. 7 of *The Gates of Paradise*, passive love or 'Luvah', smites the creative love: ' "Thy brother Luvah hath smitten me, ..." '[90] After the creative personality or mind is slain, Urizen and his 'Hosts' or natural memories rise. Urizen exults in his passive memories but his joys are based on sense-perception or the 'Abyss' in which Enion or passive personality eagerly searches for prey like the 'hungry worm'.

> 'Urizen rose from the bright Feast like a star thro' the
>   evening sky,
> Exulting at the voice that call'd him from the Feast oɪ
>   envy.
> First he beheld the body of Man, pale, cold; the horrors
>   of death
> Beneath his feet shot thro' him as he stood in the Human
>   Brain,
> And all its golden porches grew pale with his sickening
>   light,
> No more Exulting, for he saw Eternal Death beneath.
> Pale, he beheld futurity: pale, he beheld the Abyss
> Where Enion, blind & age bent, wept in direful hunger
>   craving,
> All rav'ning like the hungry worm & like the silent
>   grave.'[91]

Inside the Abyss is 'Non Existence' or 'voidness' which draws 'Existence' inside the indefinite space. The indefinite space is full of passive natural memories which, like a shell, cover Albion or the creative mind:

> ' *"Build we the Mundane Shell around the Rock of Albion"* ',[92]

Albion can see only what is inside the 'Mundane Shell'. He is shut in and has closed himself up, and applies his creative power to his limited natural memories. He sees, as we have seen in *The Marriage*, all things 'thro' narrow chinks of his cavern'. Inside the cavern Urizen weaves his 'Atmospheres' where 'Spider' and 'Worm' work together:

> '. . . all the time, in Caverns shut, the golden Looms
>   erected
> First spun, then wove the Atmospheres; there the Spider
>   & Worm
> Plied the wing'd shuttle, piping shrill thro' all the
>   list'ning threads;'[93]

The Spider and Worm correspond to the Priest and King who collaborate together. One makes his 'Heaven' by laws of restraint and the other by 'Net of Religion'.

Urizen, by expanding his flexible senses, has built his own abstract world which is divided from the rest of existence. Enitharmon or society is suffering at the hands of this character. Los, the creative or prophetic son of Enitharmon, is mocked by the 'worm' or parasitic being:

> ' "The poor forsaken Los, mock'd by the worm, the shelly snail," '94

Here the 'worm' also suggests the natural memories which correspond to Vala. The Natural or fallen Man and Vala are the same idea. Vala, like the fallen Man or Urizen, becomes a 'worm' in the womb of Enitharmon:

> ' ". . .Vala shall become a Worm in Enitharmon's Womb". '95

The 'Worm' in the 'Womb' of Enitharmon is, like Tiriel, a harmful being, feeding and living on other beings. One of the arts of Urizen is to reduce others to poverty by his 'Words of Wisdom' which teach 'Moral Duty' or the laws of 'Good and Evil' while he himself fails to do his moral duty. Urizen reads in his book of brass in 'sounding' tones:

> ' "Listen, . . . to my voice. Listen to the Words of Wisdom,
>   "So shall [you] govern over all; let Moral Duty tune your tongue.
>   "But be your hearts harder than the nether millstone.
>   "To bring the Shadow of Enitharmon beneath our wondrous tree,
>   "That Los may Evaporate like smoke & be no more,
>   "Draw down Enitharmon to the Spectre of Urthona,
>   "And let him have dominion over Los, . . .
>   "Compell the poor to live upon a Crust of bread, by soft mild arts.
>   "Smile when they frown, frown when they smile; & when a man looks pale
>   "With labour & abstinence, say he looks healthy & happy;
>   "And when his children sicken, let them die; there are enough
>   "Born, even too many, & our Earth will be overrun
>   "Without these arts . . .
>   . . . If pale, say he is ruddy.
>   "Preach temperance: . . ." '96

Mother Enitharmon and her creative soul Los have been reduced to shadow or abstraction. The Spectre of Urthona personifies the false prophet or Urizenic character who, supposedly the shepherd or protector of Los the creative personality, has instead dominated him and compelled him to live in poverty.

Enitharmon has been thus divided and the 'Worm' or Urizenic character restrains his children, compelling and binding others to his own natural memories or 'worm'. Seeing the hypocrisy of Urizen, Orc answers in protest:

' ". . . Curse thy Cold hypocrisy! already round thy Tree
  "In scales that shine with gold & rubies, thou beginnest
    to weaken
  "My divided Spirit. Like a worm I rise in peace,
    unbound
  "From wrath. Now when I rage, my fetters bind me
    more.
  "O torment! O torment! A Worm compell'd! Am I a
    worm?
  "Is it in strong deceit that man is born? In strong deceit
  "Thou dost restrain my fury that the worm may fold
    the tree.
  "Avaunt, Cold hypocrite! I am chain'd, or thou couldst
    not use me thus.
  "The Man shall rage, bound with this chain, the worm
    in silence creep." '97

To the question: 'Am I a worm?' or 'is Man a worm?' the answer is apparently positive. In *The Four Zoas* the natural memories, the 'Worm', cause the fall of man by binding or enfolding the creative mind:

' "Man is a Worm; wearied with joy, he seeks the caves of
    sleep
  "Among the Flowers of Beulah, in his selfish cold repose
  "Forsaking Brotherhood & Universal love, in selfish clay
  "Folding the pure wings of his mind. . . ." '98

In *Jerusalem*, Blake also uses the word in this sense:

' "Why wilt thou give to her a Body whose life is but a
    Shade?

> "Her joy and love, a shade, a shade of sweet repose:
> "But animated and vegetated she is a devouring
>   worm." '[99]

The words 'Woman', 'Female', 'Vala' convey the same idea. In *Jerusalem*, the passive natural memories as opposed to the creative mind are also criticized. The passive personality or mind is, as we have seen before, an unquenchable fire and never a dying 'Worm':

> ' "... thou shalt be a Non Entity for ever;
> "And if any enter into thee, thou shalt be an Unquench-
>   able Fire,
> "And he shall be a never dying Worm, ..." '[100]

The 'Unquenchable Fire' is the fury and selfrighteousness of Urizenic man. The 'never dying Worm' represents the fixity of the passive personality. According to some rationalists, like Swedenborg, the natural memories have divine origin. All memories of man from earliest infancy even to the conclusions of life are

> 're-produced when it is well-pleasing to the Lord'.[101]

The reproduction of the memories takes place by rational power and the divine acts through this rational power:

> 'Man hath Reason and Free will, or Rationality and
> Liberty; and that these two faculties are from the Lord
> in Man.'[102]

What the passive rationalist calls Divine is the 'Worm of seventy inches long' or his passive memories:

> ' "I am your Rational Power, O Albion, & that Human
>   Form
> "You call Divine is but a Worm seventy inches long
> "That creeps forth in a night. . . ." '[103]

The 'Worm of seventy inches long' conveys the mentality whose knowledge of the divine is based on the impressions that he has formed by sense-perceptions in a limited environment. The 'Worm seventy inches long' and the 'worm of sixty winters' in Tiriel convey the same idea and are the symbol of negation. The worm of 'sixty winters' is also used in *Jerusalem*:

> . . . O mortal Man, O worm of sixty winters,'

The 'mortal Man' opposes 'Immortal Man':

> 'The Immortal Man that cannot Die.'[104]

In order to realize the full potential of Immortal Man, the worm must be cut:

> 'The cut worm forgives the plow.'

Blake lived amid negation and oppression, and personally experienced these within society. Enitharmon, Los, Orc and Rintrah must be understood in this social context. Blake's use of these symbols does not spring from mere personal fancy. He had to convey his thoughts by some hidden means or starve in open opposition to false art and social oppression. In other words, telling the truth was not without trouble. In his letter to Thomas Butts (January 10, 1802) Blake writes:

> '. . . you have so generously & openly desired that I will divide my griefs with you, that I cannot hide what it is now become my duty to explain.—My unhappiness has arisen from a source which, if explor'd too narrowly, might hurt my pecuniary circumstances, As my dependence is on Engraving at present, & particularly on the Engravings I have in hand for Mr. H.: & I find on all hands great objections to my doing anything but the meer drudgery of business, & intimations that if I do not confine myself to this, I shall not live; . . . I am not ashamed, afraid, or averse to tell you what Ought to be Told: That I am under the direction of Messengers from Heaven, Daily & Nightly; but the nature of such things is not, as some suppose, without trouble or care. Temptations are on the right hand & left; behind, the sea of time & space roars & follows swiftly; he who keeps not right onward is lost, & if our footsteps slide in clay, how can we do otherwise than fear & tremble?'[105]

The conflict is within society. It is, therefore, within the artist too. It is a conflict between true and false art. In a society

where to defend the Bible, for example, was a perilous under-
taking, it is difficult for Blake to keep to the right path without
fear, not only of physical hardship, but of losing his integrity
and turning against Man. Blake, adding 'A Song of Liberty'
(plates 25–27) to *The Marriage*, concludes:

'EMPIRE IS NO MORE! AND NOW THE LION &
WOLF SHALL CEASE.

Chorus:

Let the Priests of the Raven of dawn, no longer in
deadly black, with hoarse note curse the sons of joy. Nor
his accepted brethern—whom, tyrant, he calls free—lay
the bound or build the roof. Nor pale religious letchery
call that virginity that wishes but acts not!

For every thing that lives is Holy.'[106]

Chapter Seven

JERUSALEM

Jerusalem is the vision of society that should be brought into existence on earth. In holding this vision the poet revolts against the established social system and all its intellectual culture and wholly immoral morality. To Blake Jerusalem is not a religious fantasy or utopia. Milton attempted 'to Justify the Ways of God to Men' in *Paradise Lost* and *Paradise Regained*; repudiating this limited vision Blake has attempted to depict the tragedy in human history and to build a Paradise on earth or within society. Blake believes that freedom or the gaining of Paradise on an individual level is not really freedom but is escapism and retirement from social reality into one's own limited world of passive memories. True freedom and real Paradise must exist as a whole, that is, on a social and universal level. Blake wants to justify the ways of Jerusalem, the humane society, to men. He knows that evil is within society and that men are agents of evil, and in order to build Jerusalem or Paradise we must rise against a 'Class of Men whose whole delight is in Destroying', and build this Paradise in society materially and intellectually. Opposing Milton's pacificism and his idea of 'Divine Providence' Blake writes in his Preface to *Milton*:

> 'The Stolen and Perverted Writings of Homer & Ovid, of Plato & Cicero, which all Men ought to condemn, are set up by artifice against the Sublime of the Bible; but when the New Age is at leisure to Pronounce, all will be set right, & those Grand Works of the more ancient & consciously & professedly Inspired Men will hold their proper rank, & the Daughters of Memory shall become the Daughters of Inspiration. Shakespeare & Milton were both curb'd by the general malady & infection from the silly Greek & Latin slaves of the Sword.
>
> Rouze up, O Young Men of the New Age! set your

K*

foreheads against the ignorant Hirelings! For we have Hirelings in the Camp, the Court & the University, who would, if they could, for ever depress Mental & prolong Corporeal War. Painters! on you I call. Sculptors! Architects! Suffer not the fash[i]onable Fools to depress your powers by the prices they pretend to give for contemptible works, or the expensive advertising boasts that they make of such works; believe Christ & his Apostles that there is a Class of Men whose whole delight is in Destroying. We do not want either Greek or Roman Models if we are but just & true to our own Imaginations, those Worlds of Eternity in which we shall live for ever in Jesus our Lord.'

This passage is a concise criticism of Milton and the entire established social and philosophical system; and in this criticism, Imagination, the human identity or energy, is set up against all the abstract philosophies of Plato and others. To Blake, as we have noted before, Jesus or Lord is the 'Poetic Genius' (see K. p. 90). But the historical tragedy of England has been that the 'Poetic Genius' or Imagination has been suppressed from the beginning of English history by the influence of the Greek and Roman philosophers. The human Jesus who defended the poor masses in Jerusalem revolted against the oppression of the Roman Empire and the Jewish priests, and was therefore crucified:

'Wherefore did Christ come? Was it not to abolish the Jewish Imposture? Was not Christ murder'd because he taught that God loved all Men & was Their father & forbad all contention for Worldly prosperity in opposition to the Jewish Scriptures... Christ died as an Unbeliever...'

Blake remarks in *Annotations to Watson* (K. p. 387). Again he writes in *The Laocöon* that 'There are States in which all Visionary Men are accounted Mad Men; such as Greece & Rome: Such is Empire or Tax—See Luke, Ch. 2, V. I.' (K. p. 777.) Christ was a Visionary Man and opposed the Empire. Afterwards the teachings of Christ were perverted by importations of the philosophy of Plato and others and imported into England under the name of 'Christianity'

which supported the ruling interests against the wretched mass.
It is this Christianity that Blake doubts, questions and attacks:

> 'And did those feet in ancient time
> Walk upon England's mountains green?
> And was the holy Lamb of God
> On England's pleasant pastures seen?
>
> And did the Countenance Divine
> Shine forth upon our clouded hills?
> And was Jerusalem builded here
> Among these dark Satanic Mills?'

The answer to these questions is obviously 'No'. Since the true
teachings of Jesus are not being practised and realized within
English society Blake demands that this society be changed
and a new foundation and true Jerusalem be built:

> 'Bring me my Bow of burning gold:
> Bring me my Arrows of desire:
> Bring me my Spear: O clouds unfold!
> Bring me my Chariot of fire.
>
> I will not cease from Mental Fight,
> Nor shall my Sword sleep in my hand
> Till we have built Jerusalem
> In England's green & pleasant Land.'[1]

This is the antithesis of Milton's *Paradise Regained*, which is an
indirect response to the defeat of 1660 with the moral that we
must endure till God's good time:

> 'What wise and valient man would seek to free
> These thus degenerate, by themselves enslaved,
> Or could of inward slaves make outward free?'[2]

Milton's Paradise is a product of his limited and passive God
or Imagination, but Blake's God is unlimited and active and, as
I have noted before, 'only Acts & Is in existing beings or Men'.
(K. p. 155.) Milton sees only himself, but Blake sees a whole
society where God or Imagination must be freed both physically
and spiritually. Jerusalem, the embodiment of such a society,
should be built in 'England's green & pleasant Land'. In other
words, it is the responsibility of men and not of a metaphysical

God to change evil to good and an oppressive society to a humane one. Milton leaves the freedom of man to a God whom Blake does not see as existing in this limited sense. Blake says that we must be true to our own Imagination which alone can hold a true vision of social reality. Blake sees and experiences his existing society, and comprehends its entire system of 'dark Satanic Mills'. In *Jerusalem*, calling on people to rally their own creative power and rise against the social tyranny, he writes:

> ' "... Why stand we here trembling around
> "Calling on God for help, and not ourselves, in whom God
> dwells,
> "Stretching a hand to save the falling Man? ...
> "Seeing these Heavens & Hells conglobing in the Void,
> Heavens over Hells
> "Brooding in holy hypocritic lust, drinking the cries of
> pain
> "From howling victims of Law, building Heavens Twenty-
> seven-fold." '[3]

Some critics* have suggested that by the time Blake was writing *Milton* he had changed his views regarding Plato and other philosophers whom he had opposed, and had also abandoned his former political and revolutionary ideas. This is, as the preface to *Milton* shows, far from the truth. While writing *Milton*, Blake not only did not doubt his own vision and ideas, but on the contrary, gave them new depth and sharpness by his fuller experience of a harsh life and his dependence on such unimaginative employers as Hayley, who 'came to typify to him the perverter of Art and Truth'.[3] In his *Annotations to Sir Joshua Reynolds's Discourses* (1808) Blake writes:

> 'Having spent the Vigour of my Youth & Genius under the
> Opression of Sr. Joshua & his Gang of Cunning Hired
> Knaves Without Employment & as much as could
> possibly be Without Bread, The Reader must Expect to
> Read in all my Remarks on these Books Nothing but
> Indignation & Resentment. While Sr Joshua was rolling

---

* See, for example, Kathleen Raine, *William Blake*, Thames and Hudson, London 1970, p. 52.

in Riches, Barry was Poor & Unemploy'd except by his
own Energy; . . .'

Blake had already written or was about to finish writing his
Milton (1804–08) when he wrote these lines. Following his own
human experiences, Blake wanted to bring Milton down from
his limited Deity and abstract Paradise into social reality on
earth:

'Daughters of Beulah! Muses who inspire the Poet's Song,
Record the journey of immortal Milton thro' your Realms
Of terror & mild moony lustre in soft sexual delusions
Of varied beauty, to delight the wanderer and repose
His burning thirst & freezing hunger! Come into my hand,
By your mild power descending down the Nerves of my
right arm
From out the Portals of my brain, where by your ministry
The Eternal Great Humanity Divine planted his Paradise,
And in it caus'd the Spectres of the Dead to take sweet
forms
In likeness of himself. Tell also of the False Tongue!
vegetated
Beneath your land of shadows, of its sacrifices and
Its offerings: even till Jesus, the image of the Invisible
God,
Became its prey, a curse, an offering and an atonement
For Death Eternal in the heavens of Albion & before the
Gates
Of Jerusalem his Emanation, in the heavens beneath
Beulah.'[5]

Blake satirizes Milton's Puritan deity, the limited and passive
memories—'Daughters of Beulah'—which destroy the creative
Imagination. The 'soft sexual delusions' are passive impressions
formed by the five senses where Milton is wandering and
resting. This is the 'Paradise' of Milton. Blake tells Milton that
the 'Paradise' that man must gain is the creation of the 'Poetic
Genius' or creative Imagination which is the creative power
in man. To give priority to the impressions formed in the mind
by the senses or to associate them with Divine Providence is,
in fact, to sacrifice the creative Humanity Divine or Imagina-
tion for the passive memories which Blake calls 'the Spectres

of the Dead'. Milton sets his limited memories before Imagina-
tion and is 'pond'ring the intricate mazes of Providence, . . .'[6]

In his concept of 'Paradise' and 'Hell', Milton makes a
similar mistake to that of Swedenborg in that he sets up his
idealized limited memories as his 'Paradise'. But Blake does
not put Milton and Swedenborg on the same level. Milton
was one of the great Republican poets who was misguided by
religion: ' "Milton's Religion is the cause" ',[7] whereas Swedenborg
was a religious mineowner and monarchist. Swedenborg
attempted to justify the existing social system by the idea of
'Divine Providence' but Milton wanted to change the existing
social system by 'Divine Providence'. Milton 'welcomed the
English revolution which broke out in 1640 with the same
enthusiasm as Wordsworth welcomed the French revolution;
and, unlike Wordsworth, Milton never degenerated to be a
pensioner of the revolution's enemies'.[8] Milton instead with-
drew from politics and chose religious utopia and pacificism as
his paradise. It is the revolutionary spirit and poetic genius in
Milton which made Blake interested in him and write his
Milton as a critical work:

'Say first! what mov'd Milton, who walk'd about in
    Eternity
One hundred years, pond'ring the intricate mazes of
    Providence,
Unhappy tho' in heav'n—he obey'd, he murmer'd not,
    he was silent
Viewing his Sixfold Emanation scatter'd thro' the deep
In torment—To go into the deep her to redeem & himself
    perish?
That cause at length mov'd Milton to this unexampled
    deed,
A Bard's prophetic Song? for sitting at eternal tables,
Terrific among the Sons of Albion, in chorus solemn &
    loud
A Bard broke forth: all sat attentive to the awful man.'[9]

This is a criticism of Milton's philosophy of 'Providence'.
Blake repudiates this philosophy and its assumption that a
super-human power can interfere in history and human

societies. The philosophy of 'Providence' is essentially used to endorse the existing social systems by allocating a pre-ordained class position to all men and, above all, to distract men from their social and human responsibility. To Blake this philosophy and fixed outlook is the product of a limited and passive upbringing and of a static social system which is being repeated age after age:

> 'Rolling round into two little Orbs, & closed in two little
>   Caves,
> The Eyes beheld the Abyss, lest bones of solidness freeze
>   over all;
> And a third Age passed over, & a State of dismal woe.
> . . . .
> Within labouring, beholding Without, from Particulars
>   to Generals
> Subduing his Spectre, they Builded the Looms of Genera-
>   tion;
> They builded Great Golgonooza Times on Times, Ages
>   on Ages.
> First Orc was Born, then the Shadowy Female: then All
>   Los's Family.
> At last Enitharmon brought forth Satan, Refusing Form
>   in vain,
> The Miller of Eternity made subservient to the Great
>   Harvest
> . . . .'[10]

The 'Miller of Eternity' or Satan is the symbol of selfishness and of a ruling interest which grinds its victims in the 'Mill' of class society. Satan is 'Selfhood', the ruling class. Blake is challenging the whole system of thinking and of logic that Satan has created within the 'Abyss of the five senses'. Orc, the creative Imagination in man, is replaced by the 'Shadowy Female' or passive memories. The knowledge which is based on limited impressions and passive memories is not true knowledge. The passive thinker or rationalist discovers in his own world different conditions and qualities of life. Then he looks outside the world or society and sees the same different conditions and qualities of life there. The passive reasoner's

logic says that since the world outside seems the same as the
world inside therefore the world outside is the reflection and
product of the world inside which, to the passive thinker, is
the world of 'Eternity': 'Within labouring, beholding Without,
from Particulars to Generals subduing his Spectre'. By these
passive discoveries, the 'Miller of Eternity' has built the
'Looms of Generations' which as a 'Satanic Mill' rolls over
eternally. The 'Looms of Generations' represents the whole
philosophical system of the ruling interests who make 'Moral'
laws for others from their own limited interest and outlook.
These 'moral' laws are the characteristic of class society where
the ruling interests, while living amid flesh or materialism,
deny others enjoyment of the material world:

> ' "Ah weak & wide astray! Ah shut in narrow doleful
>   form,
> "Creeping in reptile flesh upon the bosom of the ground!
> "The Eye of Man a little narrow orb, clos'd up & dark,
> "Scarcely beholding the great light, conversing with the
>   Void;
> "The Ear a little shell, in small volutions shutting out
> "All melodies & comprehending only Discord and
>   Harmony;
> "The Tongue a little moisture fills, a little food it cloys,
> "A little sound it utters & its cries are faintly heard,
> "Then brings forth Moral Virtue the cruel Virgin
>   Babylon.
> "Can such an Eye judge of the stars? . . ." '[11]

The answer to this question is negative. When man is confined
within the ratio of good and evil or love of God and love of
flesh, then the 'Eye' of Imagination becomes blind and cannot
distinguish the stars from the lamps. Milton's Imagination falls
when he sets the love of God against the love of flesh. The
falling star, in Blake's painting for *Milton*, symbolizes the
mental state of Milton. The God who is set against the material
world and love of woman is, to Blake, non-existence or 'Void'.
'Every thing that lives is holy'; but the negation of living
things, or their abstraction from the material world, is unholy
and cruel. This cruelty is peculiar to Babylon, the class society
which destroys Jerusalem. Babylon negates and restrains

Imagination by its 'Moral' laws, but Jerusalem frees Imagina-
tion by casting out these negative laws.

Blake attacks the philosophers together with such institutions
as the Church and the University because they teach abstract
moral laws which are outside the social and human context.
The divorce of philosophy, religion and University teachings
from the social context is deliberate and the work of the
Satanic system. Blake had noted that all these institutions
teach passive obedience to the ruling interests and regard
silence and obedience as wisdom and virtue. In *Public Address*
he writes: 'Obedience to the Will of the Monopolist is call'd
Virtue, and the really Industrious, Virtuous & Independent . . .
is driven out . . .'[12] To Blake passivity towards those who
violate human rights by physical exploitation and mental
suppression is, in fact, to accept and approve their system, and
to be a part of it. This state of obedience and silence in face of
the Satanic system is the state of sleep and death. Opposing
the 'Will of Monopolist' Blake writes:

> ' "If you account it Wisdom when you are angry to be
>   silent and
> "Not to shew it, I do not account that Wisdom, but Folly.
> "Every Man's Wisdom is peculiar to his own Indi-
>   viduality.
> "O Satan, my youngest born, art thou not Prince of the
>   Starry Hosts
> "And of the Wheels of Heaven, to turn the Mills day &
>   night?
> "Art thou not Newton's Pantocrator, weaving the Woof
>   of Locke?
> "To Mortals thy Mills seem every thing, & the Harrow
>   of Shaddai
> "A Scheme of Human conduct invisible & incompre-
>   hensible.
> "Get to thy Labours at the Mills & leave me to my
>   wrath." '[13]

Blake kept his 'wrath' right up to the end of his life. His anger
was directed, as I have noted in Chapter One, against the
social and philosophical atmosphere which suffocated and
suppressed human 'Individuality' or Imagination. In his

Public Address, repudiating the selfish ruling politics at the time, Blake writes:

> 'I am really sorry to see my Countrymen trouble them-
> selves about Politics. If Men were Wise, the Most arbitrary
> Princes could not hurt them. If they are not wise, the
> Freest Government is compell'd to be a Tyranny. Princes
> appear to me to be Fools. Houses of Commons & Houses
> of Lords appear to be fools; they seem to me to be some-
> thing Else besides Human Life.'[14]

If Politics are not based on 'Human Life' then they must be based on selfish interest or money which is 'the life's blood of Poor Families' and 'The Great Satan or Reason'.[15] Only by opposition to and resentment against the Satanic social system can human Imagination or 'Individuality' exist and develop. Opposing passivity and polite obedience to the selfish system Blake remarks in his *Annotations to Reynolds* that 'The Enquiry in England is not whether a Man has Talents & Genius, But whether he is Passive & Polite & a Virtuous Ass & obedient to Noblemen's Opinions in Art & Science. If he is, he is a Good Man. If Not, he must be Starved.'[16]

Blake's argument in *Milton* is mainly based on the principle that man is the creator of all religions and philosophies but should not be enslaved by his own created mythology. Human knowledge and mythology are the products of men's creative mental activity within a specific environment. Therefore any discussion about wisdom and knowledge, including religion and philosophy, in abstraction from the social and human context is like 'conversing with the Void'.[17] In other words, knowledge outside of human experience and society is a 'Void outside of Existence'. The human society or 'Jerusalem' is 'Existence':

> 'There is a Void outside of Existence, which if enter'd into
> Englobes itself & becomes a Womb; such was Albion's
> Couch,
> A pleasant Shadow of Repose call'd Albion's Lovely Land.
> His Sublime & Pathos become Two Rocks fix'd in the
> Earth;
> His reason, his Spectrous Power, covers them above.
> Jerusalem his Emanation is a Stone laying beneath.'[18]

And 'Existence' must be recognized within a social context. Blake opposes passivity and abstraction because they teach love and brotherhood but do not practise them in society. If society is selfless, and love and brotherhood are practised, there Jerusalem or God exist. But if society is selfish—dominated by those who teach love but do not practise it—then Jerusalem is suppressed and God does not dwell there. Thus to believe in a God outside the human and social context is believing in a 'Void outside Existence' or 'Vacuum'. Blake criticizes Milton's God because he is a heaven-dwelling God, outside human experience and society. In *The Marriage of Heaven and Hell* Blake writes: 'in Milton, the Father is Destiny, the Son a Ratio of the five senses, & the Holy-ghost Vacuum!' The 'Ratio of the five senses' and 'Vacuum' blind the Eye of Imagination and fetter the Poetic Genius in man; and Blake recognizes these fetters in Milton: 'The reason Milton wrote in fetters when he wrote of Angels & God, and at liberty when of Devils & Hell, is because he was a true Poet and of the Devil's party without knowing it.'[19]

The power of Poetic Genius or Imagination in Milton is perverted by abstract teaching which sees only the 'ratio'. The 'Angels & God', which represent self-centred and Urizenic power in society, fetter Imagination in the poet and negate it from embracing 'All' or 'Infinite' in society. When Imagination is free the poet sees the wretched mass or 'Devils' and 'Hell', for Milton 'wrote at liberty' when he wrote 'of Devils & Hell'. But when Imagination is divorced from society the man falls. Criticizing Milton's retirement from 'Infinite' or society to his limited deity in *Paradise Regained*, Blake writes:

'To the weak traveller confin'd beneath the moony shade.
Thus is the heaven a vortex pass'd already, and the earth
A vortex not yet pass'd by the traveller thro' Eternity.
. . . .
Hovering over the cold bosom in its vortex Milton bent
        down
To the bosom of death: what was underneath soon seem'd
        above:'[20]

The struggle between true Man or Poetic Genius and false Man or 'Ratio' in Milton and his society is still the theme of

Blake's *Milton* and *Jerusalem*. Believing that mental conflict is an articulation of social conflict Blake attempts to solve this conflict in society first. If society is not freed from the conflict of two opposing interests, Jerusalem, the land of brotherhood, cannot be built. There are two ways, one of which leads to reality or human society, and the other leads to abstraction or nonexistence. One way leads to Blake's Jerusalem and the other to Milton's Puritan deity. One is truth or objective reality and the other is falsehood or abstraction, and man has to choose one or the other: for ' "he who will not defend Truth may be compell'd to defend/A Lie" '.[21] 'Truth' is not an abstraction, but a practical demonstration of genuine human relationships: 'Truth can never be told so as to be understood, and not be believ'd.' (Proverbs of Hell.) Again in his *Annotation to Bacon* Blake remarks:

> 'Self Evident Truth is one Thing and Truth the result of Reasoning is another Thing. Rational Truth is not the Truth of Christ, but of Pilate.' (K. p. 397.)

Milton attempted to cast out his 'Selfhood' by denouncing love of the world and taking refuge in his mental deities. To Blake, 'Selfhood' is not cast out by denouncing love of the world. This rationalism is misleading because the reasoner not only fails to cast out his 'Selfhood' but, in fact, falls back into the 'Selfhood' or passive memories which form the deity of the negative reasoner. To divorce oneself from active life and society is to create 'Selfhood' which is a 'state of **Death**'. Selfhood can be cast out and annihilated only by recognizing the principle that 'Energy is from the Body' while sacrificing self-interest for others. The material world is holy in its unity and when it is used as a means for the whole society. But it becomes loathsome and unholy when possessed by a few and used as a means of exploitation of others. But in *Milton*, the redeemed imagination of Milton the true poet sees 'Selfhood' or evil within the social system. Denouncing the moral laws of Church and priests as 'Satan's holiness' he says:

> ' "Satan! my Spectre! I know my power thee to annhilate
> "And be a greater in thy place & be thy Tabernacle,
> "A covering for thee to do thy will, till one greater comes

"And smites me as I smote thee & becomes my covering.
"Such are the Laws of thy false Heav'ns; but Laws of
    Eternity
"Are not such; know thou, I come to Self Annihilation.
"Such are the Laws of Eternity, that each shall mutually
"Annihilate himself for others' good, as I for thee.
"Thy purpose & the purpose of thy Priests & of thy
    Churches
"Is to impress on men the fear of death, to teach
"Trembling & fear, terror, constriction, abject selfishness.
"Mine is to teach Men to despise death & to go on
"In fearless majesty annihilating Self, laughing to scorn
"Thy Laws & terrors, shaking down thy Synagogues as
    webs.
"I come to discover before Heav'n & Hell the Self
    righteousness
"In all its Hypocritic turpitude, opening to every eye
"These wonders of Satan's holiness, shewing to the Earth
"The Idol Virtues of the Natural Heart, . . .'[22]

The freed Imagination in Milton revolts against the social
system and its God who 'impress on men the fear of death'. It
is this kind of God who, in the *Book of Job*, is called Satan.
Blake shows that the conflict between Imagination, the true
Man, and 'Natural Man' is within society and within Milton
himself. The 'Natural Man', while desiring and devouring
worldly riches, issues his laws of virtue and morality—'The
Idol Virtues of the Natural Heart'. Blake lets Milton's Poetic
Genius speak. From the viewpoint of this Poetic Genius the
Church and State who teach selflessness and 'Negation' of the
world are the real 'Selfhood' and negator of 'Human Existence'.
The Church and State teach men 'trembling and fear', but
Poetic Genius, the true Man, teaches men 'to despise death'
and to 'scorn' the 'Laws & terrors, shaking down' the 'webs'
of the ruling interests, the 'Natural Heart'. Attacking the
hypocrisy and selfishness of the Church and her state Blake
writes in *A Vision of the Last Judgment*:

'Men are admitted into Heaven not because they have
curbed & govern'd their Passions or have No Passions, but

because they have Cultivated their Understandings. The
Treasures of Heaven are not Negations of Passion, but
Realities of Intellect, from which all the Passions Emanate
Uncurbed in their Eternal Glory. The Fool shall not enter
into Heaven let him be ever so Holy. Holiness is not The
Price of Enterance into Heaven. Those who are cast out are
All Those who, having no Passions of their own because No
Intellect, Have spent their lives in Curbing & Governing
other People's by the Various arts of Poverty & Cruelty of
all kinds. Wo, Wo, Wo to you Hypocrites. Even Murder,
the Courts of Justice, more merciful than the Church, are
compell'd to allow is not done in Passion, but in Cool
Blooded design & Intention.' (K. p. 615.)

Swedenborg's 'Heaven', as I have shown before, is an example
of 'Negations of Passion' and 'Realities of Intellect'. Blake's
'Heaven' is a society of plenty and peace where the 'Realities
of Intellect' are appreciated in 'All' men. In other words,
Blake's 'Heaven' is not exclusive to a few 'Elect'.

Blake redeems Milton's suppressed Poetic Genius by showing
him the ways of God, not through negation of the Love of the
world, but through depicting the evil of the selfish system
which teaches self-denial while serving 'Selfhood' by living
upon others. Now Milton's 'Daughters of Memory' are
replaced by the 'Daughters of Inspiration' and the 'Ways of
God to Men' are justified by giving oneself up to 'All', the
'Children of Jerusalem':

   ' "All that can be . . . annhilated must be annihilated

     "That the Children of Jerusalem may be saved from
       slavery.

     "There is a Negation, & there is a Contrary:

     "The Negation must be destroy'd to redeem the Contra-
       ries.

     "The Negation is the Spectre, the Reasoning Power in
       Man:

     "This is a false Body, an Incrustation over my Immortal

     "Spirit, a Selfhood which must be put off & annhilated
       alway.

     "To cleanse the Face of my Spirit by Self-examination,

"To bathe in the Waters of Life, to wash off the Not
    Human,
"I come in Self-annihilation & the grandeur of Inspira-
    tion,
"To cast off Rational Demonstration by Faith in the
    Saviour,
"To cast off the rotten rags of Memory by Inspiration,
"To cast off Bacon, Locke & Newton from Albion's
    covering,
"To take off his filthy garments & clothe him with
    Imagination,
"To cast aside from Poetry all that is not Inspiration,
"That it no longer shall dare to mock with the aspersion
    of Madness
"Cast on the Inspired by the tame high finisher of paltry
    Blots
"Indefinite, or paltry Rhymes, or paltry Harmonies,
"Who creeps into State Government like a catterpiller
    to destroy;
"To cast off the idiot Questioner who is always question-
    ing
"But never capable of answering, who sits with a sly grin
"Silent plotting when to question, like a thief in a cave,
"Who publishes doubt & calls it knowledge, whose
    Science is Despair," '[23]

Passive and limited memories and abstract teachings divorced
from society and human relationships form 'Selfhood' which
must be put off by Imagination, which is the source of human
'Inspiration'. The 'rotten rags of Memory' are 'Not Human'
and any knowledge based on them is not human either. The
'Reasoner's' Knowledge is limited and negative. It is limited
because it is based on limited memories, and negative because
it sees society only from its own viewpoint. The Reasoner is
'like a thief in a cave' who stabs the journeyman, the active
one, from behind and steals from him. Imagination inspires
but abstract knowledge based on passive memories fetters
creativity. It is this selfish 'Reasoning Power' and abstract
knowledge, or the 'Spectre', which causes division in society
and war and death among men:

' "Hence arose all our terrors in Eternity; & now remem-
brance

"Returns upon us; are we Contraries, O Milton, Thou
& I?

"O Immortal, how were we led to War the Wars of
Death?

"Is this the Void Outside of Existence, which if enter'd
into

"Becomes a Womb? & is this the Death Couch of
Albion?'[24]

The answers to these questions are positive. Men were once
contraries to each other but negations were created later
within society.

'. . . the three Classes of Men take their fix'd destinations.
They are the Two Contraries & the Reasoning Nega-
tive.'[25]

The 'Elect' in *Milton* represent the ruling interest or the
'Reasoning Negative' and the two 'Contraries' represent the
redeemed and reprobate, the mass and prophet, the flock and
shepherd. All of these, the 'Contraries', are living under
suppression of the Elect—the 'Negative'—as the flock live
under the terror of the wolf. The 'Negative must be destroy'd
to redeem the Contraries'. In order that the innocent lamb can
enjoy the green and pleasant land the wolf must be destroyed.
Without providing a sense of place, purpose and security for
the people in society the building of Jerusalem is impossible.
In a society where love, justice, equality, democracy and
human rights and all moral laws are only preached and not
put into practice Jerusalem cannot exist. But if these laws and
human values were put into practice then Jerusalem or the
society of 'Contraries' would 'Exist'. To Blake fine words,
such as 'love, pity and peace', which are only spoken and not
put into practice in society are 'Abstract' and 'Non-Existence',
and those who speculate and teach about abstract human
values live in the 'Void Outside of Existence'. For 'Human-
Existence' has its own specific meaning and it should be shown
and demonstrated by action in social relationships:

' "Negations are not Contraries: Contraries mutually
    Exist;
"But Negations Exist Not. Exceptions & Objections &
    Unbeliefs
"Exist not, nor shall they ever be Organized for ever &
    ever.
"If thou separate from me, thou art a Negation, a meer
"Reasoning & Derogation from me, an Objecting &
    cruel Spite
"And Malice & Envy; . . .'26

The separation of men is caused by their limited interest. One
interest negates the other but the ruling interest negates 'All',
the Jerusalem. The ruling interest has its root outside 'Himself',
what Blake considered to be the human Imagination. To fall
outside human Imagination or society is 'a Void outside
Existence', and if 'enter'd into englobes itself & becomes a
Womb' (K. p. 620). The 'Womb' represents Urizen and its
dividing system. In Urizenic society 'Heaven' seeks only to
please 'Self' by binding the people in 'Hell' and is therefore a
society of 'Negations'. But in Jerusalem, the 'Contraries
mutually Exist' by self-sacrifice and seeking to give ease for
others. The 'Emanation of the Giant Albion' can be fulfilled
and manifested only through an organic unity of men. For
'less than All cannot satisfy Man'. Man can find the sense of
place and security only among others, that is, within society,
where 'Mercy, Love, & Pity dwell'.

2. JERUSALEM THE 'RESURRECTION'

Jerusalem is the continuation of the same theme which Blake
has discussed in his early Phrophecies such as *The Four Zoas*
where he illustrated the fall of Man 'into Division & his
Resurrection to Unity'.27 The 'Division' has taken place both
in society and minds. Man lives in a split society of 'Heaven'
and 'Hell' with a split mentality and personality. The meaning
of 'Resurrection to Unity' is freedom from this state of split
mentality. Jerusalem represents the social 'Resurrection' and
without the social resurrection man cannot have a united
mind and regain his creative personality:

' "Awake! awake O sleeper of the land of shadows, wake!
      expand!
"I am in you and you in me, mutual in love divine:
"Fibres of love from man to man thro' Albion's pleasant
      land.
"In all the dark Atlantic vale down from the hills of
      Surrey
"A black water accumulates; return Albion! return!
"Thy brethren call thee, and thy fathers and thy sons,
"Thy nurses and thy mothers, thy sisters and thy
      daughters
"Weep at thy soul's disease, and the Divine Vision is
      darken'd,
"Thy Emanation that was wont to play before thy face,
"Beaming forth with her daughters into the Divine
      bosom: . . .
"Where hast thou hidden thy Emanation, lovely Jeru-
      salem,
"From the vision and fruition of the Holy-one?
"I am not a God afar off, I am a brother and friend;
"Within your bosoms I reside, and you reside in me:
"Lo! we are One, forgiving all Evil, Not seeking recom-
      pense.
"Ye are my members, O ye sleepers of Beulah, land of
      shades!" '28

The 'sleeper of the land of shadows' is the man who has fallen
from the state of unity into division, from Imagination into
limited memories and from society or 'Existence' into the land
of shadow or 'Void'. The theme of 'The Divine Image' in the
Songs of Innocence is repeated in *Jerusalem*. Blake defines his
meaning of God and society. Human society is an organic
being and the human form is divine. God is not an abstract
being but can exist and be manifested through human relation-
ships. He is a brother and friend and resides within society. To
Blake having faith in a sky God is an illusion and the sleep of
death: 'By demonstration man alone can live, and not by
faith.'29 Faith must be created in man by practical demonstra-
tion of the 'human form divine' within social relationships. In
other words, a society which is free from arrogance, self-

righteousness, suppression and exploitation of man by man is the 'Emanation' of the 'Divine'. It is to this 'Divine Vision' that Blake holds throughout his writings.

Jerusalem is the 'Emanation' of the 'Divine Vision' within society. In order to understand a nation's culture and religion we must therefore recognize them through its relationship with others. In the eighteenth century, as I have noted in Chapter Five, the philosophy of 'Reason' was proclaimed as a superior culture to the African and Asians. Before the Africans and Asians themselves started questioning the superiority of Western civilization and its philosophical systems, Blake had already questioned it. He writes in *Jerusalem*:

'I turn my eyes to the Schools & Universities of Europe
And there behold the Loom of Locke, whose Woof rages
     dire,
Wash'd by the Water-wheels of Newton: black the cloth
In heavy wreathes folds over every Nation: cruel Works
On many Wheels I view, wheel without wheel, with cogs
     tyrannic
Moving by compulsion each other, not as those in Eden,
     which,
Wheel within Wheel, in freedom revolve in harmony &
     peace.

I see in deadly fear in London Los raging round his Anvil
Of death, forming an Ax of gold; the Four Sons of Los
Stand round him cutting the Fibres from Albion's hills
That Albion's Sons may roll apart over the Nations, . . .'[30]

Blake not only opposed the selfrighteousness of 'Reason' and the British Empire of the time, but saw similar cruelties committed against humanity by Empires in the past. 'I see the Past, Present & Future existing all at once/Before me'[31] he states in *Jerusalem*. In his *Annotations to Boyd's Dante* he criticizes equally the intolerance of the Roman and Persian Empires. Boyd had written:

'Such were the effects of intolerance even in the extreme. In a more moderate degree, every well-regulated government, both ancient and modern, were *so far intolerant*, as not to admit the pollutions of every superstition and *every pernicious opinion*. It was from a regard to the morals of the people, that the Roman Magistrates expelled the Priests of Bacchus, in the first and most virtuous ages of the republic. It was on this principle that the *Persians* destroyed the *temples of Greece wherever they came.*'

Blake comments:

'If Well regulated Governments act so who can tell so well as the hireling Writer whose praise is contrary to what he Knows to be true. Persians destroy the Temples & are praised for it.'[32]

Blake opposed Empire because of its tyrannical and inhuman relationship of men with other men. The nature of cruelty and of its effects on men is the same always, all over the world, regardless of nationality. It cripples the intellectual power and ruins humanity. 'A Tyrant is the Worst disease & the Cause of all others' remarks Blake in his *Annotations to Bacon* (K. p. 402).

Jerusalem and Blake's philosophy of Imagination rise against Empire. Jerusalem and the power of Imagination defend the suppressed peoples against the exploitation which forms the driving force of all Empires. The ruling interests hide their pernicious commercial greed under the veil of religion and culture as the missionaries of love and civilization. In his *Annotations to Bacon* Blake notes the following passage:

'It is likewise to be remembered, that forasmuch as the increase of any estate must be upon the foreigner (for whatsoever is somewhere gotten is somewhere lost,) there be but three things which one nation selleth unto another: the commodity as nature yieldeth it; the manufacture; and the vecture or carriage: so that if these two wheels go, wealth will flow as in a spring tide.'

Blake writes:

'The Increase of a State as of a Man is from Internal Improvement or Intellectual Acquirement. Man is not Improved by the hurt of another. States are not Improved at the Expense of Foreigners. Bacon has no notion of anything but Mammon.'[33]

The 'Internal Improvement or Intellectual Acquirement' of a nation depends on their bodily and mental freedom. All nations, like men, equally possess creative Imagination or Poetic Genius, but they need material means and favourable social conditions to develop it. True Empire must provide peoples with means and create a favourable atmosphere for human development and not deprive them of their material needs and means for intellectual development. If Empire is based on the interest of Humanity it grows and develops eternally, but if it is based on limited interest then it falls, to leave humanity in ruins, as all Empires have done.

Blake writes in opposition to Sir Joshua Reynolds:

'The Foundation of Empire is Art & Science. Remove them or Degrade them, & the Empire is No More. Empire follows Art & Not Vice Versa as Englishmen suppose.'[34]

Blake's philosophy of Art is not separated from his social vision. Reynolds represented the art of limited memories but Blake represented the art of Imagination, the true Man. Reynolds was Royalist and a prospering figure in the Royal Society of Art. But Blake was an engraver who worked for his living and shared the insecurity and other disadvantages of the working class. They represent two different classes and two different philosophical systems. Reynolds regarded the mind as a 'barren soil' which is 'soon exhausted', whereas Blake believed that the 'Human Mind is the most Prolific of All Things & Inexhaustible'.[35] Reynolds represents the ruling interests which suppress people economically and intellectually. 'This Man was Hired to Depress Art', remarks Blake. Passive art depresses creative art in order to devalue and belittle it, on the one hand, and to exploit it on the other. This happens within society on a larger scale. Blake's Jerusalem revolts against the arrogance and exploitation of the ruling interests:

' "They mock at the Labourer's limbs: they mock at his
    starv'd Children:
"They buy his Daughters that they may have power to
    sell his Sons:
"They compell the Poor to live upon a crust of bread by
    soft mild arts:

"They reduce the Man to want, then give with pomp &
    ceremony:
"The praise of Jehovah is chaunted from lips of hunger
    & thirst." '36

The exploiter cannot exploit the labourer unless he first
destroys his creative personality, mocks at his energy and
reduces him to poverty. And all this to buy his labour cheap!

Blake's Jerusalem is neither an illusion nor based on an
idealist philosophy. He realized that evil is within society and
unless it be cast out Jerusalem cannot be built. The building
of Jerusalem is based on a radical change in social relationships
and conditions. The change is from divided class society to a
classless society of brotherhood. This brotherhood, unlike
abstract religious brotherhood, must be based on the material
conditions of life and the having of equal means for intellectual
development. Blake had no illusion that brotherhood could
exist in a society where all goods and means of life were in the
hands of a few.

The few 'Mighty Ones' control all aspects of social life:

'Satan, Worship'd as God by the Mighty Ones of the
    Earth,
    Having a white Dot call'd a Center, from which branches
    out
    A Circle in continual gyrations: this became a Heart
    From which sprang numerous branches varying their
    motions,
    Producing many heads, three or seven or ten, & hands &
    feet
    Innumerable at will of the unfortunate contemplator
    Who becomes his food: such is the way of the Devouring
    Power.'37

Jerusalem revolts against these 'Mighty Ones of the Earth'.
The 'Devouring Power' is the ruling interests who have
sprouted numerous branches 'varying their motions'. They
change governments, leaders and institutions but still remain
the body or 'Centre'. In other words, the ruling interests re-
main the same always and only the hands and jaws which
seize prey for the devouring Centre change.

Blake stresses that limited and superficial reforms do not cure social maladies. In order to cure them the 'Centre' of disease, the 'Devouring Power' must be 'cut':

> ' "The English are scatter'd over the face of the Nations: are these
> "Jerusalem's children? Hark! hear the Giants of Albion cry at night:
> "We smell the blood of the English! we delight in their blood on our Alters.
>
> . . . .
>
> "I will not endure this thing! I alone withstand to death
> "This outrage! Ah me! how sick & pale you all stand round me!
> "Ah me! pitiable ones! do you also go to death's vale?
> "All you my Friends & Brothers, all you my beloved Companions,
> "Have you also caught the infection of Sin & stern Repentance?
> "I see Disease arise upon you! yet speak to me and give
> "Me some comfort! why do you all stand silent?" '38

The merchant ships followed the Church and army who 'scatter'd over the face of the Nations'. The innocent soldiers were killed in the name of a holy war but, in fact, they lost their lives for the interests of the industrialists. War and misery are the product of the ruling interests of the 'Devouring Power'. For the 'Devouring Power', money is everything. It devours human energy and life by war and poverty; 'Satan's Wife, The Goddess Nature, is War & Misery, & Heroism a Miser'.39 Satan is guided by a self-interest opposed to organic humanity, the large single humanity embraced by Blake's concept of Jerusalem. He is the 'Devouring Power' who seeks for only his limited interest and selfish progression. In other words, his interest is divided from that of the rest of society. This division of interests hampers human progression. Opposing Sir Joshua Reynolds' idea of 'progress' and 'cultivated life' Blake writes:

> 'The Bible says That Cultivated Life Existed First.
> Uncultivated Life comes afterwards from Satan's Hire-

lings. Necessaries, Accomodations & Ornaments are the whole of Life. Satan took away Ornament first. Next he took away Accomodations, & Then he became Lord & Master of Necessaries.'[40]

A society where a few are the 'Lord & Master of Necessaries' is the society of Babylon. Blake revolts against this society and its immoral morality. Christ also opposed it, and in his address 'To the Christians' Blake writes:

> 'I stood among my valleys of the south
> And saw a flame of fire, even as a Wheel
> Of fire surrounding all the heavens: it went
> From west to east, against the current of
> Creation, and devour'd all things in its loud
> Fury & thundering course round heaven & earth.
> By it the Sun was roll'd into an orb,
> By it the Moon faded into a globe
> Travelling thro' the night; for, from its dire
> And restless fury, Man himself shrunk up
> Into a little root a fathom long.
> And I asked a Watcher & a Holy-One
> Its Name; he answered: "It is the Wheel of Religion".
> I wept & said: "Is this the law of Jesus,
> "This terrible devouring sword turning every way?"
> He answer'd: "Jesus died because he strove
> "Against the current of this Wheel; . . .'[41]

That answer could stand as Blake's epitaph.

NOTES

NOTES TO CHAPTER TWO

Page references to all citations from Blake are from *The Complete Writings of William Blake with Variant Readings*, ed. Geoffrey Keynes, London 1969.

1. *Songs of Innocence*, K. pp. 111–12.
2. *Ibid.* K. p. 112.
3. For example see E. Swedenborg, *A Treatise concerning . . . Heaven and Hell*, the chapter 'Concerning The States of Innocence of the Angels in Heaven', pp. 206–14, nos. 276–83. (Manchester 1817: originally published in London in 1758); references in all citations from *Heaven and Hell* are this edition unless stated otherwise.
4. *Songs of Experience*, K. p. 216.
5. *All Religions Are One* [Second Series], K. p. 98.
6. See, for example, 'The Little Girl Lost' and *M.H.H.*, Plates 15–17.
7. M.H.H., Plate 3.
8. *Annotations to Thornton*, K. p. 789.
9. *The First Book of Urizen*, K. p. 224.
10. *Songs of Innocence*, K. pp. 112–15.
11. See, for example, *M.H.H.*, plate 3.
12. *Tiriel*, K. p. 105.
13. *M.H.H.*, K. p. 158.
14. *Ibid.*, K. p. 121.
15. *Ibid.*, K. p. 121.
16. *Ibid.*, K. p. 121.
17. *Songs of Experience*, K. pp. 218–19.
18. *Ibid.*, K. p. 212.
19. *The First Book of Urizen*, K. p. 224.
20. *Poems From The Note-Book*, K. p. 173.
21. *Ibid.*, K. p. 172.
22. *The First Book of Urizen*, K. p. 222.
23. *M.H.H.*, K. p. 155.
24. *Ibid.*, K. p. 151.
25. *Songs of Experience*, K. p. 214.
26. *Songs of Innocence*, K. p. 111.
27. *Milton*, K. p. 488.
28. *Europe*, plate 8, K. p. 240.
29. *M.H.H.*, K. pp. 148–9.
30. *Songs of Experience*, K. p. 217.
31. *Songs of Innocence*, K. p. 117.
32. *Songs of Experience*, K. p. 212.
33. *Songs of Innocence*, K. p. 126.
34. *A Vision of The Last Judgment*, K. p. 617.
35. *Songs of Experience*, K. p. 210.
36. *Ibid.*, K. p. 213.
37. *Ibid.*, K. p. 217.
38. *M.H.H.*, K. p. 152.
39. *Songs of Experience*, K. p. 216.
40. *M.H.H.*, K. p. 151.

41. *Songs of Innocence*, K. p. 117.
42. *All Religions Are One*, K. p. 98.
43. *M.H.H.*, K. p. 155.
44. *Annotations to Lavater*, K. p. 87.
45. *M.H.H.*, K. p. 151.
46. *Ibid.*, K. p. 152.
47. *M.H.H.*, p. 151.
48. *Heaven and Hell*, p. 303, no. 368.
49. *M.H.H.*, K. p. 151.
50. See *Heaven and Hell*, chapter 'Concerning Infants in Heaven', p. 260.
51. *M.H.H.*, K. p. 152.
52. *Songs of Experience*, K. p. 215.
53. *M.H.H.*, K. p. 149.
54. *Songs of Innocence*, K. p. 124.
55. *Songs of Experience*, K. p. 213.
56. *A Vision of the Last Judgment*, K. p. 616.
57. *Ibid.*, K p. 615.
58. *Annotations to Lavater*, K. p. 80.
59. *Jerusalem*, K. p. 665.
60. *M.H.H.*, K. p. 153.
61. *Ibid.*, K. p. 153.
62. *Ibid.*, K. p. 155.
63. *Vala* K. p. 366.
64. *Annotations to Berkerley's 'Siris'*, K. p. 773.
65. *All Religions are One*, K. p. 98.
66 *Annotations to Reynolds*, K. pp. 470–1.
67. *All Religions are One*, K. p. 98.
68. *Annotations to "Poems" by William Wordsworth*, K. p. 782.
69. *Ibid.*, K. p. 782.
70. *Ibid.*, K. p. 783.
71. *The Marriage of Heaven and Hell*, K. p. 152.
72. *Annotations to Berkeley*, K. p. 775.
73. *Annotations to Lavater*, K. p. 83.
74. *A letter to Dr. Trusler 23 August 1799*, K. p. 793.
75. *M.H.H.*, K. p. 149.
76. *Vala or Four Zoas*, K. p. 281.
77. *A Descriptive Catalogue*, K. p. 581.
78. *Annotations to Reynolds*, K. p. 475.
79. *M.H.H.*, K. p. 153.
80. *M.H.H.*, K. p. 150.
81. *Milton*, K. p. 521.
82. *Milton*, K. p. 521.
83. *The Gates of Paradise*, K. p. 768.
84. *There Is No Natural Religion* [second series], K. p. 97.
85. *Ibid.*, K. p. 97.
86 *Annotations to Reynolds*, K. p. 446.
87. *Annotations to Thornton*, K. pp. 787-8.
88. *M.H.H.*, K. p. 150.
89. *Jerusalem*, K. p. 695, line 52.
90. *Annotations to Swedenborg's Divine Providence*, K. p. 131.
91. *Annotations to Reynolds*, K. p. 471.
92 *Milton*, K. p. 522.
93. *Milton*, K. p. 533.

94. *M.H.H.*, K. p. 149.
95. *Public Address*, K. pp. 594–5.
96. *Ibid.*, K. p. 600.
97. *The Laocoön*, K. p. 777.
98. *Annotations to Reynolds*, K. p. 457.
99. *A Vision of The Last Judgment*, K. p. 604.
100. *Jerusalem*, K. p. 684.
101. *Ibid.*, K. p. 685.
102. *Annotations to 'Poems' by William Wordsworth*, K. p. 782.
103. *Milton*, K. p. 484.
104. *A Vision of The Last Judgment*, K. p. 605–6.
105. *A Descriptive Catalogue*, K. pp. 565–6.
106. *Poetical Sketches*, K. p. 1.
107. *Poetical Sketches*, K. pp. 1–2.
108. *A Letter to Dr. Trusler, 23 August 1799*, K. p. 793.
109. *Poetical Sketches*, K. p. 7.
110. *Ibid.*, K. pp. 7–8.
111. *Ibid.*, K. pp. 9–10.
112. *Ibid.*, K. pp. 10–11.
113. *Poetical Sketches*, K. p. 11.
114. *Annotations to Reynolds*, K. p. 445.
115. *Tiriel*, K. p. 110.
116. *Ibid.*, K. p. 99.
117. *The Book of Thel*, K. p. 127.
118. *Vala* or *The Four Zoas*, K. p. 290.
119. *An Island In The Moon*, K. p. 44.
120. *Ibid.*, K. p. 57.
121. *An Island In The Moon*, K. p. 59.
122. *Tiriel*, K. p. 110.
123. *Vala* or *The Four Zoas*, K. p. 380.

NOTES TO CHAPTER THREE

1. See, for instance, Harold Bloom's article on 'Dialectic' In 'The Marriage' published in *English Romantics*, edited by M. H. Abrams (Oxford University Press, 1960), p. 76; D. V. Erdman, *Prophet against Empire* (Princeton 1954), p. 185 and p. 174; N. K. Nurmi, *Blake's Marriage of Heaven and Hell* (Ohio 1957), p. 29; J. M. Murry, *William Blake* (London 1933), p. 61.
2. Northrop Frye, *Fearful Symmetry, A Study of William Blake* (Princeton (1947), p. 70.
3. David E. Erdman, *op. cit.*, p. vii.
4. *Ibid.*, see, for instance, pp. 161–6.
5. D. V. Erdman, *op. cit.*, p. 160.
6. J. Bronowski, *op. cit.*, p. 47.
7. Erdman, *op. cit.*, p. 174.
8. *Ibid.*, p. 174.
9. *Ibid.*, p. 174.
10. *Ibid.*, p. 174.
11. *Ibid.*, pp. 174–5.
12. *Heaven and Hell*, *op. cit.*, p. 471, no. 543.

13. *Heaven and Hell*, p. 471, no. 543.
14. *Ibid.*, p. 471, no. 543.
15. *The Marriage of Heaven and Hell* (K. p. 148).
16. See, for instance, p. 65, no. 87; p. 86, no. 115; p. 91, no. 119; p. 128, no. 171; p. 188, no. 256; p. 189, no. 258.
17. Matt. xi. 29, 30. H.H., p. 293, no. 359.
18. *M.H.H.* (K. p. 148).
19. *A Vision of The Last Judgment* (K. p. 617).
20. K. Raine, *Blake and Tradition* (London 1969), Vol. 1, p. 8.
21. *The Note-Book* (K. p. 164).
22. *Songs of Experience* (K. p. 217).
23. *M.H.H.*, (K. p. 148).
24. *The Marriage of Heaven and Hell* (K. p. 158).
25. *Annotations to Swedenborg's Divine Love* (K. p. 92).
26. See, for instance, *Tiriel* (K. pp. 100–2) and *The Book of The* (K. pp. 129–30), and also see J. Bronowski, *op. cit.*, pp. 40–2.
27. *M.H.H.* (K. p. 149).
28. *Heaven and Hell*, p. 339, no. 412.
29. *M.H.H.*, (K. p. 149).
30. See, for example, Stewart Oakley, *The Story of Sweden* (London 1966), p. 180.
31. About 'Indra' see Jones, *Sakuntala* (London 1790), Act VII, pp. 137–55. Northrop Frye kindly wrote to me and said that he 'looked for a Hebrew source of the word once, but found nothing tangible'. He also, kindly commenting on my suggestion about the connection between Rintrah and 'the wrath of Indra', wrote saying that the connection would help to explain the association of Rintrah with India in the *Song of Los*.
32. *Milton*, p. 34 (K. p. 488).
33. *Europe*, plate 8, line 13 (K. p. 240).
34. *Annotations to Lavater* (K. p. 80).
35. *Annotations to Lavater* (K. p. 88).
36. *The Song of Los* (K. p. 246).
37. *M.H.H.* (K. p. 149).
38. E. Swedenborg, *A Treatise Concerning the Last Judgment* (London 1810: originally published in London in the year 1758), p. 67, no. 45.
39. *Ibid.*, p. 66, no. 45. See also pp. 1–28.
40. Kathleen Raine, *Blake and Tradition* (London 1969), Vol. 1, chap. 14, p. 335.
41. *Milton*, Book The Second, plate 22, line 51, p. 506.
42. *Annotations to Swedenborg's . . . Divine Providence* (K. p. 131).
43. *Ibid.*, p. 131.
44. *Ibid.*, p. 132.
45. *Ibid.*, p. 132.
46. J. Bronowski, *op. cit.*, p. 18.
47. Stewart Oakley, pp. 111–18.
48. *H.H.* p. 134, no. 180.
49. *Ibid.*, p. 135, no. 181.
50. *M.H.H.*, plate 3 (K. p. 149).
51. *The First Book of Urizen*, Chap. II, plate 4 (K. p. 224).
52. *Tiriel*, line 33 (K. p. 101).
53. *A Vision of The Last Judgment* (K. p. 604).
54. Kathleen Raine, *William Blake* (London 1970), p. 9.

55. *A Vision of The Last Judgment* (K. p. 605).
56. *Jerusalem* (K. p. 665).
57. Kathleen Raine, *op. cit.*, p. 74.
58. *A Vision of The Last Judgment* (K. p. 612).
59. *M.H.H.* (K. p. 149).
60. Martin K. Nurmi, *op. cit.*, p. 28; Kathleen Raine, *Blake and Tradition* (London 1969), Vol. 1, p. 363.
61. Martin K. Nurmi, *op. cit.*, p. 29.
62. *Ibid.*, pp. 26–7.
63. *Ibid.*, p. 25.
64. *Ibid.*, see, for example, pp. 11–14 and 15–23.
65. *Ibid.*, p. iii.
66. Nurmi, *op. cit.*, p. 28.
67. *Ibid.*, p. 26.
68. *Ibid.*, p. 28.
69. *Ibid.*, p. 31.
70. *Ibid.*, p. 31.
71. *H.H.*, p. 16, no. 18.
72. *Ibid.*, p. 17, no. 18.
73. *Ibid.*, p. 85, no. 113.
74. *Ibid.*, p. 100, no. 131.
75. *Ibid.*, p. 103, no. 135.
76. *Ibid.*, p. 153, no. 209.
77. *Ibid.*, p. 167, no. 229.
78. *Ibid.*, p. 450, no. 524.
79. *Ibid.*, p. 214, no. 283.
80. *Ibid.*, p. 508, no. 584.
81. K. Raine, *op. cit.*, p. 363.
82. *Arcana Caelestia: Or Heavenly Mysteries* (London 1825, translated from the Original Latin, first published at London in 1749), Vol. 1, no. 1366, p. 123.
83. *Ibid.*, Vol. IV, pp. 249–50, no. 3425.
84. *Ibid.*, Vol. IV, p. 351, no. 3425.
85. *Ibid.*, Vol. V, p. 314, no. 3993.
86. *Ibid.*, Vol. VII, p. 367, no. 5427.
87. *Ibid.*, Vol. VIII, p. 161, no. 6052.
88. *Ibid.*, Vol. VIII, p. 211, no. 6144.
89. *Ibid.*, Vol. VIII, p. 288, no. 6309.
90. *Ibid.*, Vol. IX, p. 536, no. 7812.
91. *Ibid.*, Vol. IX, p. 536. no. 7812,
92. *Ibid.*, Vol. II, p. 155, no. 1427.
93. *Ibid.*, Vol. II, p. 165, no. 1451.
94. *Ibid.*, Vol. II, p. 190, no. 1495.
95. *Ibid.*, Vol. II, p. 190, no. 1495.
96. *Ibid.*, Vol. III, p. 60, no. 2196.
97. *Ibid.*, Vol. III, p. 235, no. 2500.
98. *Ibid.*, Vol. III, p. 325, no. 2500.
99. *Ibid.*, Vol. III, p. 246, no. 2523.
100. *Ibid.*, Vol. III, p. 395, no. 2744.
101. *Ibid.*, Vol. IV, p. 37, no. 2950.
102. *Ibid.*, Vol. IV, p. 254, no. 3308.
103. *Ibid.*, Vol. VI, p. 118, no. 4375.
104. *Ibid.*, Vol. VI, p. 152, no. 4430.

105. *Arcana Caelestia: Or Heavenly Mysteries*, Vol. VII, p. 126, no. 5122.
106. *Milton*, Book The Second, plate 40, line 32 (K. p. 533).
107. *The Gates of Paradise* (K. p. 770).
108. *Annotations to Swedenborg's Divine Love* (K. p. 92).
109. *Annotations to Swedenborg's Divine Love* (K. p. 96).
110. *H.H.*, p. 118, no. 155.
111. *Ibid.*, p. 118, no. 155.
112. *M.H.H.* (K. p. 152).
113. *H.H.*, p. 123, no. 164.
114. *Ibid.*, p. 125, no. 167.
115. *Ibid.*, pp. 123–7, no. 162–9.
116. *Ibid.*, p. 124, no. 165.
117. *Ibid.*, p. 141, no. 192.
118. *Ibid.*, p. 117, no. 154.
119. *Ibid.*, p. 349, no. 422
120. *Ibid.*, p. 141, no. 192.
121. *Ibid.*, p. 142, no. 193.
122. *M.H.H.* (K. ed. p. 149).
123. *H.H.*, no. 9, p. 10.
124. *Ibid.*, no. 9, p. 10.
125. *New Statesman*, August 22, 1969, p. 250.
126. Kathleen Raine, *op. cit.*, Vol. I, p. 368.
127. *Ibid.*, Vol. I, p. 364.
128. *Annotations to Lavater* (K. p. 80).
129. *Ibid.* (K. p. 82).
130. *Ibid.*, p. 80.
131. *Annotations to Swedenborg's Divine Love* (K. p. 89).
132. *Blake Complete Writings* (Oxford University Press 1969) (K p. 89).
133. *Annotations to Lavater* (K. p. 77).
134. *Annotations to Berkeley* (K. p. 774).
135. K. Raine, *op. cit.*, p. 368.
136. *H.H. op. cit.*, p. 411, no. 485.
137. *Ibid.*, pp. 411–2, no. 486,
138. *Ibid.*, p. 414, no. 488.
139. *Ibid.*, p. 326, no. 396.
140. *Ibid.*, p. 327, no. 398.
141. *Ibid.*, p. 329, no. 400.
142. *Ibid.*, p. 326, no. 396.
143. *Ibid.*, p. 330, no. 400.
144. *Ibid.*, p. 331, no. 401.
145. *M.H.H.* (K. p. 149).
146. *Visions of The Daughters of Albion* (K. p. 192).
147. *Songs of Experience* (K. p. 216).
148. *H.H. op. cit.*, p. 30, no. 39.
149. *Ibid.*, p. 31, no. 43.
150. E. Swedenborg, *The Wisdom of Angels Concerning the Divine Providence*, Manchester 1820 (originally published at Amsterdam).
151. *The Book of Urizen*, reproduced in facsimile (London 1929), p. 17.
152. *The Divine Providence, op. cit.*, p. 90, no. 71.
153. *The Divine Providence, op. cit.*, p. 101, no. 79.
154. *H.H.*, p. 161, no. 218.
155. *Ibid.*, p. 366, no. 449.
156. *M.H.H.*, plates 5–6 (K. pp. 149–50). Italics are mine.

157. See, for instance, *H.H. op. cit.*, pp. 430–6, 458–9, 467, 471, 487, 498, 505 and pp. 517–20. For the word 'governor' see pp. 156–62.
158. *Ibid.*, p. 436, no. 509.
159. *Ibid.*, p. 458, no. 530.
160. *Ibid.*, p. 459, no. 531.
161. *Ibid.*, p. 467, no. 536.
162. *Ibid.*, p. 469, no. 538.
163. *Ibid.*, p. 471, no. 543.
164. *Ibid.*, p. 471, no. 543.
165. *Ibid.*, p. 471, no. 543.
166. *Ibid.*, p. 505, no. 581.
167. *Ibid.*, p. 517, no. 592.
168. *Ibid.*, p. 520, no. 595.
169. See, for instance, K. Raine, *op. cit.*, pp. 366–7.
170. *H.H.*, p. 16, no. 18.
171. *Ibid.*, p. 142, no. 195.
172. *Ibid.*, p. 143, no. 194.
173. *Ibid.*, p. 275, no. 349.
174. *Ibid.*, p. 279, no. 352.
175. *Ibid.*, p. 294, no. 360.
176. *Ibid.*, p. 299, no. 365.
177. *Ibid.*, p. 299, no. 365.
178. *Ibid.*, p. 329, no. 400.
179. *Ibid.*, p. 347, no. 420.
180. *Ibid.*, p. 497, no. 571 (see also pp. 498–9, nos. 572–5).
181. Northrope Frye *Fearful Symmetry* (Princeton 1947), p. 55. See also pp. 55–60.
182. *Ibid.*, p. 293.
183. *M.H.H.*, plates 5–6 (K. p. 150).
184. D. V. *Erdman, op. cit.*, pp. 163–4.
185. Northrope Frye, *op. cit.*, p. 134–5.
186. *A Vision of The Last Judgment.* (K. pp. 615–17).
187. *M.H.H.*, plates 21–2 (K. p. 157).
188. *Heaven & Hell*, p. 471, no. 543; see also p. 242, no. 311.
189. *M.H.H.*, plates 22–24 (K. p. 158).
190. R. W. Harris, *Romanticism and Social Order, op. cit.*, p. 155.
191. *M.H.H.*, plates 15–17 (K. p. 155).
192. *Ibid.* (K. p. 150).
193. *Ibid.* (K. p. 154).
194. *The Gates of Paradise* (K. p. 771).
195. *M.H.H.* (K. p. 150). The phrase 'A Memorable Fancy' which Blake uses as a title for plates 6–7 and the following plates in *The M.H.H.* is apparently taken ironically from Swedenborg's 'Memorable Relation'. See, for example, *The Apocalypse Revealed.* Vol. 1, pp. 565–9, no. 484.
196. *H.H.*, p. 102, no. 134.
197. *Ibid.*, pp. 164–5, no. 224.
198. *Ibid.*, p. 497, no. 571.
199. *Ibid.*, p. 500, no. 574.
200. *Ibid.*, p. 325, no. 395.
201. *Ibid.*, p. 325, no. 315.
202. *Ibid.*, p. 341, no. 413.
203. *Ibid.*, p. 329, no. 400.

204. *H.H.*, p. 339, no. 412.
205. *Ibid.*, p. 339, no. 412.
206. *Ibid.*, p. 282, no. 354.
207. *Ibid.*, pp. 329–30, n. 400.
208. *Ibid.*, p. 451, no. 525.
209. *Ibid.*, p. 497, no. 572.
210. *Ibid.*, p. 500, no. 574.
211. *Ibid.*, p. 135, no. 182.
212. *Ibid.*, p. 221, no. 290.
213. *Ibid.*, p. 433, no. 508.
214. *Ibid.*, pp. 467–8, no. 536.
215. *Ibid.*, p. 497, no. 571.
216. *Ibid.*, p. 179, no. 245.
217. *Ibid.*, p. 244, no. 312.
218. *Ibid.*, p. 282, no. 354.
219. *Ibid.*, p. 410, no. 484.
220. *Ibid.*, p. 410, no. 484.
221. *Ibid.*, p. 436, no. 510.
222. *Ibid.*, p. 438, no. 512.
223. *Ibid.*, p. 479, no. 552.
224. *Ibid.*, p. 193, no. 265.
225. *Ibid.*, p. 200, no. 269.
226. *Ibid.*, p. 202, no. 270.
227. *Ibid.*, p. 324, no. 393.
228. *Ibid.*, p. 10, no. 9.
229. *Ibid.*, p. 26, no. 35.
230. *Ibid.*, p. 176, no. 341.
231. *Ibid.*, p. 178, no. 244.
232. *Ibid.*, p. 324, no. 393.
233. *Ibid.*, p. 100, no. 131.
234. *Ibid.*, p. 502, no. 577.
235. *Ibid.*, p. 392, no. 469.
236. *Ibid.*, p. 136, no. 183.
237. *Ibid.*, p. 137, no. 183.
238. *Ibid.*, p. 138, no. 185.
239. *Ibid.*, p. 324, no. 393.
240. *Ibid.*, p. 295, no. 361.
241. *Ibid.*, pp. 508–9, no. 594–5.
242. *Ibid.*, p. 509, no. 586.
243. *Ibid.*, p. 131, no. 177.
244. *Ibid.*, p. 132, no. 179.
245. *Ibid.*, p. 132, no. 178.
246. *Ibid.*, p. 132, no. 178.
247. *Ibid.*, p. 132, no. 178.
248. *Ibid.*, p. 134, no. 180.
249. *Ibid.*, p. 135, no. 181.
250. *Ibid.*, pp. 329–30, no. 400.
251. *M.H.H.*, 'Proverbs of Hell' (K. p. 152).
252. See David V. Erdman, *Blake Prophet Against Empire* (Princeton 1954), p. 160.
253. *H.H.*, p. 379, no. 461.
254. *Ibid.*, p. 384, no. 463.

255. The contents of this chapter are similar to Locke's account of memory and his idea of 'tabula rasa'.
256. *H.H.*, pp. 429–30, no. 505.
257. *Ibid.*, p. 430, no. 505.
258. *Ibid.*, p. 363, no. 445. 'The bones of the dead'.
259. *Ibid.*, p. 379, no. 461.
260. *Ibid.*, p. 388, no. 464. Swedenborg uses words like 'cultivate', 'plough', 'seed' and 'ground' to explain his 'rational principle of man'. Thus the word 'plow' is also possibly inspired by the text of *H.H.* See, for instance, pp. 388–9, nos. 464–6.
261. *Ibid.*, p. 128, no. 171.
262. *Ibid.*, p. 327, no. 398.
263. *Ibid.*, p. 53, no. 75. See also p. 380, no. 462.
264. *Ibid.*, p. 338, no. 411.
265. *Ibid.*, p. 339, no. 411.
266. *Ibid.*, p. 339, no. 412.
267. *Ibid.*, p. 132, no. 177.
268. *Ibid.*, p. 197, no. 267.
269. *Ibid.*, p. 202, no. 270.
270. *Ibid.*, p. 202, no. 270.
271. *Ibid.*, p. 202, no. 270.
272. *H.H.*, p. 202, no. 270.
273. *The Book of Thel* (K. p. 127).
274. *Annotations to Swedenborg's . . . Divine Love and Divine Wisdom* (K. p. 89).
275. *H.H.*, pp. 143–6, no. 187–200.
276. 'Proverbs of Hell', plate 7, p. 150. Italics are mine.
277. *H.H.*, p. 128, no. 171.
278. *Ibid.*, p. 338, no. 411.
279. *M.H.H.*, plates 15–17 (K. p. 155).
280. *Ibid.*, plate 10 (K. p. 152).
281. *H.H.*, p. 100, no. 131.
282. *Ibid.*, p. 74, no. 99.
283. *Ibid.*, p. 100, no. 131.
284. *Annotations To Lavater* (K. p. 81 Aphorism 532.)
285. 'Proverbs of Hell', plate 9 (K. p. 152).
286. Letter to Dr. Trusler (1799) (K. p. 793).
287. 'Proverbs of Hell' (K. p. 151).
288. *H.H.*, p. 291, no. 358.
289. *Ibid.*, p. 291, no. 358.
290. *Ibid.*, p. 291, no. 358.
291. *Annotations to Swedenborg's. . . . Divine Love and Divine Wisdom* (K. ed. 1969, p. 89).
292. *Annotations to Lavater* (K. p. 88).

NOTES TO CHAPTER FOUR

1. *M.H.H.*, plate II (K. p. 153).
2. *H.H.*, p. 58, no. 82.
3. *Ibid.*, p. 59, no. 84.
4. *Ibid.*, p. 66, no. 87.
5. *Ibid.*, p. 67, no. 87.
6. *Ibid.*, p. 82, no. 111.

L*

7. *H.H.* p. 87, no. 115.
8. *Ibid.*, p. 91, no. 119.
9. *Ibid.*, p. 188, no. 256.
10. *Ibid.*, p. 59, no. 84.
11. *Ibid.*, p. 86, no. 115.
12. *Ibid.*, p. 68, no. 89.
13. Swedenborg's concept of the 'Grand Man' is in some ways similar to Hobbes' 'Leviathan'.
14. *H.H.*, p. 72, no. 97.
15. 'Proverbs of Hell', plate 10 (K. p. 152).
16. *H.H.*, p. 72, no. 96.
17. 'Proverbs of Hell', plate 9 (K. p. 152).
18. *Ibid.*, plate 9 (K. p. 152).
19. *H.H.*, p. 68, no. 89.
20. *Ibid.*, p. 82, no. 111.
21. *Ibid.*, p. 83, no. 111.
22. *Ibid.*, p. 81, no. 110.
23. *Ibid.*, pp. 78–9, no. 108.
24. *H.H.*, p. 78, no. 107.
25. *Ibid.*, p. 78, no. 107.
26. See, for example, *There is no Natural Religion* (K. pp. 97–8).
27. *Ibid.*, p. 97.
28. *H.H.*, p. 85, no. 112.
29. *Ibid.*, p. 272, no. 346.
30. *Ibid.*, pp. 130–1, no. 176.
31. *Ibid.*, p. 128, no. 171.
32. *Ibid.*, p. 6–7, no. 3.
33. See *Hume on Religion* (ed. by Richard Wollheim, London 1963), pp. 143–4.
34. *Ibid.*, p. 145.
35. *Ibid.*, p. 18.
36. *Ibid.*, pp. 149–50.
37. *Then She Bore Pale Desire* (K. p. 42).
38. *The Four Zoas*, Night The First (K. edition, lines 83–5, p. 266).
39. *Ibid.*, Night the Eighth, lines 469–70, p. 353.
40. *Ibid.*, Night the Eighth, lines 618–20.
41. *Jerusalem*, plate 12, lines 1–5 (K. p. 631).
42. *Ibid.*, plate 82, line 14 (K. p. 725).
43. *The Complete Poetical Works of William Wordsworth*, 'The Excursion Book First (Macmillan ed., London 1902) p. 421.
44. 'Poetical Sketches' (K. p. 1).
45. *Ibid.*, pp. 1–2.
46. *Ibid.*, p. 2.
47. *Ibid.*, p. 2.
48. *H.H.*, p. 87, no. 117.
49. *Ibid.*, p. 88, no. 118.
50. *Ibid.*, p. 90, no. 118.
51. *Ibid.*, p. 93, no. 122.
52. *Ibid.*, p. 90, no. 119.
53. 'Poetical Sketches' (K. pp. 3–4).
54. *The Complete Poetical Works of Percy Bysshe Shelley*, ed. by Thomas Hutchinson, 1845, p. 33.
55. *Ibid.*, p. 35.

56. 'Principle 7th' of *All Religions are One* (K. p. 98).
57. Northrop Frye, *op. cit.*, p. 61.
58. Sir Edward Burnett Tylor, *Religion in Primitive Culture* (Harper & Row ed., New York 1958), vol. 2, p. 61.
59. *A Vision of the Last Judgment* (K. pp. 606–7).
60. *Milton, Book the Second*, plate 32, lines 30–8.
61. Claude Levi-Strauss, *Structural Anthropology*. Translated from the French by Claire Jacobson and Brooke Grundfest Schoepf (London 1963), p. 230. I acknowledge Mr. H. Philsooph's help, who kindly suggested that I should read this book.
62. John Beer, *Blake's Humanism* (Manchester University Press 1968), p. 54.
63. *H.H.*, p. 179, no. 245.
64. *Ibid.*, p. 185, no. 254.
65. *M.H.H.*, plates 12–13 (K. pp. 153–4).
66. *H.H.*, p. 93, no. 122.
67. *Ibid.*, p. 159, no. 216.
68. *Ibid.*, p. 168, no. 229.
69. *Ibid.*, p. 185, no. 254.
70. *Ibid.*, p. 186, no. 254.
71. *Ibid.*, p. 189, no. 258.
72. *Ibid.*, p. 179, no. 246.
73. *Ibid.*, p. 180, no. 246.
74. *Ibid.*, pp. 180–1, no. 247.
75. *Ibid.*, p. 10, no. 9.
76. *Ibid.*, p. 182, no. 249.
77. *Ibid.*, pp. 182–3, no. 249.
78. *Ibid.*, p. 181, no. 249.
79. *Ibid.*, p. 183, no. 250.
80. *Ibid.*, p. 184, no. 252.
81. *Ibid.*, p. 185, no. 254.
82. Max Weber, *The Sociology of Religion*. First published in Germany in 1922.
83. *Ibid.* (London 1966), p. 46.
84. *All Religions are One* (K. p. 98).
85. John Locke, *An Essay Concerning Human Understanding*, edited by A. S. Pringle-Pattison (Oxford 1928), p. 42.
86. *Visions of The Daughters of Albion* (K. p. 191).
87. *Ibid.*, plate 4, line 21 (K. p. 192).
88. *H.H.*, p. 166, no. 228.
89. *Ibid.*, p. 167, no. 228.
90. *Ibid.*, p. 167, no. 228.
91. *Ibid.*, p. 168, no. 229.
92. *Ibid.*, p. 168, no. 229.
93. See, for example, *H.H.*, p. 511, no. 537, and p. 443, no. 442; for further details see also *The Last Judgment*, 'Mahomet': p. 45, no. 68–70; 'Quakers': pp. 56–7, no. 83–5; 'Moravians': pp. 57–9, no. 88.
94. *Annotations to Swedenborg's Divine Love* (K. p. 90).
95. *M.H.H.*, plate 14 (K. p. 154).
96. *H.H.*, p. 188, no. 256.
97. *Ibid.*, p. 187, no. 256.
98. *Ibid.*, p. 322, no. 391.
99. *Ibid.*, p. 354, no. 428.

100. *M.H.H.*, *op. cit.* (K. p. 149).
101. *The First Book of Urizen*, plate 19, lines 5–10 (K. p. 231).
102. *Annotations to Swedenborg's Divine Love* (K. p. 93).
103. *Annotations to Swedenborg's Divine Providence* (K. p. 131).
104. See, for example, E. D. Hirsch, Jr., *op. cit.*, p. 54 and pp. 58–9.
105. *The French Revolution*, line 95 (K. p. 138).
106. *America*, plate 11, line 10 (K. p. 200).
107. *The First Book of Urizen*, para. 5, line 16 (K. p. 224).
108. *Ibid.*, para 4, line 10 (K. p. 224).
109. *The Book of Ahania*, Chap. I, para. 7, line 30 (K. p. 249).
110. *The Book of Los*, plate 5, para. 12, lines 29–34 (K. p. 255).
111. *The Four Zoas*, Night the Sixth, lines 180–7 (K. p. 316).
112. *M.H.H.* (K. pp. 154–5).
113. *The Four Zoas*, Night the Ninth, lines 626 (K. p. 374).
114. *Ibid.*, Night the Second, line 99 *et seq.*
115. *Ibid.*, Night the Sixth, line 83 *et. seq.*
116. *Ibid.*, Night the Second, line 368 *et seq.*
117. *Ibid.*, Night the Ninth, lines 846–55 (K. p. 379).
118. *Annotations to Sir Joshua Reynolds' Discourses* (K. p. 445).
119. *M.H.H.*, plates 15–17 (K. p. 155).
120. *H.H.*, p. 491, no. 564.
121. *Ibid.*, p. 480, no. 553.
122. *Ibid.*, p. 492, no. 566.
123. *M.H.H.*, plates 15–17, p. 155.
124. *Ibid.*, plate 14, p. 154.
125. *Ibid.*, plates 15–17, p. 155.
126. *There Is No Natural Religion*, VII, p. 97.
127. *M.H.H.*, plates 15–17, p. 155.
128. *Ibid.*, p. 155.
129. J. Middleton Murry, *William Blake* (London 1933), pp. 80–1.
130. *Songs of Experience* (K. p. 210).
131. *M.H.H.*, plates 17–20 (K. p. 157).
132. 'Proverbs of Hell', plate 8 (K. ed. p. 151).
133. *H.H.*, p. 509, no. 585.
134. See, for instance, *There is No Natural Religion*, IV [Second Series] (K. p. 97) and *M.H.H.*, plates 17–20 (K. p. 155).
135. *Songs of Experience* (K. p. 211).
136. *H.H.*, p. 215, no. 285.
137. *Ibid.*, p. 215, no. 284.
138. *Ibid.*, pp. 220–1, no. 290.
139. *Ibid.*, p. 208, no. 278.
140. *Ibid.*, p. 210, no. 280.
141. *Ibid.*, p. 214, no. 283.
142. *Ibid.*, p. 214, no. 283.
143. *Ibid.*, p. 221, no. 290.
144. 'Proverbs of Hell', plate 7, line 16 (K. p. 151).
145. *H.H.*, pp. 216–17, no. 287.
146. *M.H.H.*, plates 15–17 (K. p. 155).
147. *H.H.*, p. 477, no. 550.
148. *Ibid.*, p. 473, no. 545.
149. *Ibid.*, p. 505, no. 581.
150. *The First Book of Urizen*, Chapter II, paras. 7–8 (K. p. 224).
151. *H.H.*, p. 157, no. 214.

152. *H.H.*, p. 157, no. 214.
153. *Ibid.*, p. 157, no. 214.
154. *Ibid.*, p. 157, no. 214.
155. *Ibid.*, p. 158, no. 215.
156. *Ibid.*, p. 161, no. 218.
157. *M.H.H.*, plates 22–4 (K. p. 158).
158. *Ibid.*, plates 22–4 (K. p. 158).
159. E. D. Hirsch, *Innocence and Experience. An Introduction to Blake* (Yale University Press, 1964), p. 68.
160. *H.H.*, p. 302, no. 367.
161. *Ibid.*, p. 302, no. 367.
162. *Ibid.*, p. 303, no. 368.
163. *Ibid.*, p. 307, no. 374.
164. *Ibid.*, p. 303, no. 368.
165. *Ibid.*, p. 309, no. 376.
166. *Ibid.*, p. 310, no. 378.
167. *Ibid.*, p. 310, no. 378.
168. *Ibid.*, p. 310, no. 378.
169. *Ibid.*, p. 316, no. 383.
170. *Ibid.*, pp. 309–10, no. 377.
171. *Ibid.*, p. 314, no. 382.
172. *Ibid.*, p. 315, no. 382.
173. *Ibid.*, p. 315, no. 382.
174. *Ibid.*, p. 318, no. 385.
175. *Ibid.*, p. 317, no. 384.
176. *Ibid.*, p. 510, no. 586.
177. *Ibid.*, p. 416, no. 488.
178. *Songs of Experience* (K. p. 216).
179. *M.H.H.*, plates 17–20 (K. p. 155).
180. *Ibid.* (K. p. 155).
181. *H.H.*, pp. 437–8, no. 512.
182. *The First Book of Urizen.* Chap. II, plate 4, line 16 (K. p. 224).
183. *H.H.*, p. 10, no. 9.
184. *M.H.H.*, plates 17–20 (K. p. 156).
185. *H.H.*, pp. 354–5, no. 429.
186. *Ibid.*, p. 354, no. 429.
187. *Ibid.*, p. 514, no. 589.
188. *M.H.H.* (K. p. 156).
189. *Ibid.*, plates 17–20 (K. p. 156).
190. *Ibid.* (K. p. 157).
191. *M.H.H.*, pp. 157–8.
192. *H.H.*, p. 165, no. 224.

NOTES TO CHAPTER FIVE

1. *Annotation to Watson*, K. p. 392.
2. *M.H.H.*, K. p. 154.
3. *Ibid.*, K. p. 149.
4. *Ibid.*, K. p. 149.
5. *Jerusalem*, K. p. 624.
6. *Annotations to Reynolds*, K. p. 460.

7. *M.H.H.*, K. p. 160.
8. *Visions of the Daughters of Albion*, K. p. 189.
9. *Ibid.*, K. p. 194.
10. *Ibid.*, K. p. 189.
11. *Ibid.*, K. p. 191.
12. *Visions of the Daughters of Albion*, K. p. 189.
13. *Ibid.*, K. p. 190.
14. *Ibid.*, K. p. 191.
15. *Ibid.*, K. p. 191.
16. *Ibid.*, K. pp. 193–4.
17. *A Man Without a Mask*, 1947, p. 57.
18. *The French Revolution*, K. p. 134.
19. *Ibid.*, K. p. 198.
20. *America*, K. p. 198.
21. *America*, K. pp. 198–9.
22. *Ibid.*, K. p. 202.
23. *Europe*, K. p. 240.
24. *Ibid.*, K. p. 240.
25. *Ibid.*, K. p. 242.
26. *Ibid.*, K. p. 243.
27. *Ibid.*, K. p. 243.
28. *Poems From The Note-Book*, K. p. 187.
29. Letter 'To George Cumberland', 26 August 1799 (K. p. 795).
30. Letter 'To Thomas Butts', 10 January 1802, K. p. 812.
31. *Africa*, K. p. 245.
32. H. Javadi-Tabrizi, 'The idea of Persia and Persian literary influence in English literature, with special reference to the nineteenth century', Ph.D. Thesis presented to Pembroke College, Cambridge, in 1964, p. 178.
33. *The Book of Los*, K. p. 258–60.
34. *The Book of Los*, K. p. 260.
35. *Vala*, K. p. 264.
36. *Ibid.*, K. p. 272.
37. *Ibid.*, K. p. 264.
38. *Ibid.*, K. p. 264.
39. *Ibid.*, K. p. 265.
40. *Ibid.*, K. p. 265.
41. *Ibid.*, K. pp. 266–7.
42. *Ibid.*, K. p. 269.
43. *Ibid.*, K. p. 271.
44. *Ibid.*, K. p. 271.
45. *Ibid.*, K. p. 272.
46. See, for example, *Vala*, pp. 325, 329, 348, 361, 375.
47. *Ibid.*, K. p. 275.
48. *Ibid.*, K. p. 275.
49. *Ibid.*, K. pp. 274–5.
50. *Ibid.*, K. p. 274.
51. *Ibid.*, K. p. 276.
52. *Ibid.*, K. pp. 276–7.
53. *M.H.H.*, K. p. 160.
54. *Vala*, K. p. 276.
55. *Songs of Experience*, K. p. 217.
56. *Songs of Innocence*, K. p. 117.

57. *Vala*, K. p. 277.
58. *M.H.H.*, K. p. 155.
59. *The Everlasting Gospel*, K. p. 748.
60. *Songs of Experience*, K. p. 211.
61. *Vala*, K. pp. 277–9.
62. *Ibid.*, K. p. 280.
63. *Ibid.*, K. p. 281.
64. *Ibid.*, K. p. 281.
65. *Ibid.*, K. pp. 282–3.
66. *Ibid.*, K. p. 283.
67. *Jerusalem*, K. p. 651.
68. *Vala*, K. p. 284.
69. *Ibid.*, K. pp. 285–6.
70. *Ibid.*, K. p. 290.
71. *Ibid.*, K. pp. 290–1.
72. *Ibid.*, K. p. 293.

NOTES TO CHAPTER SIX

1. *Tiriel*, plate 1, line 22 (K. p. 99).
2. *Ibid.*, plate 8, line 24 (K. p. 110).
3. *Ibid.*, plate 2, line 13 (K. p. 101).
4. *Ibid.*, plate 4, line 30 (K. p. 104).
5. *Ibid.*, plate 2, line 24 (K. p. 101).
6. *The Book of Thel*, 'Thel's Motto' (K. p. 127).
7. *Ibid.*, plate 3, line 18 (K. p. 129).
8. *Ibid.*, plate 3, line 21 (K. p. 129).
9. *Ibid.*, plate 1, line 6 (K. p. 127).
10. *Tiriel*, plate 5, line 8 (K. p. 106).
11. *The Book of Thel*, plate 1, line 12 (K. p. 127).
12. *Ibid.*, plate 6, line 10, p. 130.
13. *Ibid.*, plate 3, line 25, p. 129.
14. *Ibid.*, plate 4, line 2, p. 129.
15. *Ibid.*, plate 4, line 8 (K. p. 129).
16. *Ibid.*, plate 4, line 12 (K. p. 129).
17. *Ibid.*, plate 6, line 1 (K. p. 130).
18. *Songs of Experience* (K. p. 213).
19. *Songs of Innocence*, 'A Dream' (K. p. 112).
20. S. Foster Damon. *A Blake Dictionary. The Ideas and Symbols of William Blake* (Brown University Press, 1965), p. 149.
21. *The Notes* (K. p. 922).
22. *The Notes* (K. p. 888).
23. *The Dance of Albion* (K. p. 160).
24. *The Book of Thel*, plate 4, line 10 (K. p. 129).
25. Swedenborg also uses animals and insects as symbols. He refers to the caterpillar as follows:

> 'How extraordinary is the *case of caterpillars*, which are the vilest things in the animal kingdom! They have the sagacity to nourish themselves with the juice extracted from *leaves* of the peculiar plants . . . lay *eggs* and provide . . .'

As comment on this passage, Blake wrote the proverb:

'As the *catterpiller* chooses the fairest *leaves* to lay her *eggs* on, so the priest lays his curse on the fairest joys.'

26. *The Gates of Paradise* (K. p. 770).
27. *The Four Zoas*, Night the First, line 21 (K. p. 264).
28. See, for instance, *Visions of the Daughters of Albion*, plate 6, line 6 (K. p. 193).
29. *Ibid.*, p. 189.
30. *The Gates of Paradise* (K. p. 770).
31. *Ibid.*, pp. 770–1.
32. *Ibid.*, p. 771.
33. *Ibid.*, p. 771
34. The two children in the illustration also, apparently, echo the traditional story of Cain and Abel. Abel is slain by his brother Cain.
35. *The Gates of Paradise*, illustration No. 7 (K. p. 765).
36. *Ibid.* (K. p. 771).
37. *Ibid.* p. 771.
38. *Proverbs of Hell*, Plates 8–9.
39. *There Is No Natural Religion* (First Series), Principle III (K. p. 97).
40. *The First Book of Urizen*, Chap. I, para. I (K. p. 222).
41. *Ibid.*, Chap. I, para. 4 (K. p. 223).
42. *Ibid.*, Chap. I, Para. 5 (K. p. 223).
43. *Ibid.*, Chap. I, para. 6 (K. p. 223).
44. For discussion of 'wheel' and 'mill' in relation to the industrial revolution see J. Bronowski, *op. cit.*, pp. 58–94.
45. *First Book of Urizen*, Chap. 2, p. 223.
46. *Ibid.*, Chap. 2, p. 223.
47. *Ibid.*, Chap. 3, para. 7 (K. p. 225).
48. *Ibid.*, Chap. I, para. 3, p. 222.
49. *Ibid.*, Chap. 5, plate 15 (K. pp. 230–1).
50. The 'invisible worm', as we have seen before represents society and the dark hypocrisy of Urizenic mentality.
51. *The First Book of Urizen*, Chap. 6, para. 3, p. 232.
52. *Ibid.*, Chap. 6, para. 4, p. 232.
53. *Ibid.*, Chap. 8, para. 3 (K. p. 234).
54. *Vala or The Four Zoas*, line 368 (K. p. 289).
55. *The First Book of Urizen*, Chap. 6, para. 5 (K. p. 232).
56. *Ibid.*, para. 6 (K. p. 232).
57. *Ibid.*, para. 8 (K. p. 232).
58. *Ibid.*, Chap. 7, para. 4 (K. p. 233).
59. *Ibid.*, para. 9 (K. p. 234).
60. *Ibid.*, Chap. 8, para. 7 (K. p. 235).
61. *Europe* (K. pp. 237–8).
62. *Ibid.*, line 14 (K. p. 237).
63. *Annotations to Swedenborg's Divine Love* (K. p. 92).
64. *Europe*, plate 1, line 8 (K. p. 238).
65. *Ibid.*, plate 2, line 2 (K. p. 238).
66. *Ibid.*, plate 1, line 6 (K. p. 238).
67. *Ibid.*, plate 1, line 4 (K. p. 238).
68. *Ibid.*, plate 5, line 2 (K. p. 240).
69. *Ibid.*, plate 5, line 4 (K. p. 240).
70. *Ibid.*, plate 8, line 8 (K. p. 240).

71. *Europe*, plate 9, line 1 (K. p. 240).
72. *Ibid.*, plate 10, line 17 (K. p. 241).
73. *Ibid.*, plate 13, line 4 (K. p. 243).
74. *Ibid.*, plate 13, line 9 (K. p. 243).
75. *Ibid.*, plate 13, line 16 (K. p. 243).
76. *Ibid.*, plate 14, line 4 (K. p. 243).
77. *Ibid.*, plate 12, line 11 (K. p. 242).
78. *The Song of Los*, lines 26–8 (K. p. 243).
79. For details see J. Bronowski, chap. on 'The Seditious Writings', *op. cit.*, pp. 44–57.
80. *Ibid.*, p. 52.
81. *The Song of Los*, line 2 (K. p. 245).
82. *Ibid.*, line 10 (K. p. 245).
83. *Ibid.*, plate 4, line 13 (K. p. 246).
84. *Ibid.*, plate 7, line 1 (K. p. 247).
85. *Annotations to Lavater* (K. p. 87).
86. *Tiriel*, line 24 (K. p. 110).
87. *Annotations to Lavater* (K. p. 87).
88. See, for example, *The Four Zoas*, 'Night the Second', line 1 (K. p. 280).
89. *Ibid.*, line 3 (K. p. 280).
90. *Ibid.*, line 7 (K. p. 280).
91. *Ibid.*, line 9. (K. p. 280).
92. *Ibid.*, line 25 (K. p. 280).
93. *Ibid.* (K. p. 284).
94. *Ibid.* (K. p. 288).
95. *Ibid.* (K. p. 292).
96. *Ibid.*, 'Night the Seventh' (K. p. 323).
97. *Ibid.* (K. p. 323).
98. *Ibid.*, 'Night the Ninth', line 627 (K. p. 374).
99. *Jerusalem*, Chap. 1, plate 12, line 1 (K. p. 631).
100. *Ibid.*, plate 17, line 44 (K. p. 639).
101. *H.H.*, *op. cit.*, p. 379, no. 461.
102. *The Wisdom of Angels concerning the Divine Providence*, *op. cit.*, p. 90, no. 71.
103. *Jerusalem*, Chap. 2, plate 33, line 5 (K. p. 659).
104. *The Gates of Paradise*, line 40 (K. p. 771).
105. *The Letters* (to Thomas Butts, January 10, 1802), (K. pp. 811–3).
106. *M.H.H.*, K. p. 160.

NOTES TO CHAPTER SEVEN

1. *Milton* (K. pp. 480–2).
2. See Christopher Hill, 'The Politics of John Milton', *The Listener*, September 12, 1963.
3. *Jerusalem*, K. p. 672.
4. *The Notes* (K. p. 909).
5. *Milton* (K. p. 481).
6. *Ibid.* (K. p. 481). Abstract ideas are called spectres by Blake, and Spectres is Selfhood. This Selfhood guards love, and breeds diseases and sickness in society.
7. *Ibid.* (K. p. 506).
8. Christopher Hill, *loc. cit.*

9. *Milton* (K. pp. 481–2).
10. *Ibid.* (K. pp. 482–3).
11. *Ibid.* (K. pp. 484–5).
12. *Public Address*, K. p. 595.
13. *Milton* (K. p. 483).
14. *Public Address* (K. p. 600).
15. *Laocoön* (K. p. 776).
16. *Annotations to Reynolds* (K. pp. 452–3).
17. *Milton* (K. p. 484).
18. *Jerusalem* (K. p. 620).
19. *M.H.H.* (K. p. 150).
20. *Milton* (K. p. 497).
21. *Jerusalem* (K. p. 628).
22. *Milton* (K. pp. 529–30).
23. *Ibid.* (K. pp. 532–3). This quotation also, probably, refers to Edmund Burke who represented the ruling interests and conservatism. About Burke, as an assassin, see D. V. Erdman, *Blake, Prophet Against Empire*, *op. cit.* pp. 201–202.
24. *Ibid.* (K. p. 534).
25. *Ibid.* (K. p. 484).
26. *Jerusalem* (K. p. 639).
27. *Vala or The Four Zoas* (K. p. 264).
28. *Jerusalem* (K. p. 622).
29. *Ibid.* (K. p. 622).
30. *Ibid.* (K. p. 636).
31. *Ibid.* (K. p. 635).
32. *Annotations to Boyd* (K. p. 413).
33. *Annotations to Bacon* (K. p. 402).
34. *Annotations to Reynolds* (K. p. 445).
35. *Ibid.* (K. p. 471).
36. *Jerusalem* (K. p. 656).
37. *Ibid.* (K. p. 659).
38. *Ibid.* (K. p. 673).
39. *Laocoön* (K. p. 777).
40. *Annotations to Reynolds* (K. p. 446).
41. *Jerusalem* (K. pp. 717–18).

BIBLIOGRAPHY

1. WORKS OF WILLIAM BLAKE

All Religions are One (1788), reproduced in facsimile, published by Frederick Hollyer. London 1926.

Tiriel (1789), facsimile and transcript of the manuscript, ed. by G. E. Bentley. Oxford 1967.

Songs of Innocence and of Experience (1789–94), reproduction in the original size of Blake's Illuminated Book. The Trianon Press, 1967.

The Book of Thel (1789), facsimile, published by Frederick Hollyer. London 1924.

The Marriage of Heaven and Hell (1790–93), reproduction in facsimile. London 1960.

Inscription to 'The Dance of Albion' (1793).

Visions of the Daughters of Albion (1793), facsimile, ed. by J. M. Murry. London 1932.

America, a facsimile of the edition of 1793. With description and bibliographical statement by Sir Geoffrey Keynes. The Trianon Press, 1963.

The First Book of Urizen (1794), facsimile, ed. by D. L. Plowman. London 1929.

Vala, or The Four Zoas (1795–1804), a facsimile of the poem and a study of its growth and significance by G. E. Bentley. Oxford 1963.

The Book of Job, facsimile. London 1937.

Milton, a Poem in 2 Books (1804–08), an Exhibition of Illuminated Books of William Blake arranged by the National Library of Scotland, 1969.

An illustrative talk and a commemorative handbook with a study by Geoffrey Keynes. Edinburgh 1969.

Jerusalem (1804–20), a facsimile of the illustrated book. London 1951.

William Blake's Engravings, ed. with an introduction by Geoffrey Keynes. London 1950.

Engravings of William Blake (reproduction). The separate plates, by Geoffrey Keynes. Dublin 1956.

William Blake Works—*Poetical, Symbolic and Prophetical*, 3 vol. ed. by Edwin J. Ellis and W. B. Yeats. London 1893.

Poetical Works of William Blake, 2 vols. London 1906.

A Selection of Poems and Letters, ed. with an introduction by J. Bronowski.

The Portable Blake, selected and arranged with an introduction by A. Kazin. New York 1946.

The Writings of William Blake, ed. by Geoffrey Keynes, 3 vols. London 1925.

Poetry and Prose of William Blake, ed. by Geoffrey Keynes. London 1927.

Blake Complete Writings, with variant readings, ed. by Geoffrey Keynes. London 1957.

Blake Complete Writings, with variant readings, ed. by Geoffrey Keynes. Oxford 1969.

The Poems and Prophecies of William Blake, ed. by Max Plowman. London 1926. (Everyman's Library.)

The Prophetical Writings of William Blake, ed. with a general introduction, glossarial index of symbols by D. S. Sloss and J. P. R. Wallis. 2 vols. Oxford 1926.

The Poetical Works of William Blake, ed. by J. Sampson. Oxford 1905.

The Poetical Works of William Blake, ed. with an introduction by J. Sampson. Oxford 1913.

2. BOOKS ON WILLIAM BLAKE

Ansari (Asloob Ahmad). *Arrows of Intellect; a study in W. Blake's gospel oj imagination.* Aligarh 1965.

Beer, John. *Blake's Humanism.* Manchester 1968.

Bentley, G. E., and Martin K. Nurmi. A Blake Bibliography. Minneapolis 1964.

Blackstone, Bernard. *English Blake.* Cambridge 1949.

Bloom, Harold. Blake's Apocalypse: *A Study in Poetic Argument.* London 1963.

—— 'Dialectic in The Marriage'; *English Romantic Poets; Modern Essays in Criticism,* ed. by M. H. Abrams. New York 1964.

Bronowski, Jacob. *William Blake. A Man Without a Mask.* London 1947.

Chesterton, G. K. *William Blake.* London 1910.

Damon S. Foster. *William Blake, his Philosophy and Symbols,* London 1924.

—— *A Blake Dictionary.*

—— *The Ideas and Symbols of William Blake.* 1965.

Davies, J. G. *Theology of William Blake.* Oxford 1948.

Eliot, T. S., *The Sacred Wood* (University Paperback). London 1964.

Erdman, D. V. *Prophet Against Empire.* Princeton 1954.

—— *A Concordance to the Writings of William Blake.* 2 vols. New York 1967.

Fisher, P. F. *The Valley of Vision,* ed. by N. Frye. Toronto 1961.

Frye, Northrop. *Fearful Symmetry,* Princeton 1947.

—— *Blake* (A Collection of Critical Essays), ed. by N. Frye. Englewood Cliffs, N.J. 1966.

Gardner, Stanley. *Infinity on the Anvil.* London 1954.

Gaunt, William. *Arrows of Desire; a Study of William Blake and his Romatic World,* London 1956.

Gilchrist, Alexander. *Life of William Blake.* London 1942. (Everyman's Library.)

Gillham, D. G., *Blake's Contrary States.* Cambridge 1966.

Grant, John E. *Blake: Original and New.* Modern Language Quarterly. U.S.A. September 1964.

Harper, George Mills. *The Neoplatonism of William Blake.* Chapel Hill 1961.

Hirst, Desiree. *Hidden Riches.* London 1964.

Hirsch, E. D., Jr. *Innocence and Experience. An Introduction to Blake.* Yale 1966.

Holloway, John. *Blake: The Lyric Poetry.* London 1968.

Keynes, Geoffrey. *William Blake, Poet, Printer, Prophet.* The Trianon Press, 1964.

—— *A Bibliography of William Blake.* New York 1921.

Margolionth, H. M. *William Blake.* London 1951.

Murry, J. M. *William Blake.* London 1933.

Morton, Arthur Leslie. *The Everlasting Gospel, a Study in the Sources of William Blake.* London 1958.

Nurmi, M. K. *Blake's Marriage of Heaven and Hell.* Kent 1957.

Pinto, V. de Sola (ed.). *The Divine Vision.* London 1957.

Plowman, Max. *An Introduction to the Study of Blake.* London 1927.

Raine, Kathleen. *Blake and Tradition.* London 1969.

—— *William Blake.* London 1970.

Schorer, Mark. *The Politics of Vision.* New York 1959.

Saurat, D. *Blake and Modern Thought.* London 1929.

—— *Blake and Milton.* Bordeaux 1920.

Wilson, Mona. *The Life of William Blake.* London 1948.

Wicksteed, J. H. *William Blake's Jerusalem* (with plates including a portrait and facsimiles). London 1954.
—— *Blake's Innocence and Experience* (with plates). London 1928.
—— *Blake's Vision of the Book of Job.* London 1910.
Rose, Edward J. 'Mental Forms Creating', *The Journal of Aesthetics and Art Criticism.* U.S.A. Winter 1964.
Rudd, Margaret. *Divided Image.* London 1953.
—— *Organiz'd Innocence.* London 1956.

3. THE WORKS OF SWEDENBORG

Swedenborg, Emmanuel. *Apocalpyse Revealed.* 2 vols. Manchester 1791 (Amsterdam 1766).
—— *Arcana Caelestia:* 12 vols. London 1825 (translated from the original Latin, first published in London in 1749).
—— *The Divine Providence.* Second edition London 1810 (originally published in Amsterdam 1767).
—— *Heaven and Hell.* Manchester 1817 (originally published in London 1758).
—— *A Treatise Concerning the Last Judgement.* Second edition London 1810 (originally published in London 1758).
—— *Wisdom of Angels Concerning Divine Love and Divine Wisdom.* Second edition 1816 (originally published in Amsterdam 1763).
—— *The Delights of Wisdom Concerning Conjugial Love.* 2 vols. Manchester 1811 (originally published in Amsterdam 1768).
—— *The Doctrine of The New Church.* Manchester 1818 (originally published in Amsterdam 1769).
—— *The Doctrine of New Jerusalem respecting the Lord.* London 1812 (original 1758).
—— *The True Christian Religion.* 2 vols. London 1781 (original 1771).

4. BOOKS ON SWEDENBORG AND SWEDEN

Faulkner, J. *The Swedenborg Concordance.* London 1888.
Murray, Robert. *A Brief History of the Church of Sweden.* Stockholm 1961.
Oakley, Stewart. *The Story of Sweden.* London 1960.
Sigstedt, C. O. *The Swedenborg Epic.* New York 1952.
Swedenborg Society. *Bibliographical Index of Swedenborg's Writings.* London 1897.
—— *Minutes of the New Church.* London 1885.
Stomberg, A. A. *A History of Sweden.* New York 1931.
Trobridge, G. *Life of Emanual Swedenborg.* London 1932.

5. THE EIGHTEENTH AND EARLY NINETEENTH CENTURY BACKGROUND

Abrams, M. H. *The Mirror and the Lamp: Romantic Theory and the Critical Tradition.* New York 1958.
Berkeley, G. *The Works.* London 1837.
Blair, Robert. *The Grave.* (A Poem Illustrated by Twelve Etchings from the original of William Blake 1808.) London 1903.

Bowra, M. *The Romantic Imagination*. London 1950.
Brailsford, H. N. *Shelley, Godwin, and their Circle*. London 1913.
Bronowski, J. and B. Mazlish. *The Western Intellectual Tradition* (Penguin). London 1963.
Burton, Elizabeth. *The Georgians at Home* (1814–1830). London 1897.
Butler, Joseph. *The Works*. London 1896.
Carnall, Geoffrey. *Robert Southey and His Age*. Oxford 1960.
Clive, Geoffrey. *The Romantic Enlightenment*. New York, 1960.
Cobbett, William. *Rural Rides*. London 1958.
Ford, Boris. *From Blake to Byron* (Pelican). London 1957.
George, Dorothy. *England in Transition* (Pelican). London 1953.
Godwin, William. *Political Justice*. Ed. by H. S. Salt. London 1890.
—— *Thoughts on Man*. London 1831.
Hammond, J. L. and Barbara. *The Town Labourer*. 1760–1832. London 1917.
Harris, R. W. *Romanticism and the Social Order*. 1778–1830. London 1969.
Hobbes, Thomas. *Leviathan*. Ed. by M. Oakeshott. Oxford 1957.
Hobshawm, E. J. *The Age of Revolution*. London 1964.
Horn, D. B. *Great Britain and Europe in the Eighteenth Century*. London 1967.
Hume, David. *On Religion*. Selected and Introduced by Richard Wollheim, London 1963.
Keats, J. *Poems* (Everyman's Library). Ed. by E. Rhys. 1906.
Locke, John. *An Essay Concerning Human Understanding*. Ed. by A. S. Pringle-Pattison. London 1924.
Marshal, Dorothy. *English People in the Eighteenth Century*. London 1962.
Paine, Thomas. *The Complete Writings*. Ed. by Philip S. Foner. New York 1945.
Pinson, K. *Pietism as a Factor in the Rise of German Nationalism*. New York 1934.
Shelley, P. B. *The Complete Poetical Works*. Ed. T. Hutchinson. London 1945.
Stephen, Leslie. *English Literature and Society in the 18th Century*. London 1904.
Stauffer, Ward. *Doorways to Poetry*. New York 1938.
Trevelyan, G. M. *English Social History*. London 1948.
Willey, Basil. *The Eighteenth Century Background*. London 1962.
—— *The Seventeenth Century Background*. London 1962.
Wordsworth, William. *The Excursion*. Ed. E. de Selincourt and H. Darbishire. Oxford 1949.
Wollstonecraft, Mary. *Memories*. (Plates by Blake.) Ed. by W. C. Durant 1927. London.
—— *Vindications of the Rights of Women*. London 1792.

6. OTHER WORKS CONSULTED

Aryanpour, H. *Stylistic Study of Poetry*. Ph.D. Thesis. Tehran 1959.
—— *A Study of Static Style*. Article, Sokhan Literary Review, No. 11–12. Tehran 1961.
Bernbaum, E. *Guide Through the Romantic Movement*. New York 1949.
Bronowski, J. *Science and Human Values* (Pelican). London 1964.
Calidas. *Sakuntala* or *The Fatal Ring*. Translated by Sir William Jones. London 1789.
Chadwick, N. K. *Poetry and Prophecy*. Cambridge 1942.
Chiari, Joseph. *Realism and Imagination*. London 1960.

Courthope, W. J. *The Liberal Movement in English Literature*. London 1885.

Eliot, T. S. *Selected Essays*. London 1932.

—— *The Use of Poetry and The Use of Criticism*. London 1952.

Hauser, Arnold. *The Social History of Art*. 4 vols. London 1962.

Hegel, G. W. F. *Selections*. Ed. by J. Loewenberg. New York 1927.

Karner, S. *Kant* (Pelican). London 1960.

Kettle, Arnold. *William Blake*. The Open University Press 1972.

Levi-Strauss, Claude. *Structural Anthropology*. Translated from the French by Chaire Jacobson and B. G. Schoepf. New York 1963.

Mahood, M. M. *Poetry and Humanism*. London 1950.

Philsooph, H. *A Re-consideration of Frazer's Concept of Magic with Special Reference to More Recent Research*. M.Sc. thesis, University of Edinburgh 1968.

Piaget, Jean. *Language and Thought of the Child*. London 1959.

—— *The Child's Conception of the World*. London 1929.

Read, Herbert. *The Meaning of Art* (Penguin). London 1949.

Storr, Anthony. *The Integrity of the Personality* (Pelican). London 1963.

Tylor, Sir Edward. *Primitive Culture*. Vol. 1 (London 1871). Third edition 1891.

Weber, Max. *The Sociology of Religion*. London 1966.

Williams, Raymond. *Culture and Society 1780–1950* (Penguin). London 1961.

INDEX